baac

BBC THE LOST DIMENSION EVE...

DOCTOR WHO

BOOK TWO

"A fast-paced story that will keep your attention."
CLEARING OUT THE CLUTTER

"Every time a new Doctor appeared so did a smile on my face. This series should be a cracker."
NERDLY

"If you have any love of the show of all, The Lost Dimension is definitely worth checking out. 4 out of 5"
MYM BUZZ

"A fan pleasing, joyride full of spectacular spirit, color, exploration, and drama. 10 out of 10"
BLOGTOR WHO

"If you haven't given *Doctor Who* a chance, you couldn't do better than making this book your entryway into a bigger universe. The story is fantastic and the artwork stunning. 5 out of 5."
KABOOM

"The art of Rachael Stott and the coloring of Rodrigo Fernandes is impeccable. With beautiful, well-drawn pages full of color, the aesthetics are amazing and help bring the story to life. This issue was, as one Doctor would say, 'Fantastic!'"
GAMERS SPHERE

"This is the best way a *Doctor Who* fan can pass the time until Christmas Day."
COMICOSITY

"A very satisfying read with some great artwork provided by Rachael Stott."
COMICON

"Expansive, charming, and gorgeous. 9 out of 10."
NEWSARAMA

"If you need a *Doctor Who* fix, this is about as concentrated a dose as you're likely to find."
IGN

TITAN COMICS

SENIOR COMICS EDITOR
Andrew James

ASSISTANT EDITORS
Lauren Bowes, Amoona Saohin

COLLECTION DESIGNER
Andrew Leung

PRODUCTION ASSISTANT
Natalie Bolger

PRODUCTION SUPERVISOR
Maria Pearson

PRODUCTION CONTROLLER
Peter James

SENIOR PRODUCTION CONTROLLER
Jackie Flook

ART DIRECTOR
Oz Browne

SENIOR SALES MANAGER
Steve Tothill

PRESS OFFICER
Will O'Mullane

COMICS BRAND MANAGER
Chris Thompson

ADS & MARKETING ASSISTANT
Tom Miller

DIRECT SALES & MARKETING MANAGER
Ricky Claydon

COMMERCIAL MANAGER
Michelle Fairlamb

HEAD OF RIGHTS
Jenny Boyce

PUBLISHING MANAGER
Darryl Tothill

PUBLISHING DIRECTOR
Chris Teather

OPERATIONS DIRECTOR
Leigh Baulch

EXECUTIVE DIRECTOR
Vivian Cheung

PUBLISHER
Nick Landau

For rights information contact Jenny Boyce
jenny.boyce@titanemail.com

Special thanks to: Steven Moffat, Brian Minchin, Mandy
Thwaites, James Dudley, Edward Russell, Sally De St Croix,
Sarah Bold, Phillip Raperport, Kate Bush, and Ed Casey for their
invaluable assistance.

BBC WORLDWIDE

PRESIDENT OF UK AND ANZ
Marcus Arthur

**DIRECTOR OF
EDITORIAL GOVERNANCE**
Nicholas Brett

**PUBLISHER MAGAZINES
AND NPD**
Mandy Thwaites

**DIRECTOR FOR CONSUMER
PRODUCTS AND PUBLISHING**
Andrew Moultrie

PUBLISHING DIRECTOR
Chris Kerwin

PUBLISHING CO-ORDINATOR
Eva Abramik

DOCTOR WHO - THE LOST DIMENSION
BOOK TWO
HB ISBN: 9781785863479
SB ISBN: 9781785865916
FP SC ISBN: 9781785866609
Published by Titan Comics, a division of
Titan Publishing Group, Ltd. 144 Southwark Street,
London, SE1 0UP.

A CIP catalogue record for this title is
available from the British Library.
First edition: March 2018.

10 9 8 7 6 5 4 3 2

Printed in China.

Titan Comics does
not read or accept
unsolicited
DOCTOR WHO
submissions of ideas,
stories or artwork.

www.titan-comics.com

DOCTOR WHO

THE LOST DIMENSION

BOOK TWO

**WRITERS: GORDON RENNIE, EMMA BEEBY,
GEORGE MANN & CAVAN SCOTT**

**ARTISTS: IVAN RODRIGUEZ, WELLINGTON DIAZ,
RACHAEL STOTT & MARIANO LACLAUSTRA**

WITH ANDERSON CABRAL, MARCELO SALAZA
& FER CENTURION

**COLORISTS: THIAGO RIBEIRO,
MAURICIO WALLACE, ROD FERNANDES
& CARLOS CABRERA**

WITH MONY CASTILLO

**LETTERS: RICHARD STARKINGS AND
COMICRAFT'S JIMMY BETANCOURT**

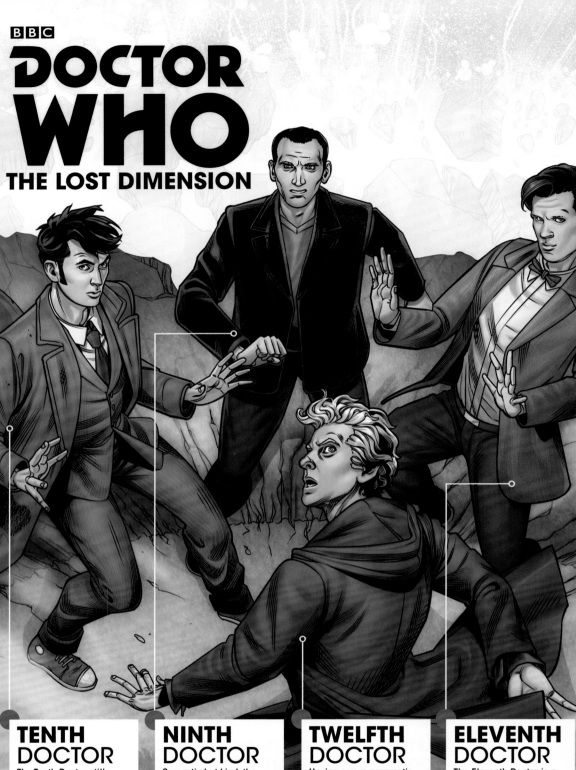

DOCTOR WHO
THE LOST DIMENSION

TENTH
DOCTOR
The Tenth Doctor still hides his post-Time War guilt beneath a happy-go-lucky guise. Never cruel or cowardly, he champions the oppressed across time and space – but is that enough to save everyone he cares for?!

NINTH
DOCTOR
Sarcastic but kind, the Ninth Doctor is beginning to have his rough edges sanded off by Rose, and to trust the scoundrel Jack. However, that doesn't mean he isn't occasionally prone to the odd lapse in judgement...

TWELFTH
DOCTOR
Having grown pragmatic with age, the Twelfth Doctor is careful with his companions. Even without a regular partner to show off to, the Doctor still manages to find adventure – and danger – wherever he goes!

ELEVENTH
DOCTOR
The Eleventh Doctor is a gangly boy professor with an old soul, who occasionally needs to be brought down to earth! He is deeply empathetic, and has made many mistakes in his time – but owns all of them.

FOURTH DOCTOR

The Fourth Doctor is a charming, unpredictable force of insatiable curiosity, let loose upon the cosmos. Filled with a new wanderlust after years exiled to Earth, this manlike mass of teeth and curls baffles friends and flummoxes foes in equal measure!

JENNY

Created from the Doctor's DNA, Jenny is part Time Lord and full maverick. Dauntless, independent, and a master with a toolbox, when the Doctor last saw his "daughter", she was briefly dead, before she revived herself and headed off in a spaceship to explore the universe. They grow up so fast...

RIVER SONG

Child of the TARDIS and wife of the Doctor, River Song spends her days as a Professor of Archaeology, although her teaching methods are sometimes questionable. Her timeline occasionally overlaps with the Doctor's, where she has to be careful to not reveal any "spoilers"...

PREVIOUSLY...

The Doctor is an immortal time traveler who champions the oppressed across time and space. He has helped the inhabitants of Earth time and time again, regenerating and changing his face many times along the way.

An unknown force is spreading throughout the whole universe, attacking the Doctor in his all of his various incarnations with an immense and destructive power.

The Doctor's friends and companions are also in grave danger, including Jenny, his daughter – who crashed back into the life of the Twelfth Doctor – and the infamous archaeologist, River Song!

The white holes striking through creation have the potential to destroy all of space and time, and to erase every version of the Doctor that has ever existed.

In the meantime, they've corrupted the forces of UNIT – along with the rest of humanity – and turned them against the Doctor, in the name of 'Peace'...

It's going to take all of the Doctors' gifts – as well as a lot of help from his friends – to uncover the truth behind the attacks, and to set the universe right.

But before all that, where is the Fourth Doctor in all of this...?

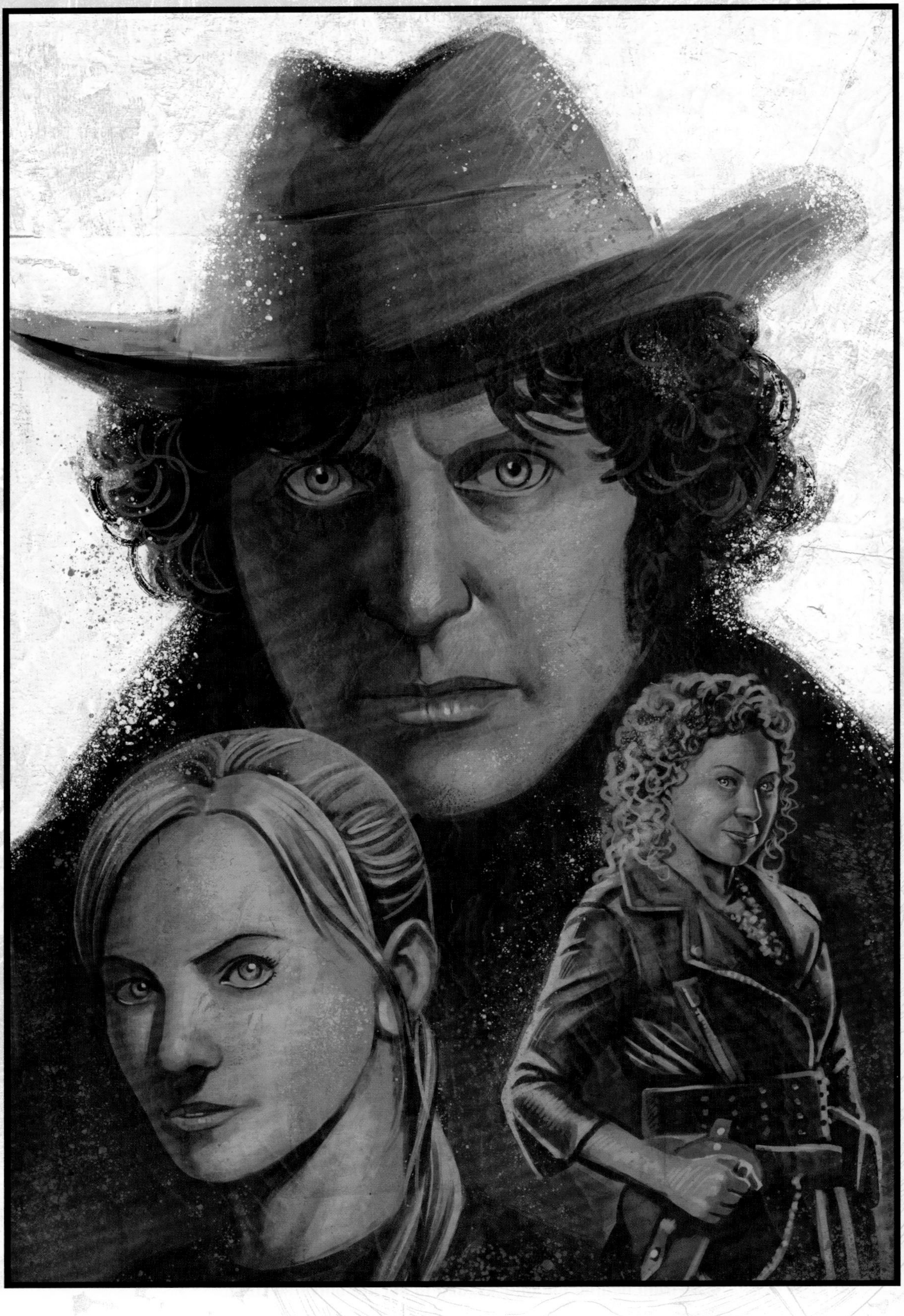

Special #1 Cover A: MARIANO LACLAUSTRA

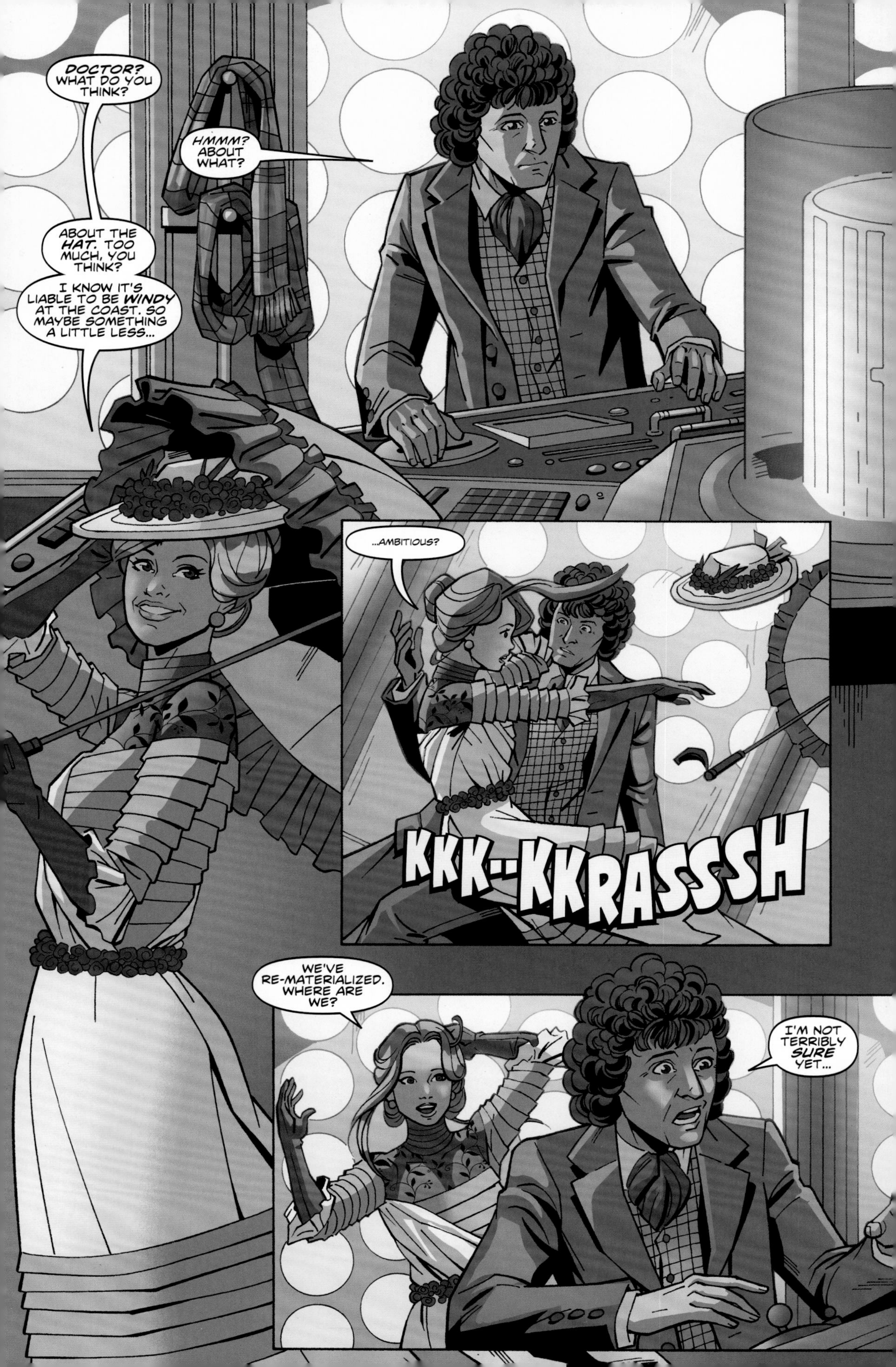
DOCTOR? WHAT DO YOU THINK?
HMMM? ABOUT WHAT?
ABOUT THE HAT. TOO MUCH, YOU THINK?
I KNOW IT'S LIABLE TO BE WINDY AT THE COAST. SO MAYBE SOMETHING A LITTLE LESS...
...AMBITIOUS?
KKK--KKRASSSH
WE'VE RE-MATERIALIZED. WHERE ARE WE?
I'M NOT TERRIBLY SURE YET...

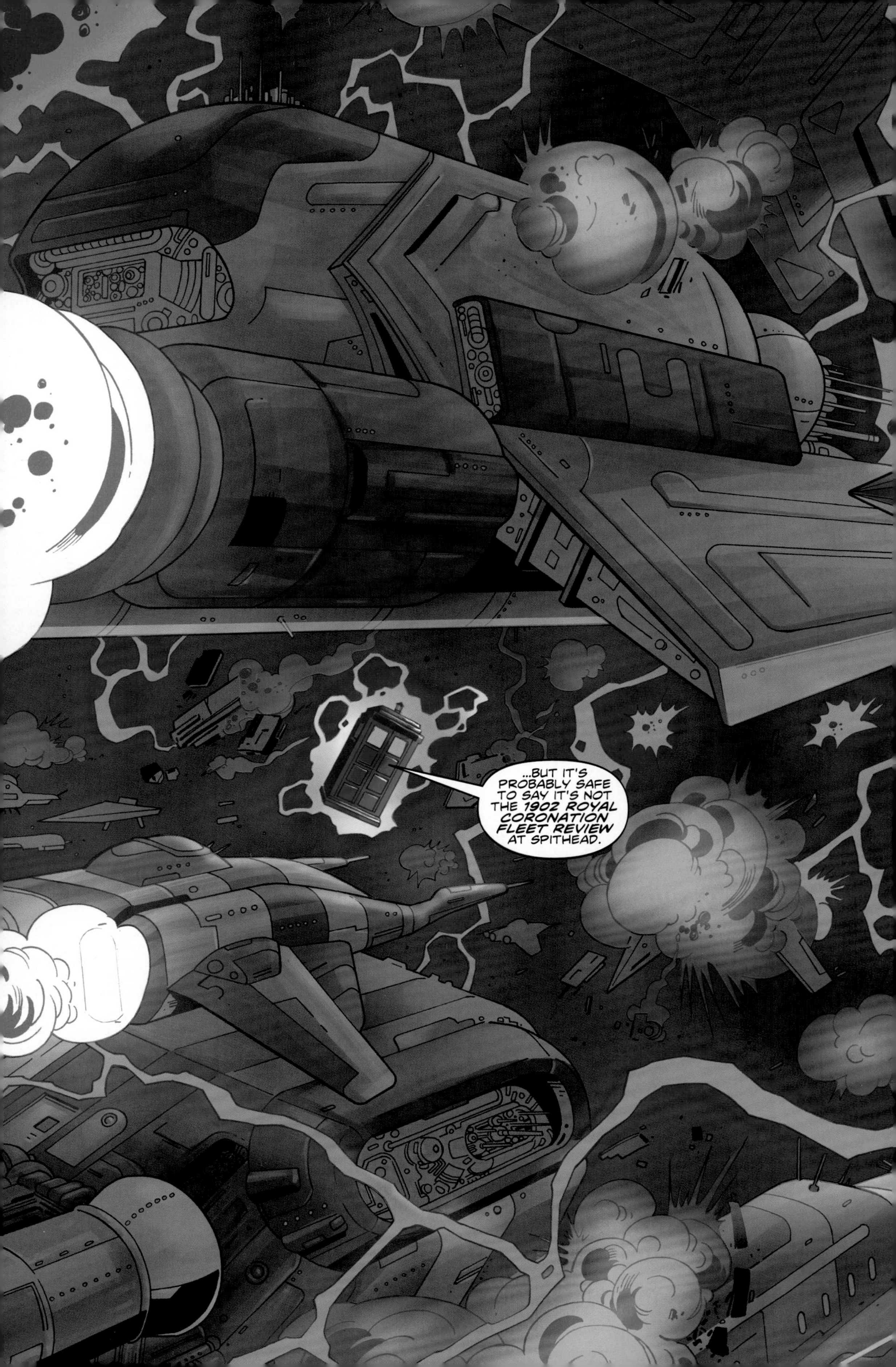
...BUT IT'S PROBABLY SAFE TO SAY IT'S NOT THE *1902 ROYAL CORONATION FLEET REVIEW* AT SPITHEAD.

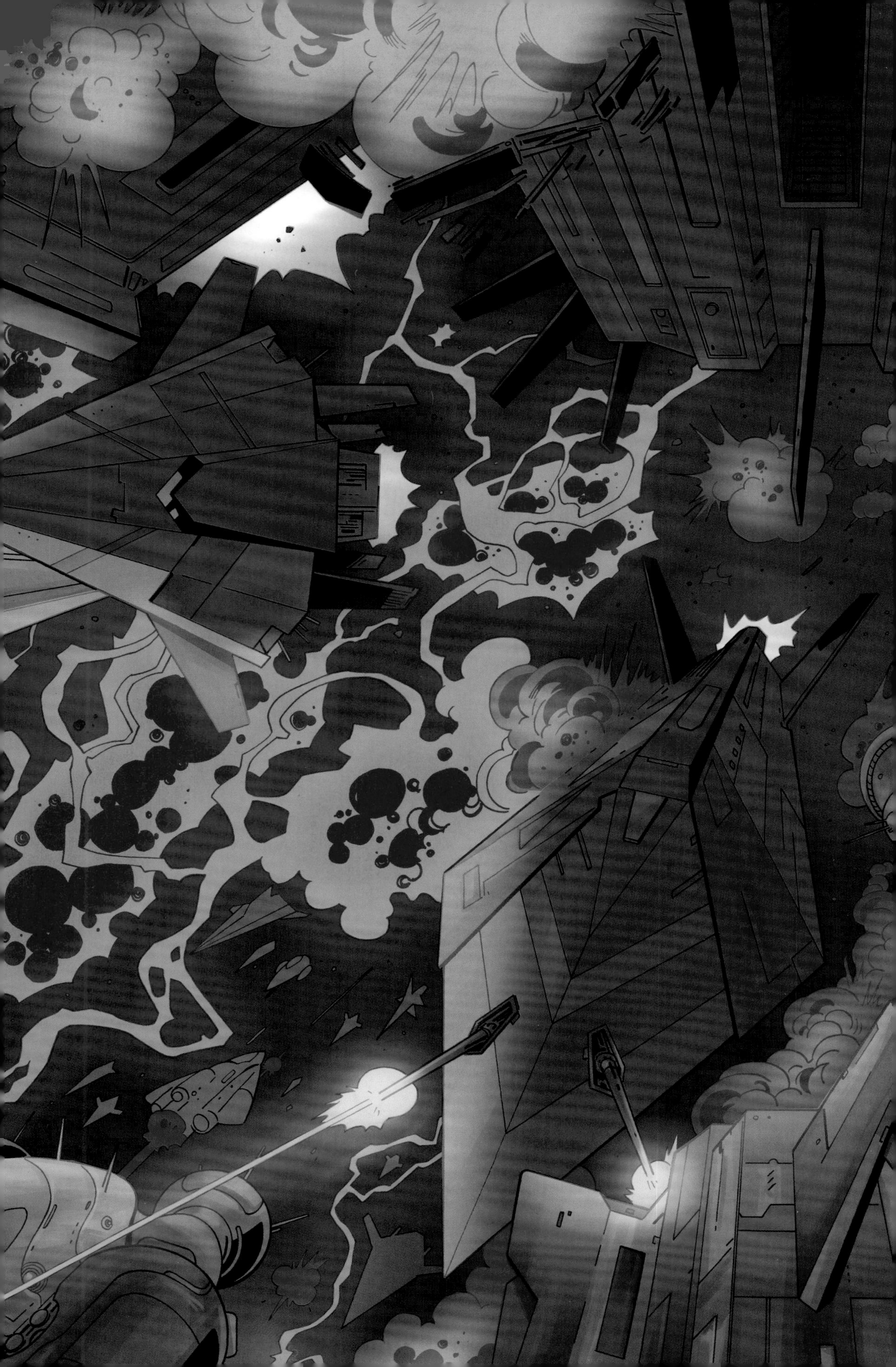

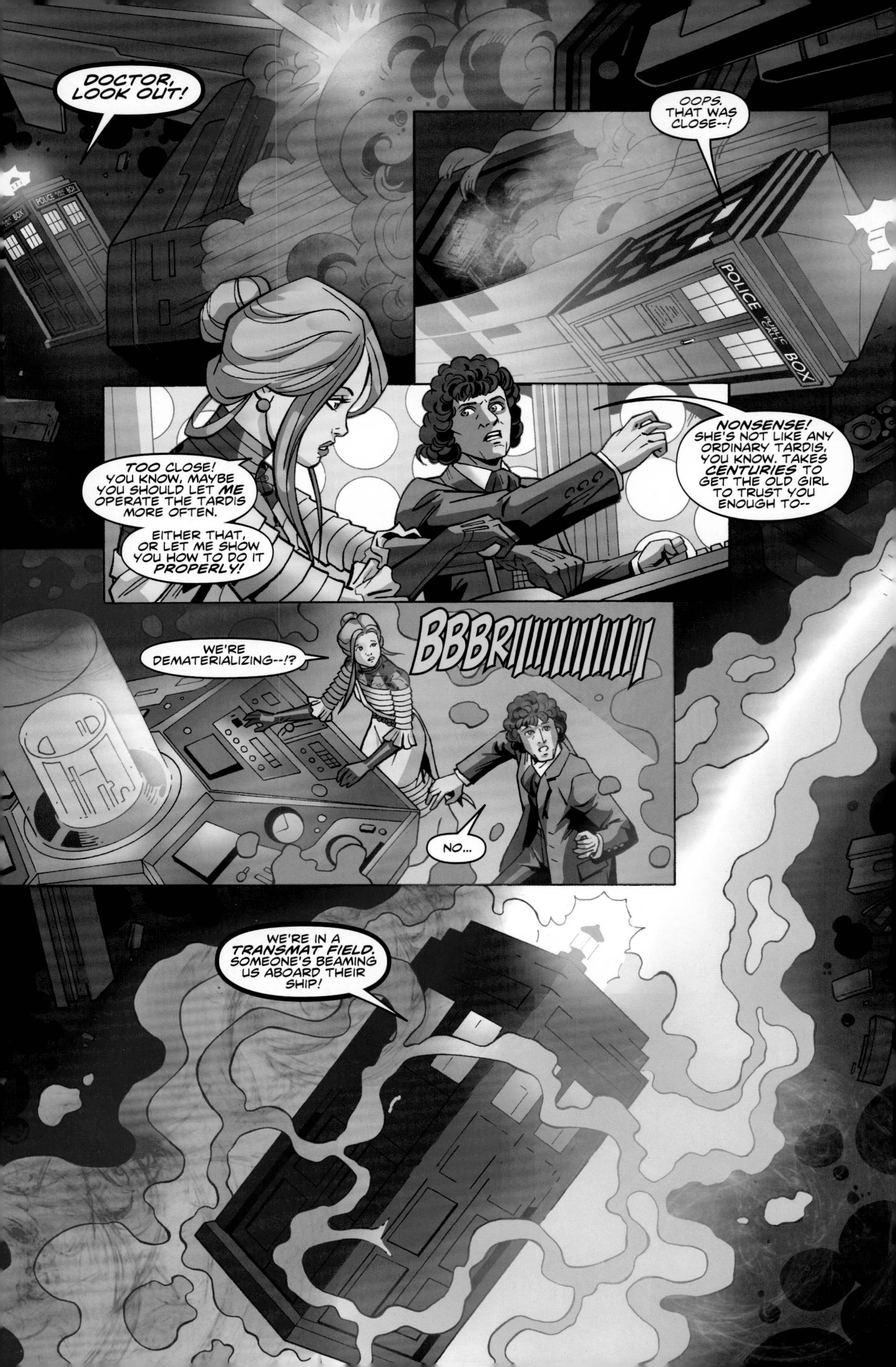
DOCTOR, LOOK OUT!
POLICE PUBLIC BOX
OOPS. THAT WAS CLOSE--!
POLICE PUBLIC CALL BOX
TOO CLOSE! YOU KNOW, MAYBE YOU SHOULD LET ME OPERATE THE TARDIS MORE OFTEN.
EITHER THAT, OR LET ME SHOW YOU HOW TO DO IT PROPERLY!
NONSENSE! SHE'S NOT LIKE ANY ORDINARY TARDIS, YOU KNOW. TAKES CENTURIES TO GET THE OLD GIRL TO TRUST YOU ENOUGH TO--
WE'RE DEMATERIALIZING--!?
BBBRIIIIIIIIIIIII
NO...
WE'RE IN A TRANSMAT FIELD. SOMEONE'S BEAMING US ABOARD THEIR SHIP!

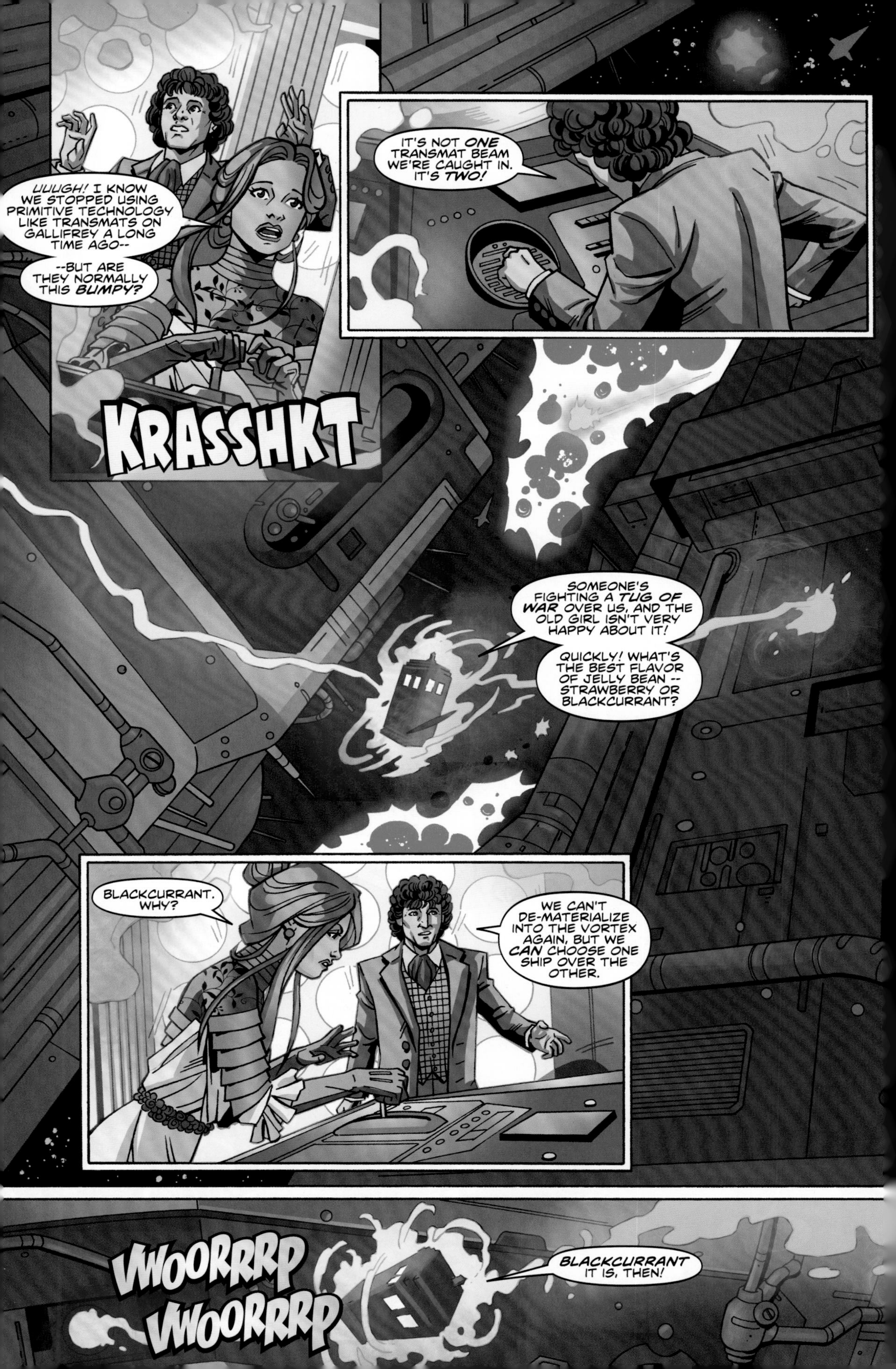
UUUGH! I KNOW WE STOPPED USING PRIMITIVE TECHNOLOGY LIKE TRANSMATS ON GALLIFREY A LONG TIME AGO--
--BUT ARE THEY NORMALLY THIS BUMPY?
IT'S NOT ONE TRANSMAT BEAM WE'RE CAUGHT IN. IT'S TWO!
KRASSHKT
SOMEONE'S FIGHTING A TUG OF WAR OVER US, AND THE OLD GIRL ISN'T VERY HAPPY ABOUT IT!
QUICKLY! WHAT'S THE BEST FLAVOR OF JELLY BEAN -- STRAWBERRY OR BLACKCURRANT?
BLACKCURRANT. WHY?
WE CAN'T DE-MATERIALIZE INTO THE VORTEX AGAIN, BUT WE CAN CHOOSE ONE SHIP OVER THE OTHER.
VWOORRRP VWOORRRP
BLACKCURRANT IT IS, THEN!

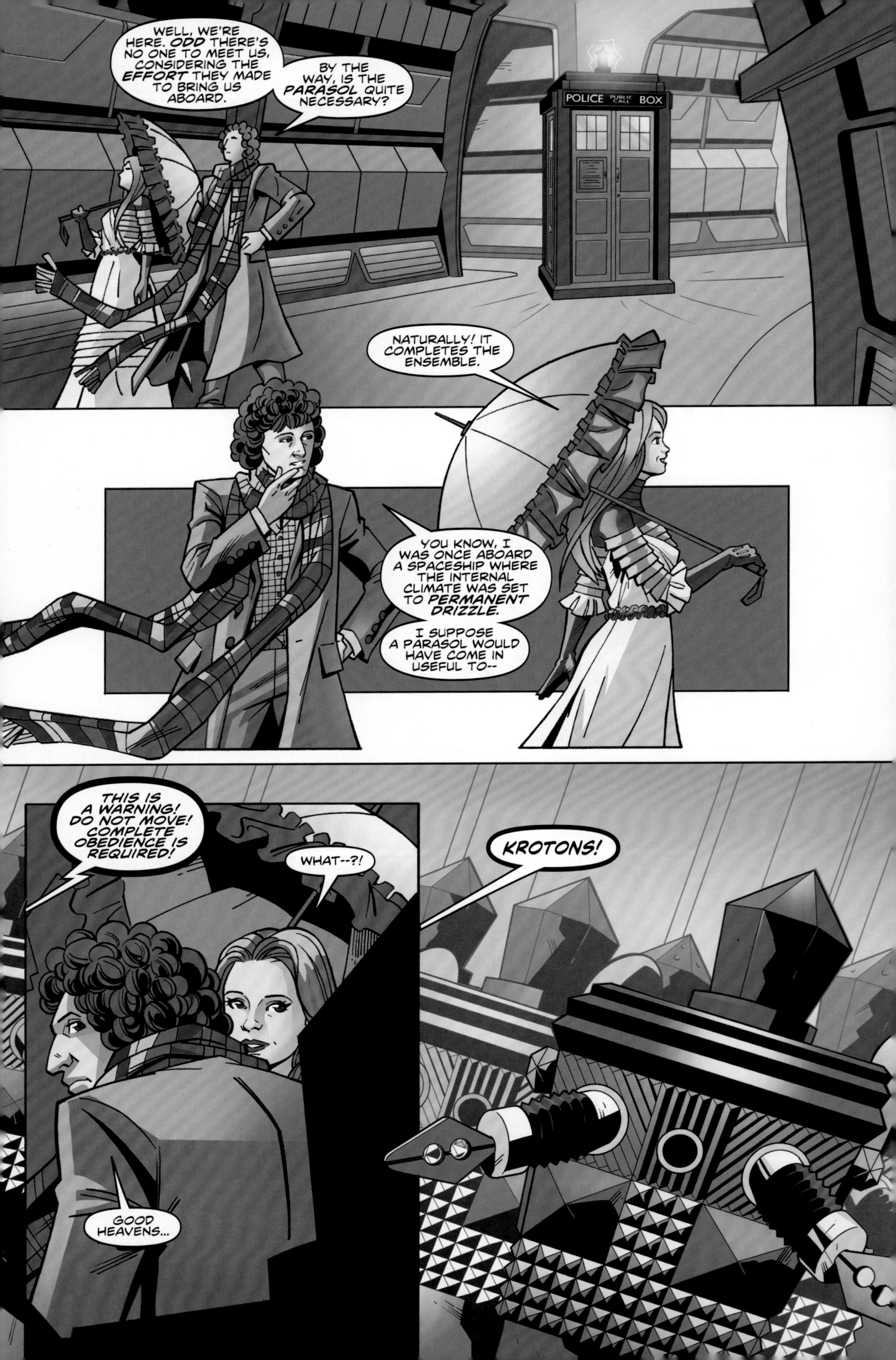
WELL, WE'RE HERE. ODD THERE'S NO ONE TO MEET US, CONSIDERING THE EFFORT THEY MADE TO BRING US ABOARD.
BY THE WAY, IS THE PARASOL QUITE NECESSARY?
POLICE PUBLIC CALL BOX
NATURALLY! IT COMPLETES THE ENSEMBLE.
YOU KNOW, I WAS ONCE ABOARD A SPACESHIP WHERE THE INTERNAL CLIMATE WAS SET TO PERMANENT DRIZZLE.
I SUPPOSE A PARASOL WOULD HAVE COME IN USEFUL TO--
THIS IS A WARNING! DO NOT MOVE! COMPLETE OBEDIENCE IS REQUIRED!
WHAT--?!
KROTONS!
GOOD HEAVENS...

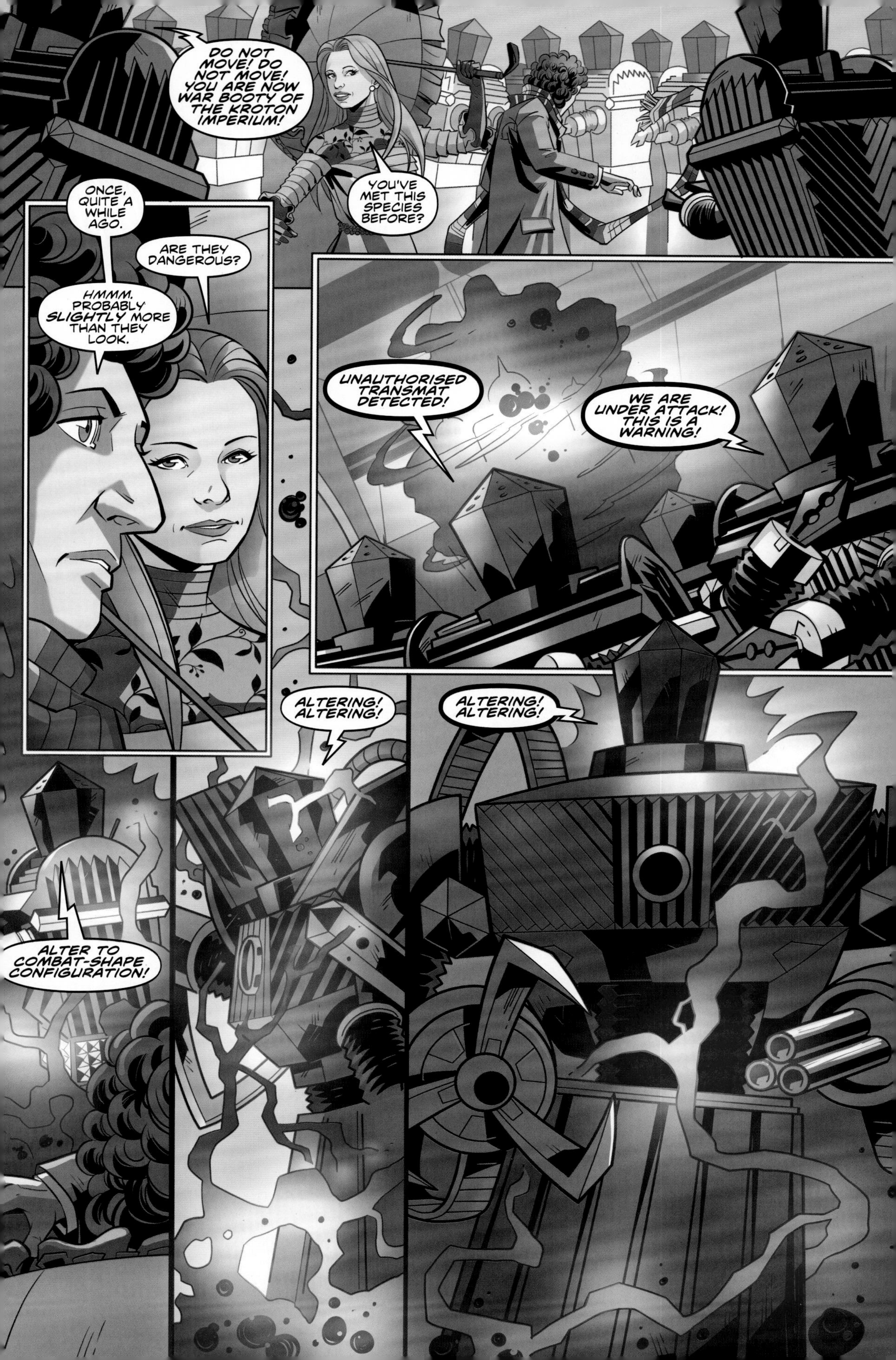
DO NOT MOVE! DO NOT MOVE! YOU ARE NOW WAR BOOTY OF THE KROTON IMPERIUM!
YOU'VE MET THIS SPECIES BEFORE?
ONCE, QUITE A WHILE AGO.
ARE THEY DANGEROUS?
HMMM. PROBABLY SLIGHTLY MORE THAN THEY LOOK.
UNAUTHORISED TRANSMAT DETECTED!
WE ARE UNDER ATTACK! THIS IS A WARNING!
ALTER TO COMBAT-SHAPE CONFIGURATION!
ALTERING! ALTERING!
ALTERING! ALTERING!

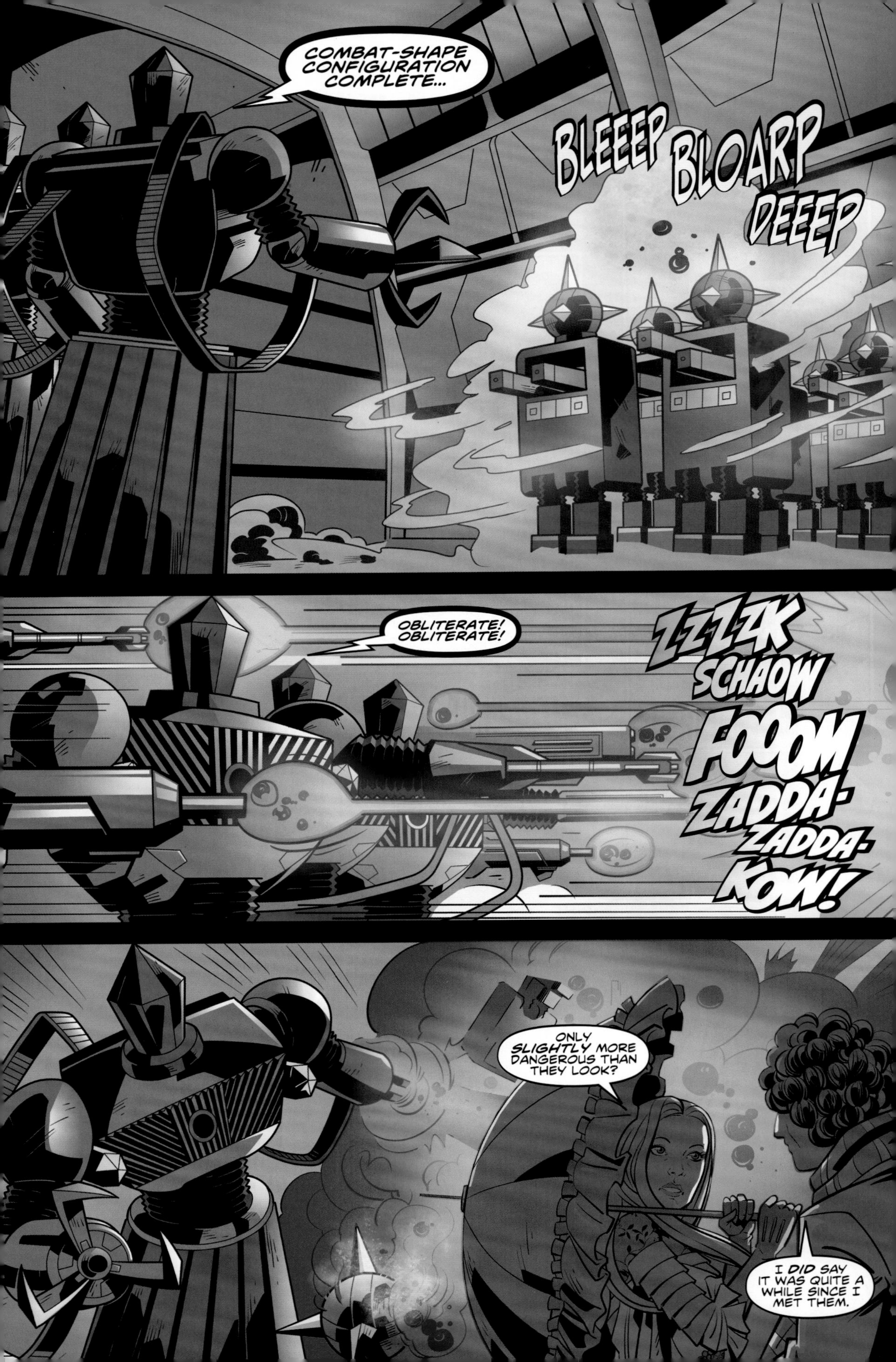
COMBAT-SHAPE CONFIGURATION COMPLETE...
BLEEEP
BLOARP
DEEEP
OBLITERATE! OBLITERATE!
ZZZZK
SCHAOW
FOOOM
ZADDA-
ZADDA-
KOW!
ONLY SLIGHTLY MORE DANGEROUS THAN THEY LOOK?
I DID SAY IT WAS QUITE A WHILE SINCE I MET THEM.

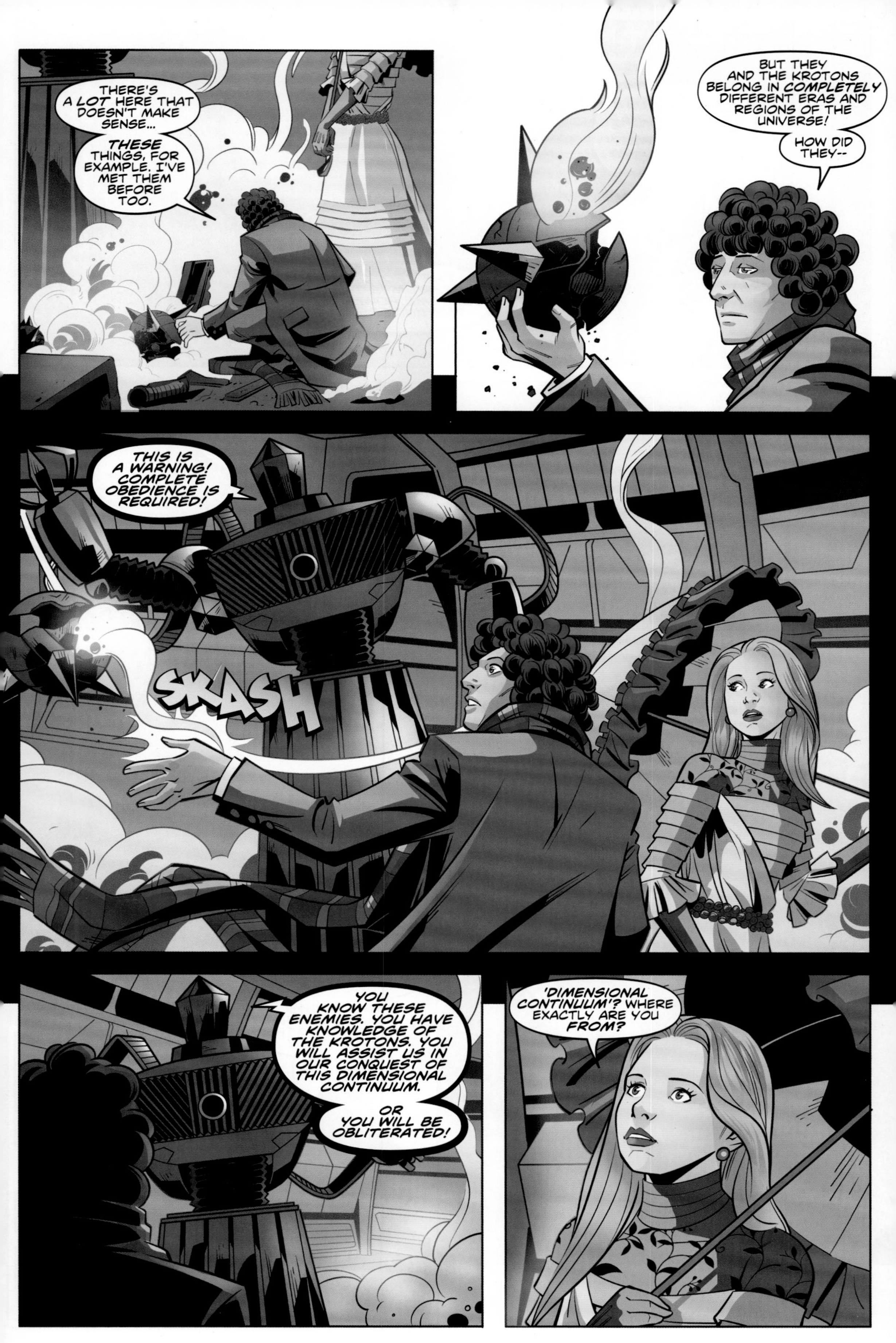
THERE'S A LOT HERE THAT DOESN'T MAKE SENSE...
THESE THINGS, FOR EXAMPLE. I'VE MET THEM BEFORE TOO.
BUT THEY AND THE KROTONS BELONG IN COMPLETELY DIFFERENT ERAS AND REGIONS OF THE UNIVERSE!
HOW DID THEY--
THIS IS A WARNING! COMPLETE OBEDIENCE IS REQUIRED!
SKASH
YOU KNOW THESE ENEMIES. YOU HAVE KNOWLEDGE OF THE KROTONS. YOU WILL ASSIST US IN OUR CONQUEST OF THIS DIMENSIONAL CONTINUUM.
OR YOU WILL BE OBLITERATED!
'DIMENSIONAL CONTINUUM'? WHERE EXACTLY ARE YOU FROM?

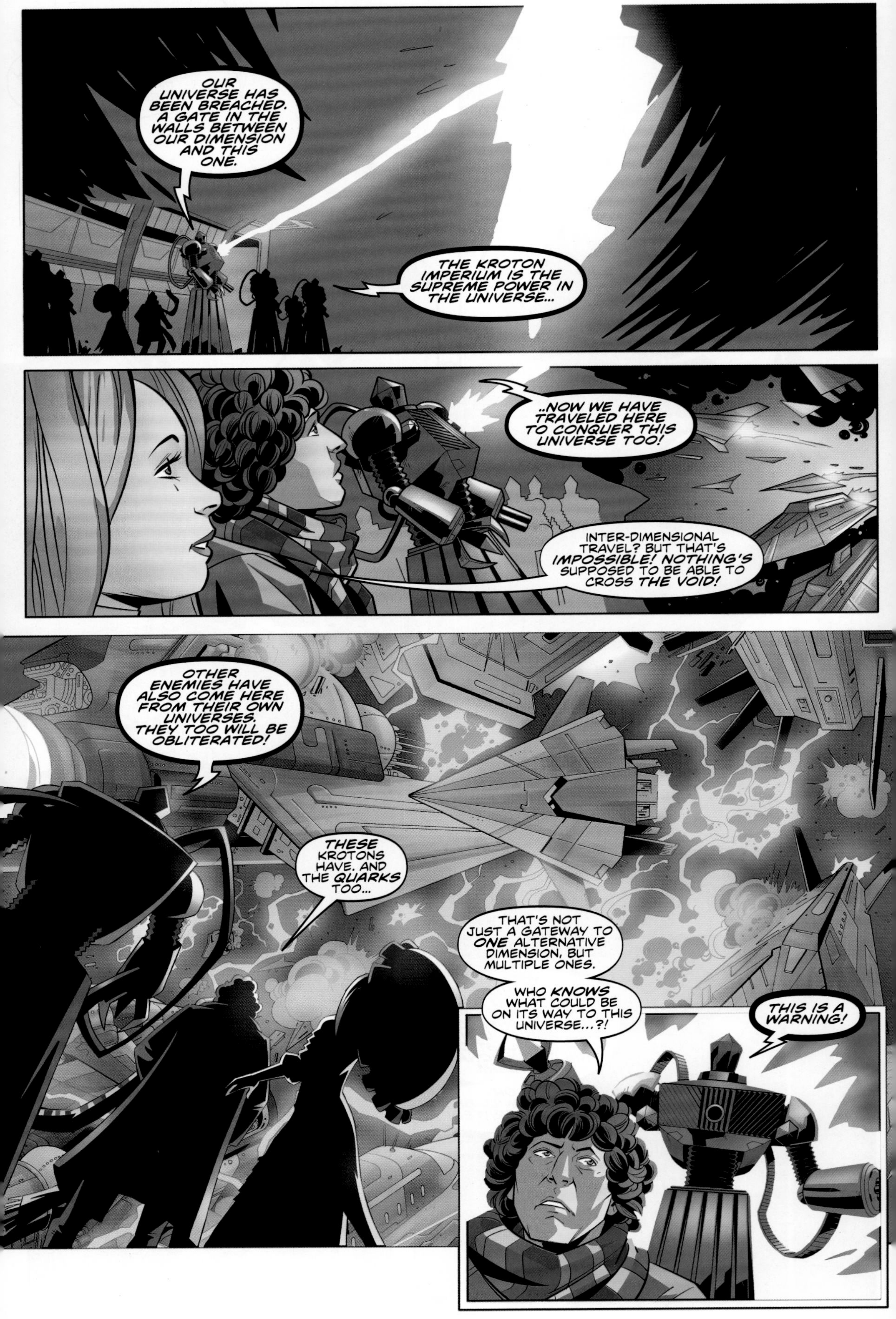
OUR UNIVERSE HAS BEEN BREACHED. A GATE IN THE WALLS BETWEEN OUR DIMENSION AND THIS ONE.
THE KROTON IMPERIUM IS THE SUPREME POWER IN THE UNIVERSE...
..NOW WE HAVE TRAVELED HERE TO CONQUER THIS UNIVERSE TOO!
INTER-DIMENSIONAL TRAVEL? BUT THAT'S IMPOSSIBLE! NOTHING'S SUPPOSED TO BE ABLE TO CROSS THE VOID!
OTHER ENEMIES HAVE ALSO COME HERE FROM THEIR OWN UNIVERSES. THEY TOO WILL BE OBLITERATED!
THESE KROTONS HAVE. AND THE QUARKS TOO...
THAT'S NOT JUST A GATEWAY TO ONE ALTERNATIVE DIMENSION, BUT MULTIPLE ONES.
WHO KNOWS WHAT COULD BE ON ITS WAY TO THIS UNIVERSE...?!
THIS IS A WARNING!

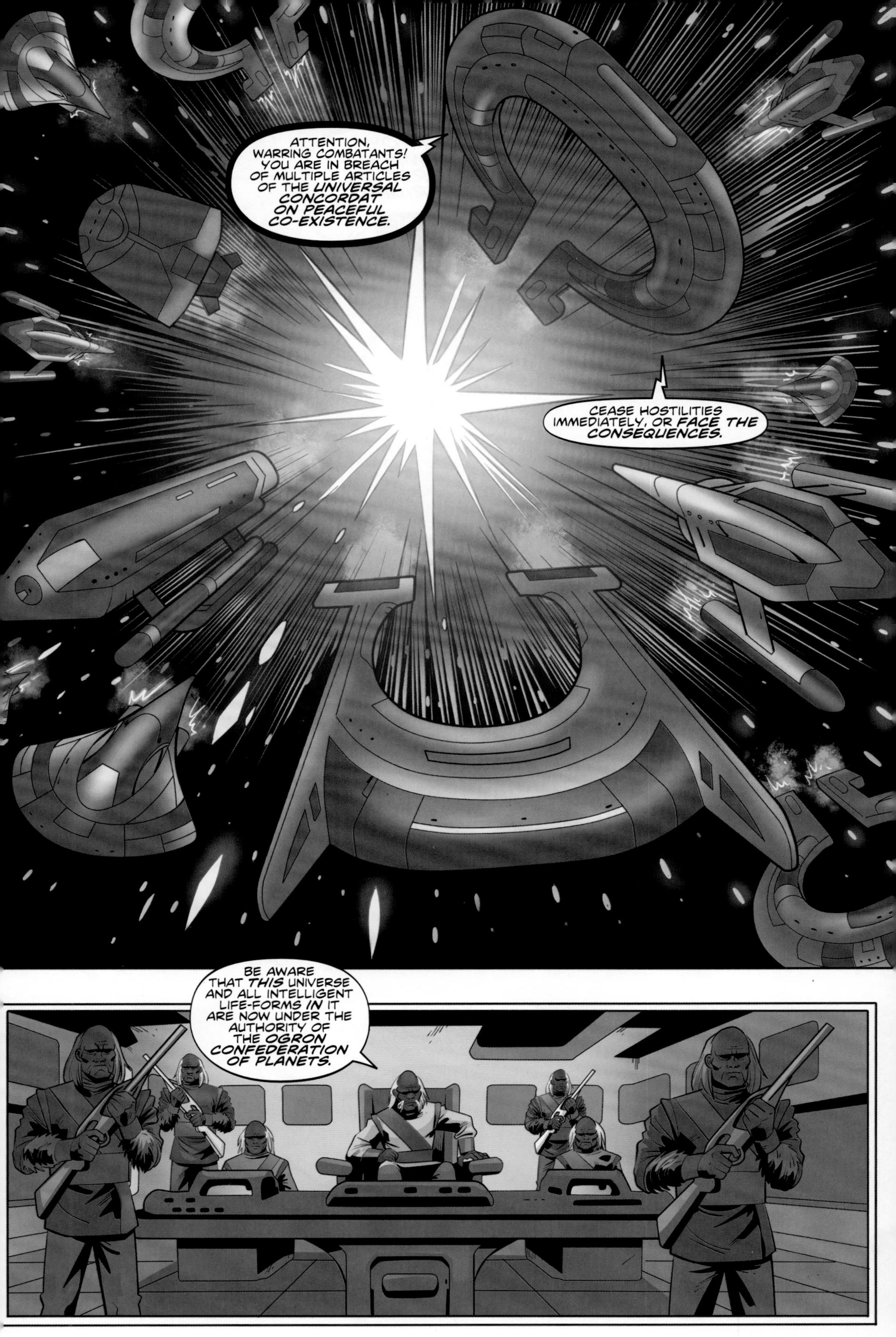
ATTENTION, WARRING COMBATANTS! YOU ARE IN BREACH OF MULTIPLE ARTICLES OF THE *UNIVERSAL CONCORDAT ON PEACEFUL CO-EXISTENCE.*
CEASE HOSTILITIES IMMEDIATELY, OR *FACE THE CONSEQUENCES.*
BE AWARE THAT *THIS* UNIVERSE AND ALL INTELLIGENT LIFE-FORMS *IN* IT ARE NOW UNDER THE AUTHORITY OF THE *OGRON CONFEDERATION OF PLANETS.*

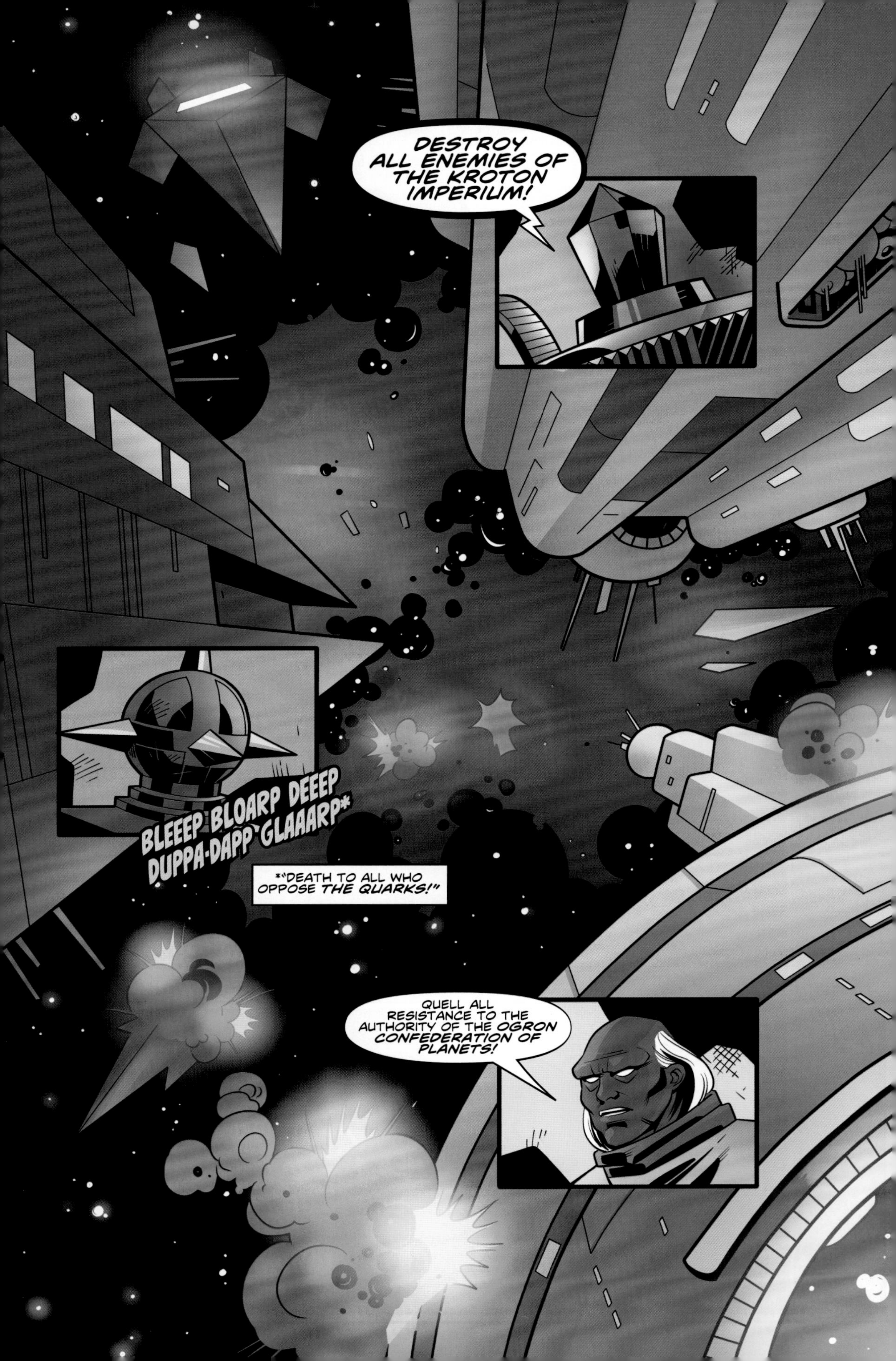
DESTROY ALL ENEMIES OF THE KROTON IMPERIUM!
BLEEEP BLOARP DEEEP DUPPA-DAPP GLAAARP*
*"DEATH TO ALL WHO OPPOSE THE QUARKS!"
QUELL ALL RESISTANCE TO THE AUTHORITY OF THE OGRON CONFEDERATION OF PLANETS!

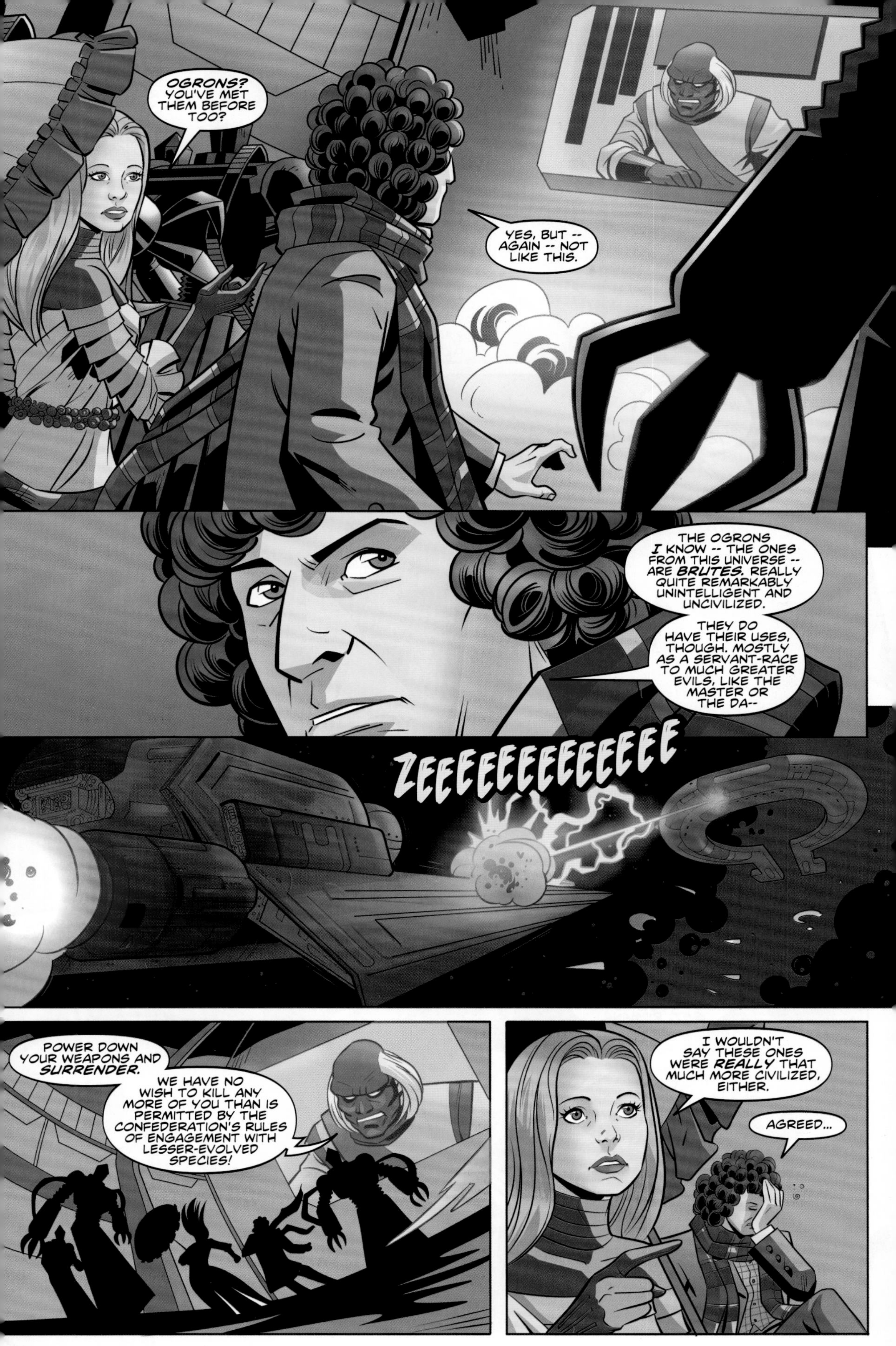
OGRONS? YOU'VE MET THEM BEFORE TOO?
YES, BUT -- AGAIN -- NOT LIKE THIS.
THE OGRONS I KNOW -- THE ONES FROM THIS UNIVERSE -- ARE BRUTES. REALLY QUITE REMARKABLY UNINTELLIGENT AND UNCIVILIZED.
THEY DO HAVE THEIR USES, THOUGH. MOSTLY AS A SERVANT-RACE TO MUCH GREATER EVILS, LIKE THE MASTER OR THE DA--
ZEEEEEEEEEEEEE
POWER DOWN YOUR WEAPONS AND SURRENDER.
WE HAVE NO WISH TO KILL ANY MORE OF YOU THAN IS PERMITTED BY THE CONFEDERATION'S RULES OF ENGAGEMENT WITH LESSER-EVOLVED SPECIES!
I WOULDN'T SAY THESE ONES WERE REALLY THAT MUCH MORE CIVILIZED, EITHER.
AGREED...

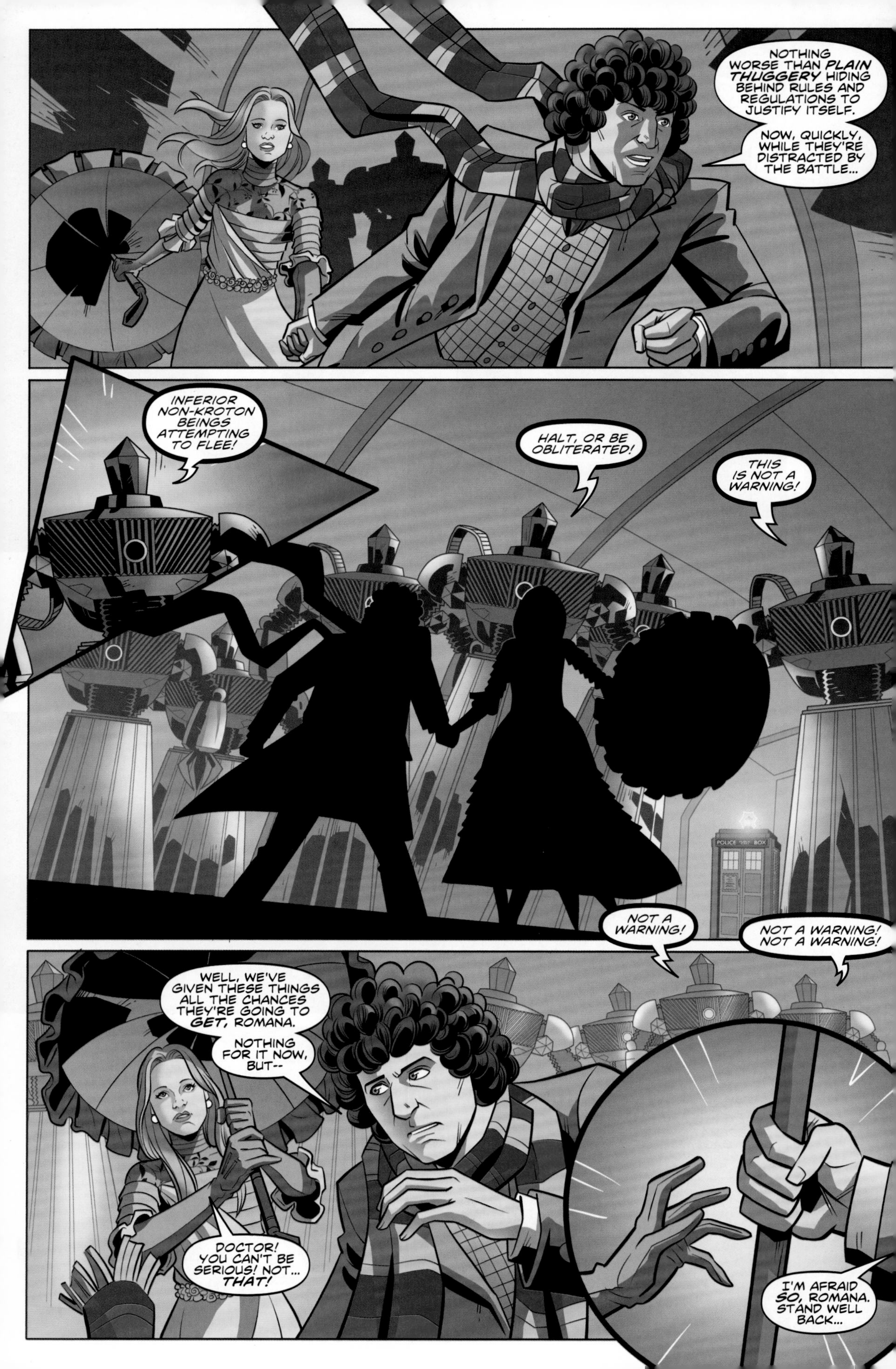
NOTHING WORSE THAN PLAIN THUGGERY HIDING BEHIND RULES AND REGULATIONS TO JUSTIFY ITSELF.
NOW, QUICKLY, WHILE THEY'RE DISTRACTED BY THE BATTLE...
INFERIOR NON-KROTON BEINGS ATTEMPTING TO FLEE!
HALT, OR BE OBLITERATED!
THIS IS NOT A WARNING!
POLICE BOX
NOT A WARNING!
NOT A WARNING! NOT A WARNING!
WELL, WE'VE GIVEN THESE THINGS ALL THE CHANCES THEY'RE GOING TO GET, ROMANA.
NOTHING FOR IT NOW, BUT--
DOCTOR! YOU CAN'T BE SERIOUS! NOT... THAT!
I'M AFRAID SO, ROMANA. STAND WELL BACK...

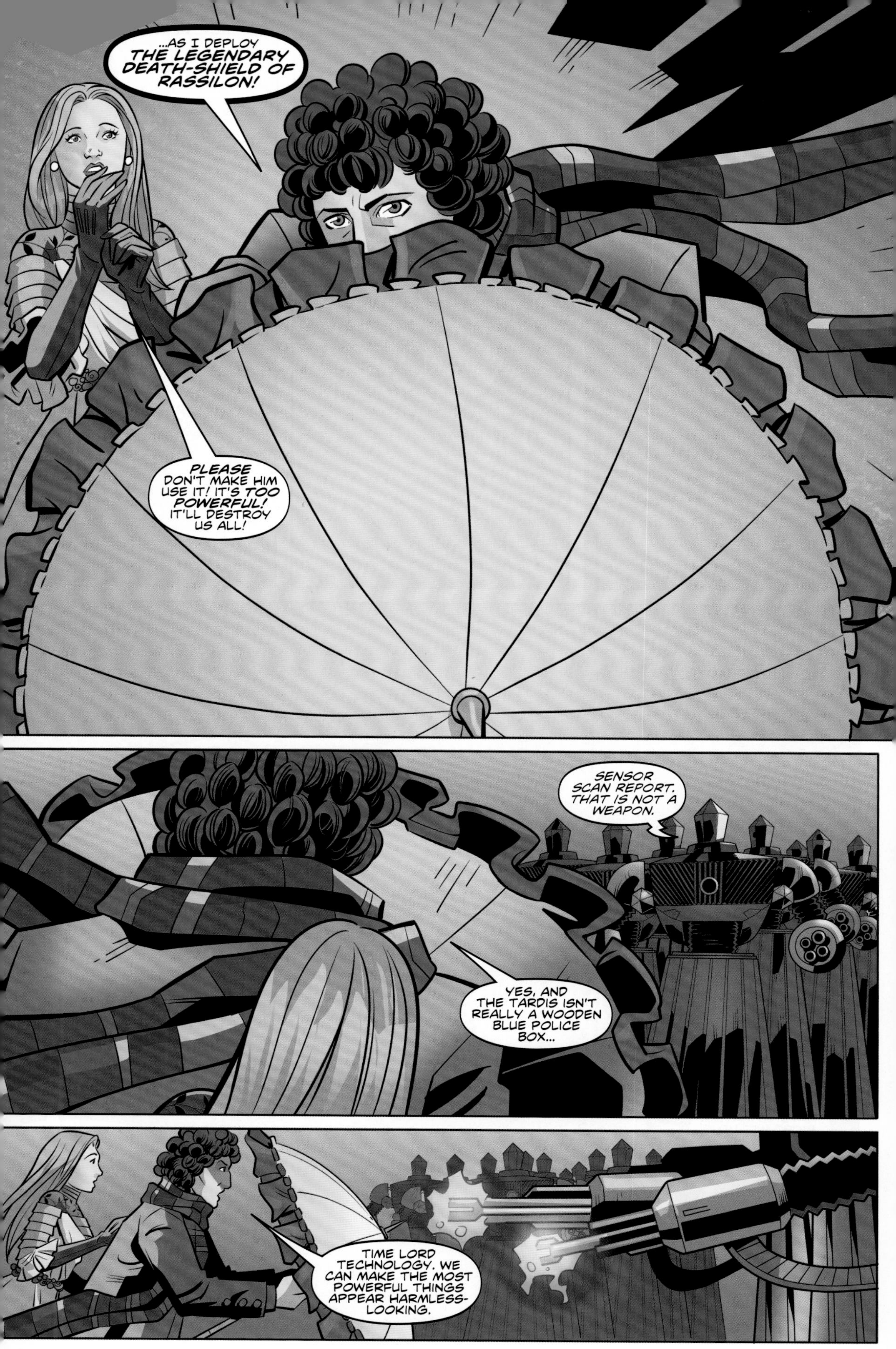
...AS I DEPLOY THE LEGENDARY DEATH-SHIELD OF RASSILON!
PLEASE DON'T MAKE HIM USE IT! IT'S TOO POWERFUL! IT'LL DESTROY US ALL!
SENSOR SCAN REPORT. THAT IS NOT A WEAPON.
YES, AND THE TARDIS ISN'T REALLY A WOODEN BLUE POLICE BOX...
TIME LORD TECHNOLOGY. WE CAN MAKE THE MOST POWERFUL THINGS APPEAR HARMLESS-LOOKING.

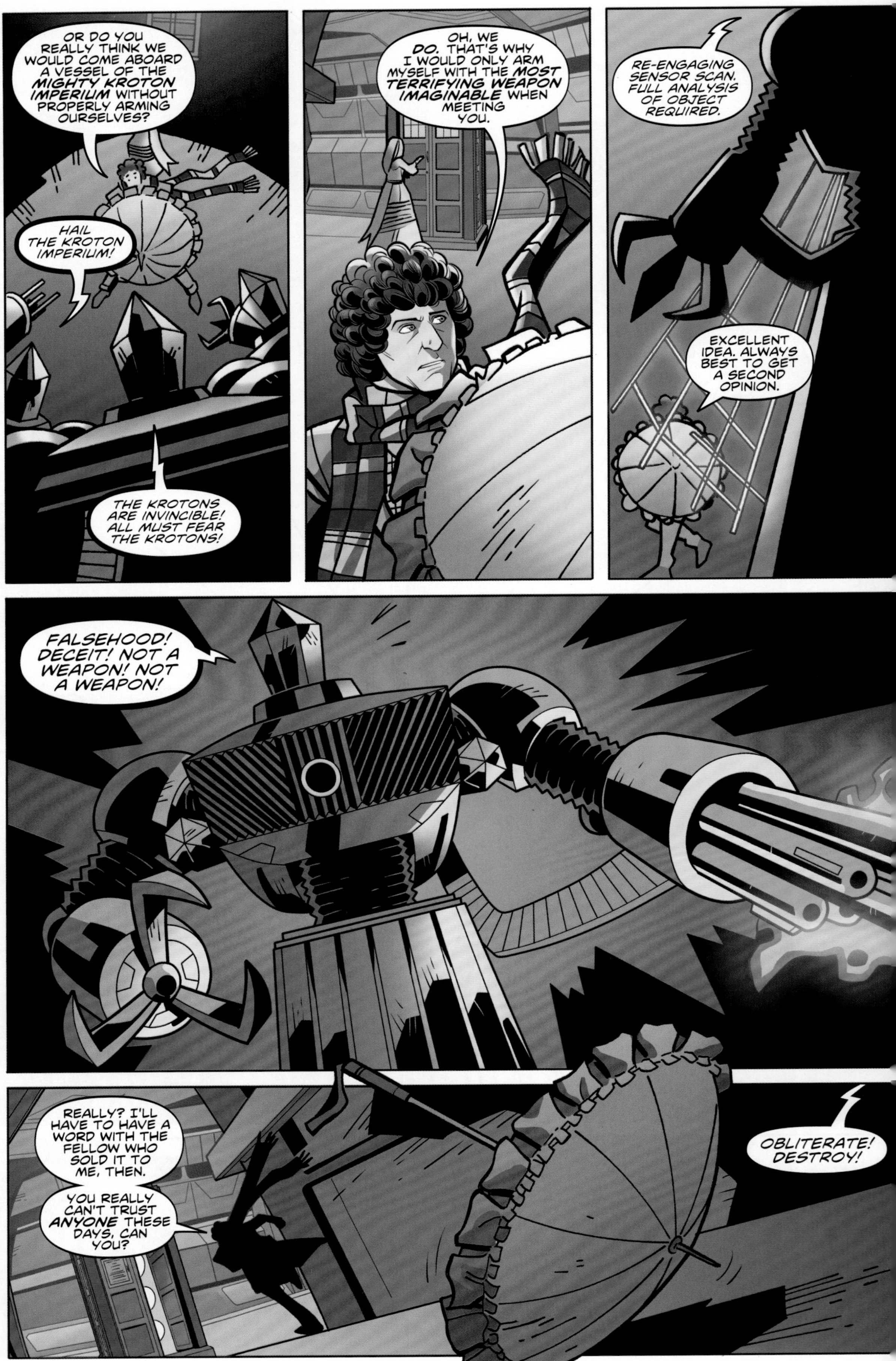
OR DO YOU REALLY THINK WE WOULD COME ABOARD A VESSEL OF THE MIGHTY KROTON IMPERIUM WITHOUT PROPERLY ARMING OURSELVES?
HAIL THE KROTON IMPERIUM!
THE KROTONS ARE INVINCIBLE! ALL MUST FEAR THE KROTONS!
OH, WE DO. THAT'S WHY I WOULD ONLY ARM MYSELF WITH THE MOST TERRIFYING WEAPON IMAGINABLE WHEN MEETING YOU.
RE-ENGAGING SENSOR SCAN. FULL ANALYSIS OF OBJECT REQUIRED.
EXCELLENT IDEA. ALWAYS BEST TO GET A SECOND OPINION.
FALSEHOOD! DECEIT! NOT A WEAPON! NOT A WEAPON!
REALLY? I'LL HAVE TO HAVE A WORD WITH THE FELLOW WHO SOLD IT TO ME, THEN.
YOU REALLY CAN'T TRUST ANYONE THESE DAYS, CAN YOU?
OBLITERATE! DESTROY!

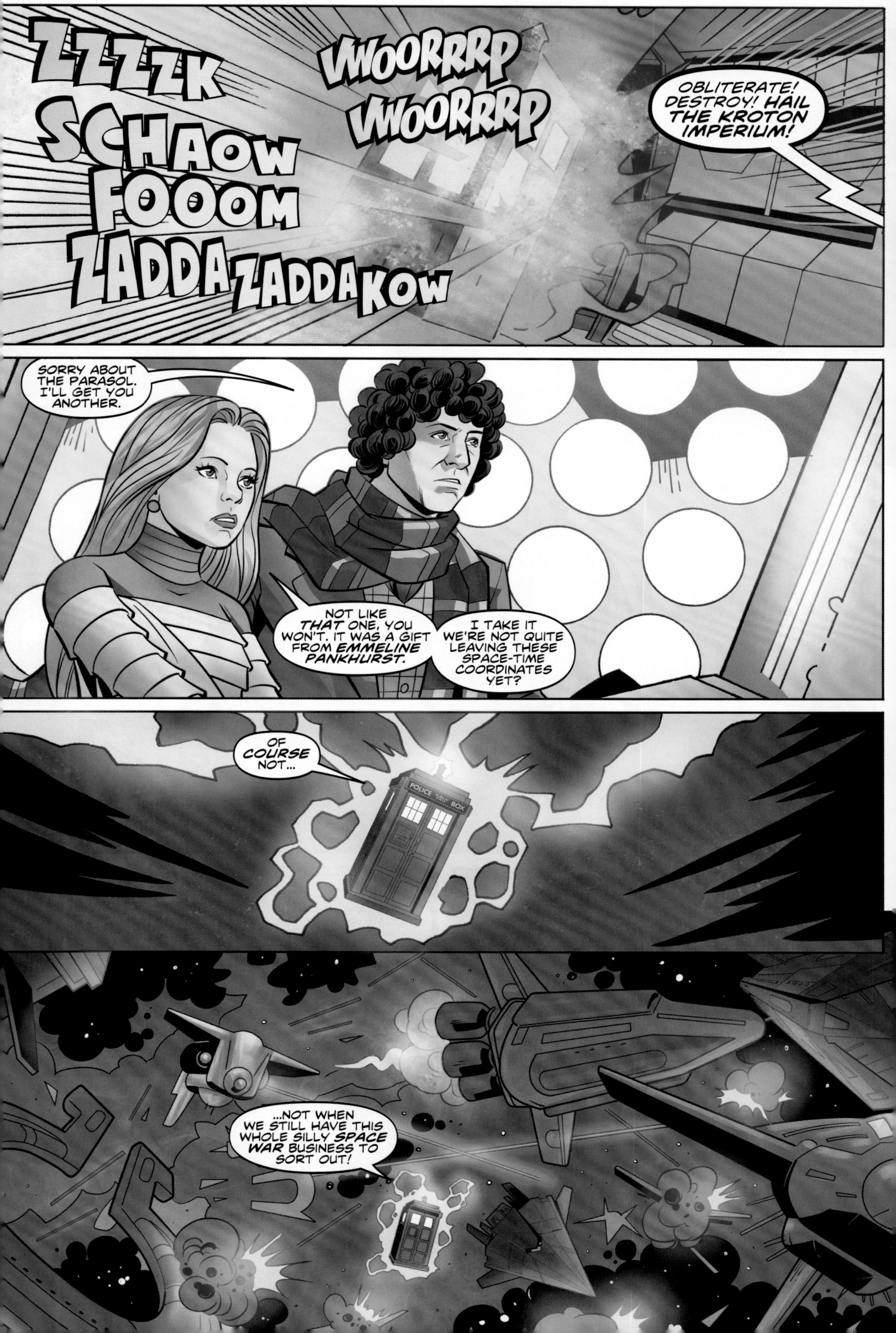
ZZZZK
SCHAOW
FOOOM
ZADDA ZADDA KOW
VWOORRRP
VWOORRRP
OBLITERATE! DESTROY! HAIL THE KROTON IMPERIUM!
SORRY ABOUT THE PARASOL. I'LL GET YOU ANOTHER.
NOT LIKE THAT ONE, YOU WON'T. IT WAS A GIFT FROM EMMELINE PANKHURST.
I TAKE IT WE'RE NOT QUITE LEAVING THESE SPACE-TIME COORDINATES YET?
OF COURSE NOT...
POLICE BOX
...NOT WHEN WE STILL HAVE THIS WHOLE SILLY SPACE WAR BUSINESS TO SORT OUT!

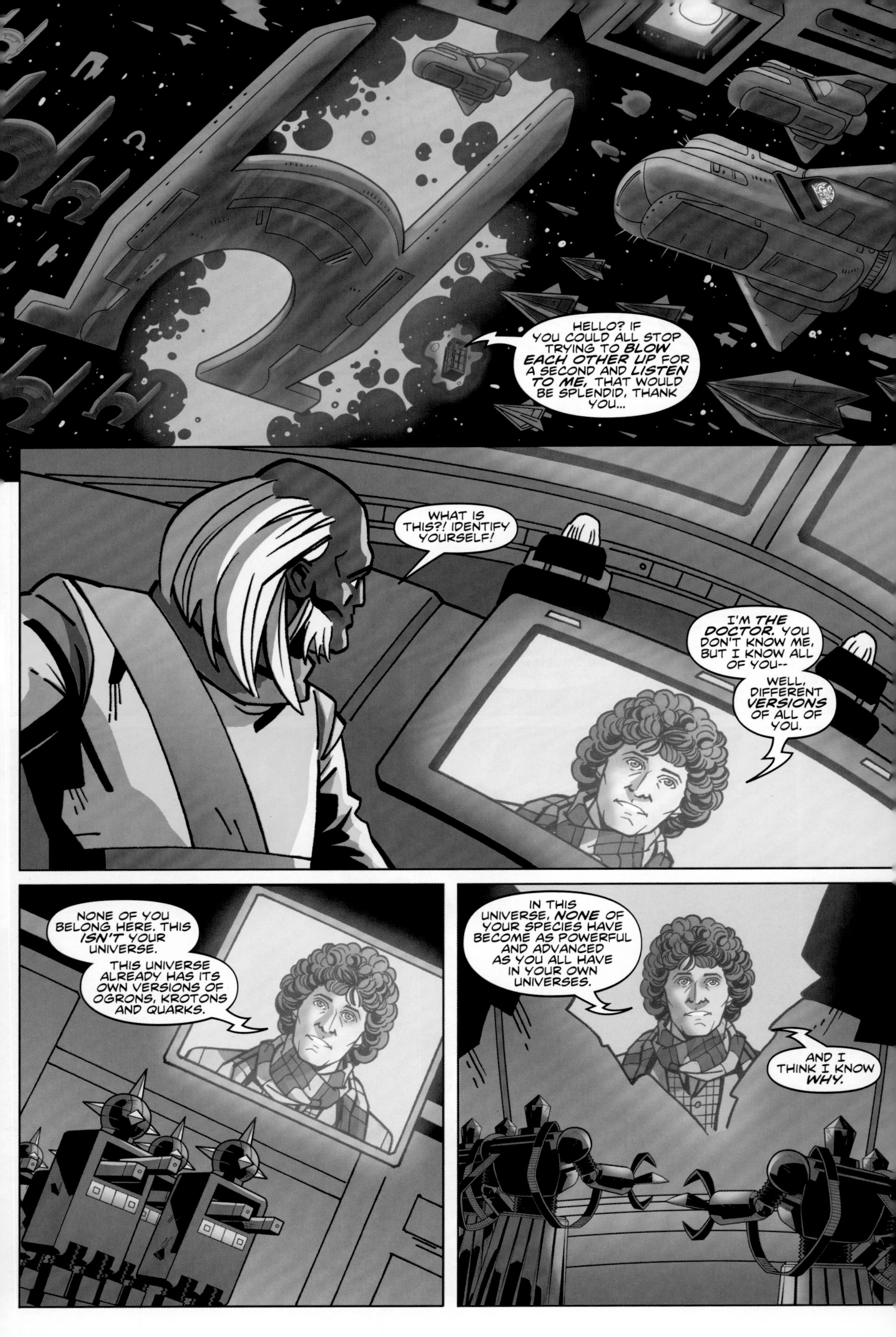
HELLO? IF YOU COULD ALL STOP TRYING TO BLOW EACH OTHER UP FOR A SECOND AND LISTEN TO ME, THAT WOULD BE SPLENDID, THANK YOU...
WHAT IS THIS?! IDENTIFY YOURSELF!
I'M THE DOCTOR. YOU DON'T KNOW ME, BUT I KNOW ALL OF YOU--
WELL, DIFFERENT VERSIONS OF ALL OF YOU.
NONE OF YOU BELONG HERE. THIS ISN'T YOUR UNIVERSE.
THIS UNIVERSE ALREADY HAS ITS OWN VERSIONS OF OGRONS, KROTONS AND QUARKS.
IN THIS UNIVERSE, NONE OF YOUR SPECIES HAVE BECOME AS POWERFUL AND ADVANCED AS YOU ALL HAVE IN YOUR OWN UNIVERSES.
AND I THINK I KNOW WHY.

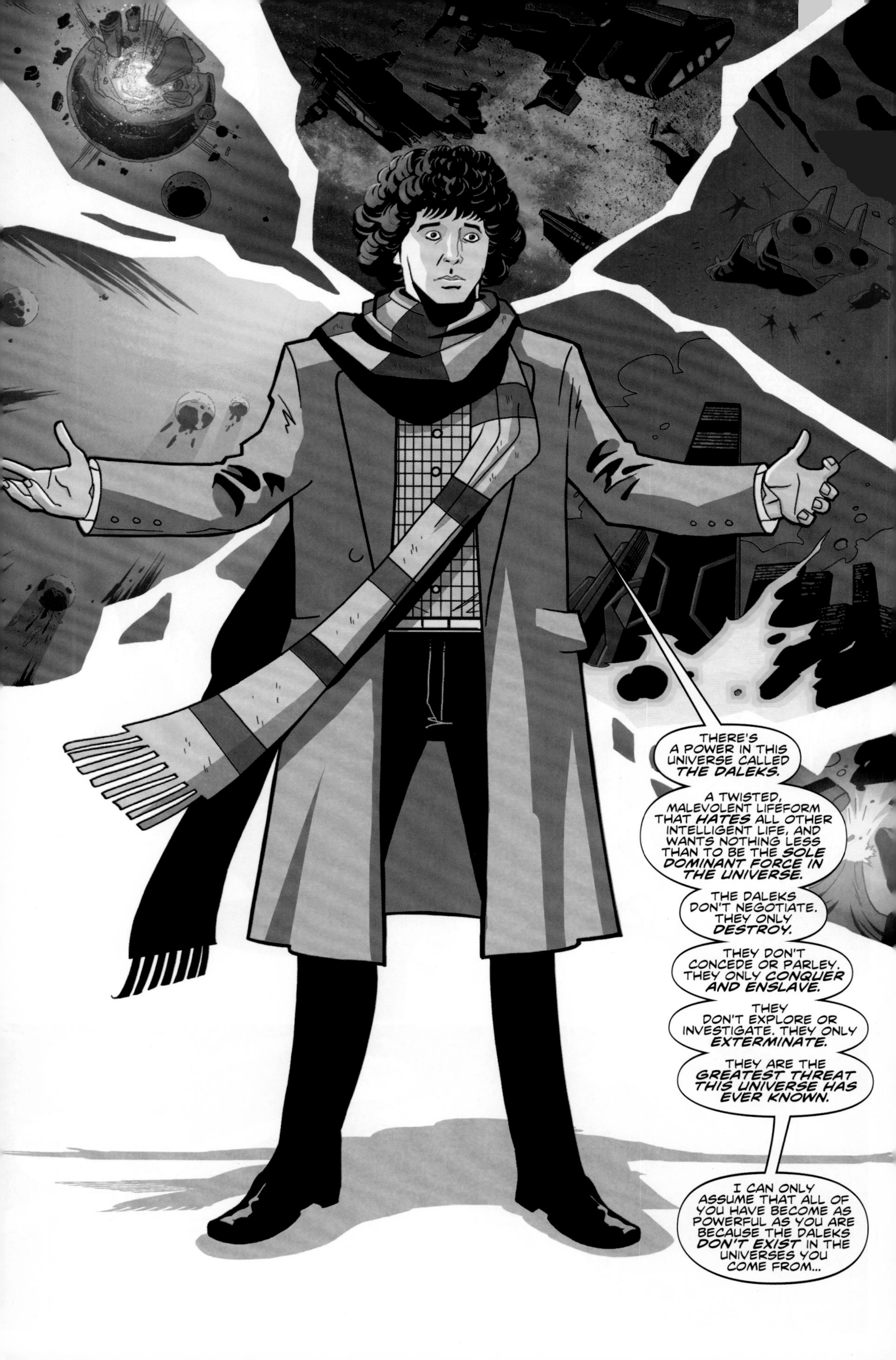
THERE'S A POWER IN THIS UNIVERSE CALLED THE DALEKS.
A TWISTED, MALEVOLENT LIFEFORM THAT HATES ALL OTHER INTELLIGENT LIFE, AND WANTS NOTHING LESS THAN TO BE THE SOLE DOMINANT FORCE IN THE UNIVERSE.
THE DALEKS DON'T NEGOTIATE. THEY ONLY DESTROY.
THEY DON'T CONCEDE OR PARLEY. THEY ONLY CONQUER AND ENSLAVE.
THEY DON'T EXPLORE OR INVESTIGATE. THEY ONLY EXTERMINATE.
THEY ARE THE GREATEST THREAT THIS UNIVERSE HAS EVER KNOWN.
I CAN ONLY ASSUME THAT ALL OF YOU HAVE BECOME AS POWERFUL AS YOU ARE BECAUSE THE DALEKS DON'T EXIST IN THE UNIVERSES YOU COME FROM...

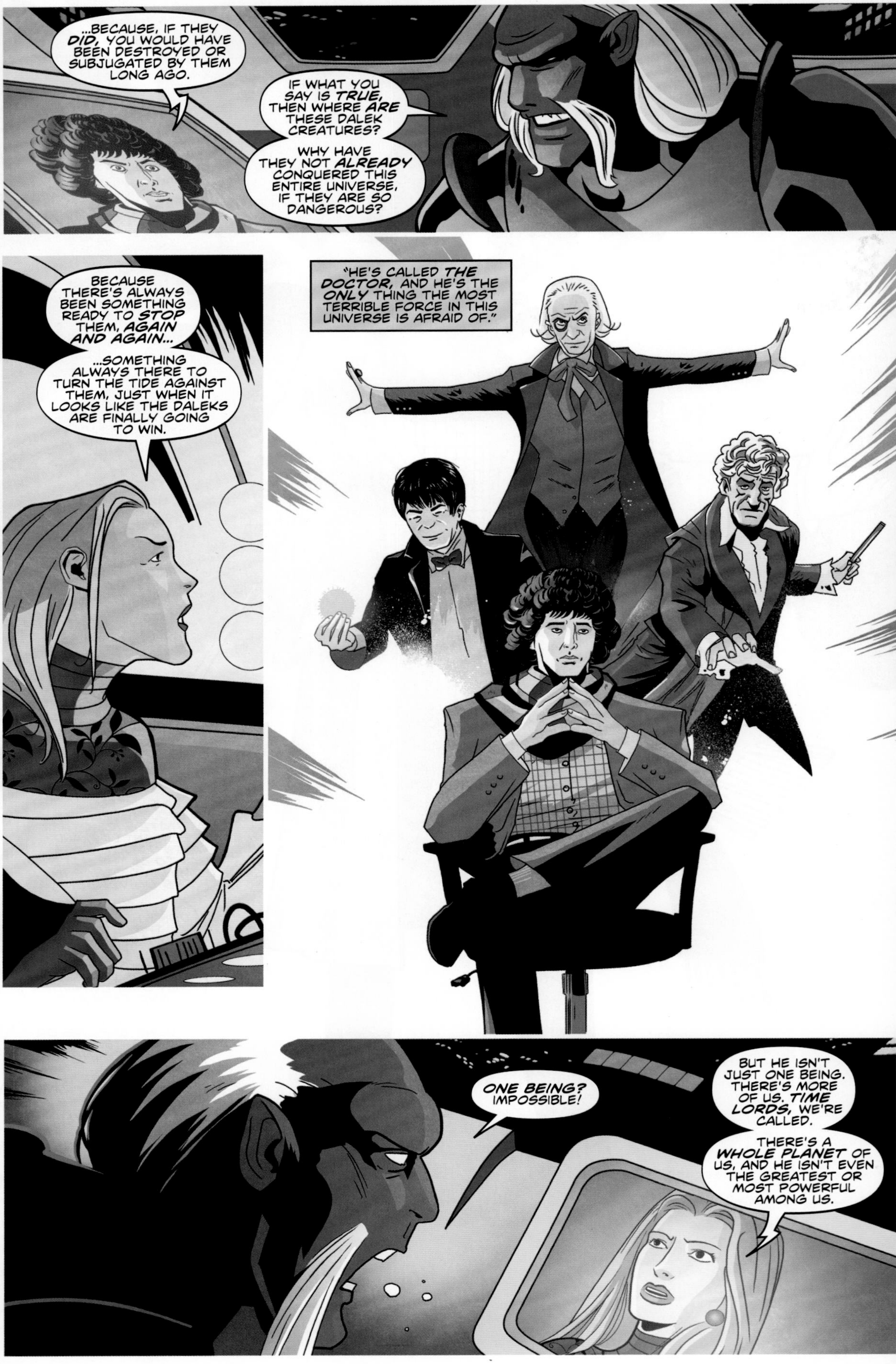
...BECAUSE, IF THEY *DID*, YOU WOULD HAVE BEEN DESTROYED OR SUBJUGATED BY THEM LONG AGO.
IF WHAT YOU SAY IS *TRUE*, THEN WHERE *ARE* THESE DALEK CREATURES?
WHY HAVE THEY NOT *ALREADY* CONQUERED THIS ENTIRE UNIVERSE, IF THEY ARE SO DANGEROUS?
BECAUSE THERE'S ALWAYS BEEN SOMETHING READY TO *STOP* THEM, *AGAIN AND AGAIN...*
...SOMETHING ALWAYS THERE TO TURN THE TIDE AGAINST THEM, JUST WHEN IT LOOKS LIKE THE DALEKS ARE FINALLY GOING TO WIN.
"HE'S CALLED *THE DOCTOR*, AND HE'S THE *ONLY* THING THE MOST TERRIBLE FORCE IN THIS UNIVERSE IS AFRAID OF."
ONE BEING? IMPOSSIBLE!
BUT HE ISN'T JUST ONE BEING. THERE'S MORE OF US. *TIME LORDS*, WE'RE CALLED.
THERE'S A *WHOLE PLANET* OF US, AND HE ISN'T EVEN THE GREATEST OR MOST POWERFUL AMONG US.

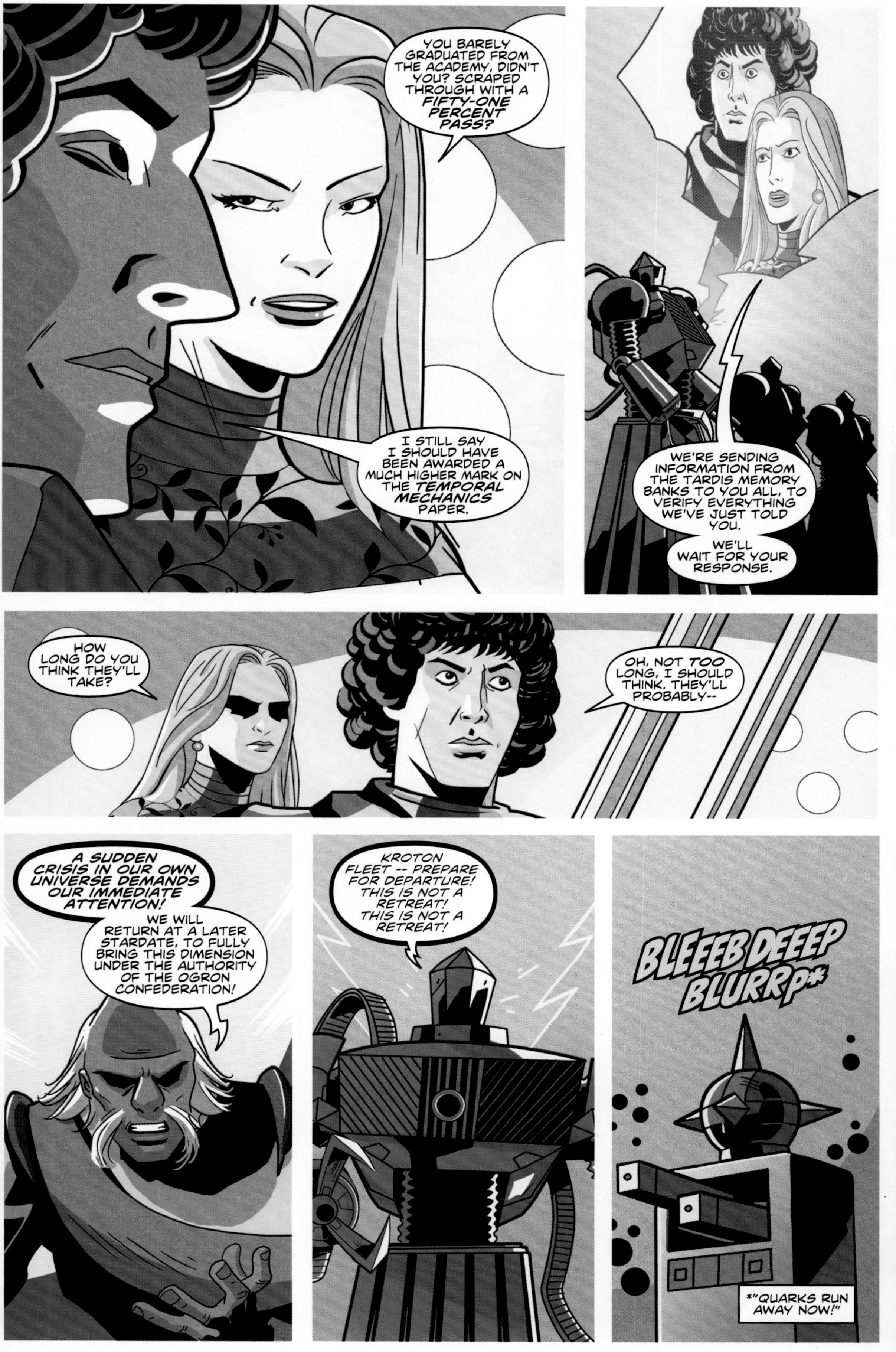
YOU BARELY GRADUATED FROM THE ACADEMY, DIDN'T YOU? SCRAPED THROUGH WITH A *FIFTY-ONE PERCENT PASS?*
I STILL SAY I SHOULD HAVE BEEN AWARDED A MUCH HIGHER MARK ON THE *TEMPORAL MECHANICS* PAPER.
WE'RE SENDING INFORMATION FROM THE TARDIS MEMORY BANKS TO YOU ALL, TO VERIFY EVERYTHING WE'VE JUST TOLD YOU.
WE'LL WAIT FOR YOUR RESPONSE.
HOW LONG DO YOU THINK THEY'LL TAKE?
OH, NOT *TOO* LONG, I SHOULD THINK. THEY'LL PROBABLY--
A SUDDEN CRISIS IN OUR OWN UNIVERSE DEMANDS OUR IMMEDIATE ATTENTION!
WE WILL RETURN AT A LATER STARDATE, TO FULLY BRING THIS DIMENSION UNDER THE AUTHORITY OF THE OGRON CONFEDERATION!
KROTON FLEET -- PREPARE FOR DEPARTURE! THIS IS NOT A RETREAT! THIS IS NOT A RETREAT!
BLEEEB DEEEP BLURRP*
*"QUARKS RUN AWAY NOW!"

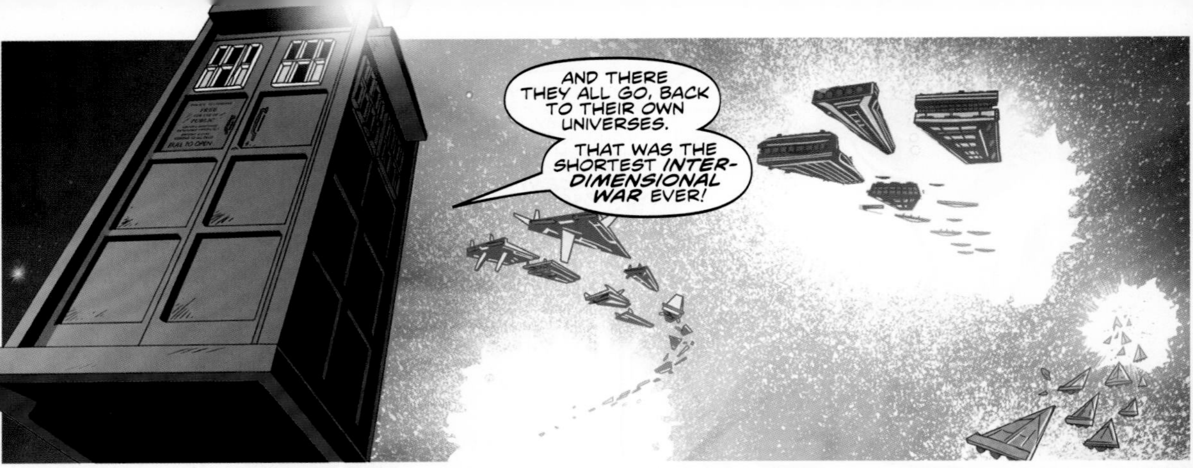
AND THERE THEY ALL GO, BACK TO THEIR OWN UNIVERSES.
THAT WAS THE SHORTEST *INTER-DIMENSIONAL WAR* EVER!

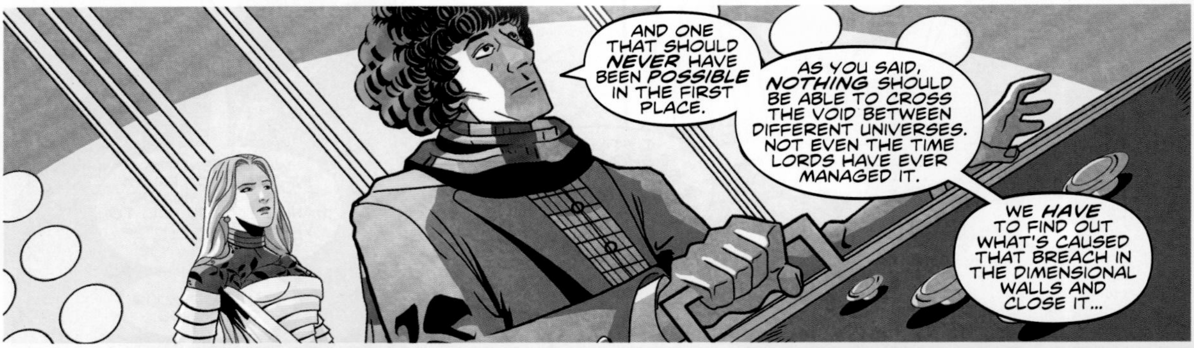
AND ONE THAT SHOULD *NEVER* HAVE BEEN *POSSIBLE* IN THE FIRST PLACE.
AS YOU SAID, *NOTHING* SHOULD BE ABLE TO CROSS THE VOID BETWEEN DIFFERENT UNIVERSES. NOT EVEN THE TIME LORDS HAVE EVER MANAGED IT.
WE *HAVE* TO FIND OUT WHAT'S CAUSED THAT BREACH IN THE DIMENSIONAL WALLS AND CLOSE IT...

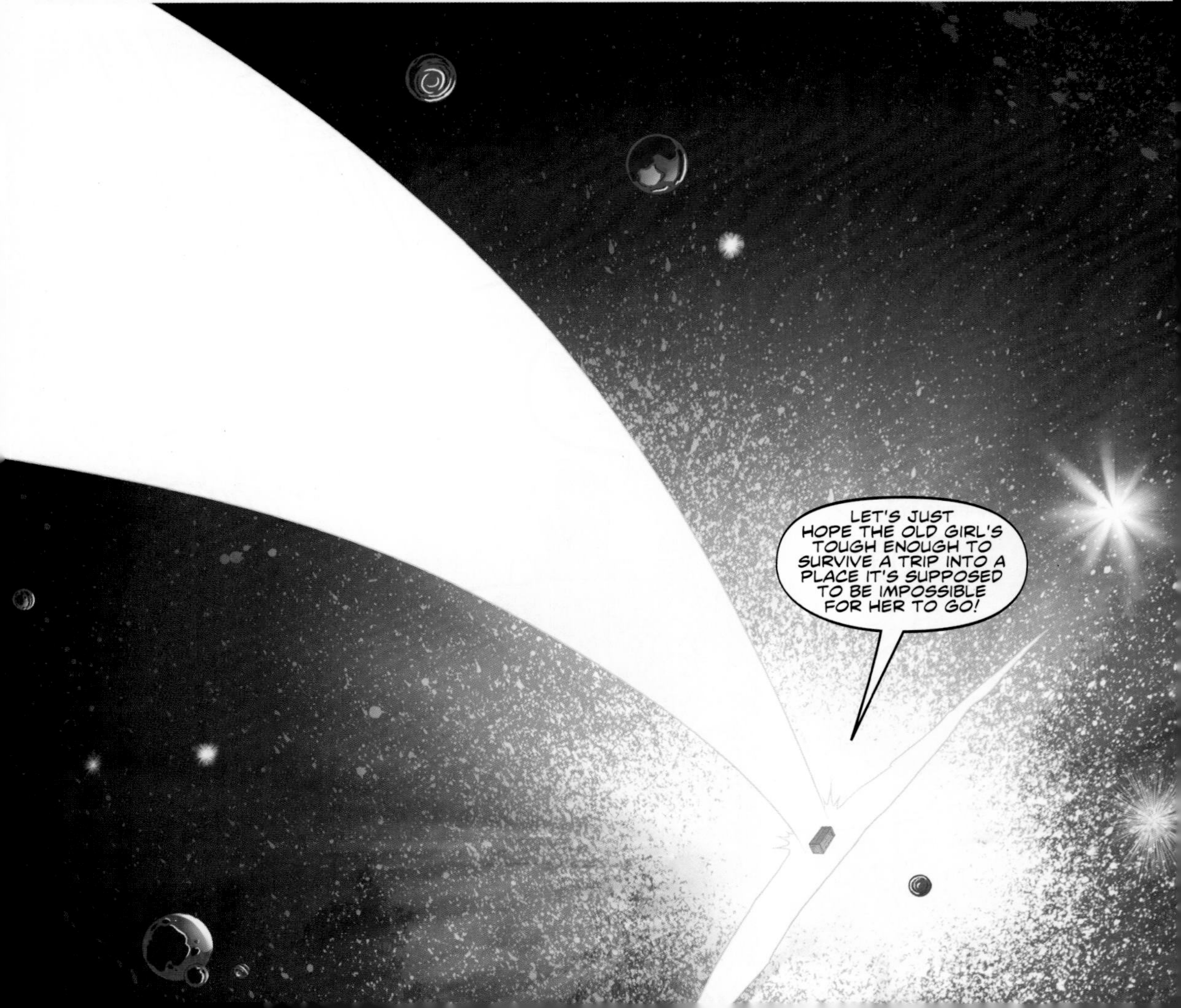
LET'S JUST HOPE THE OLD GIRL'S TOUGH ENOUGH TO SURVIVE A TRIP INTO A PLACE IT'S SUPPOSED TO BE IMPOSSIBLE FOR HER TO GO!

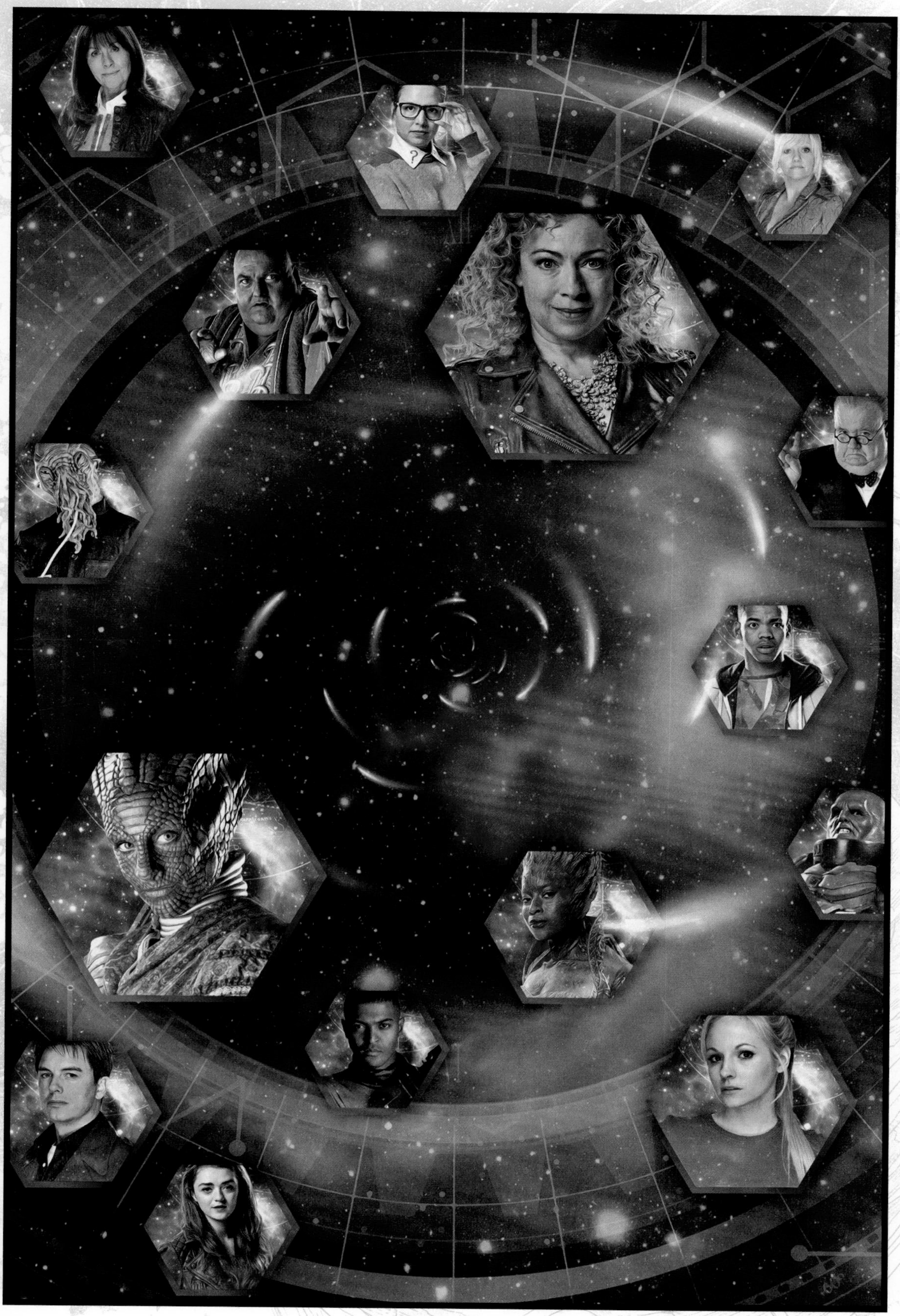

Special #1 Cover B: WILL BROOKS

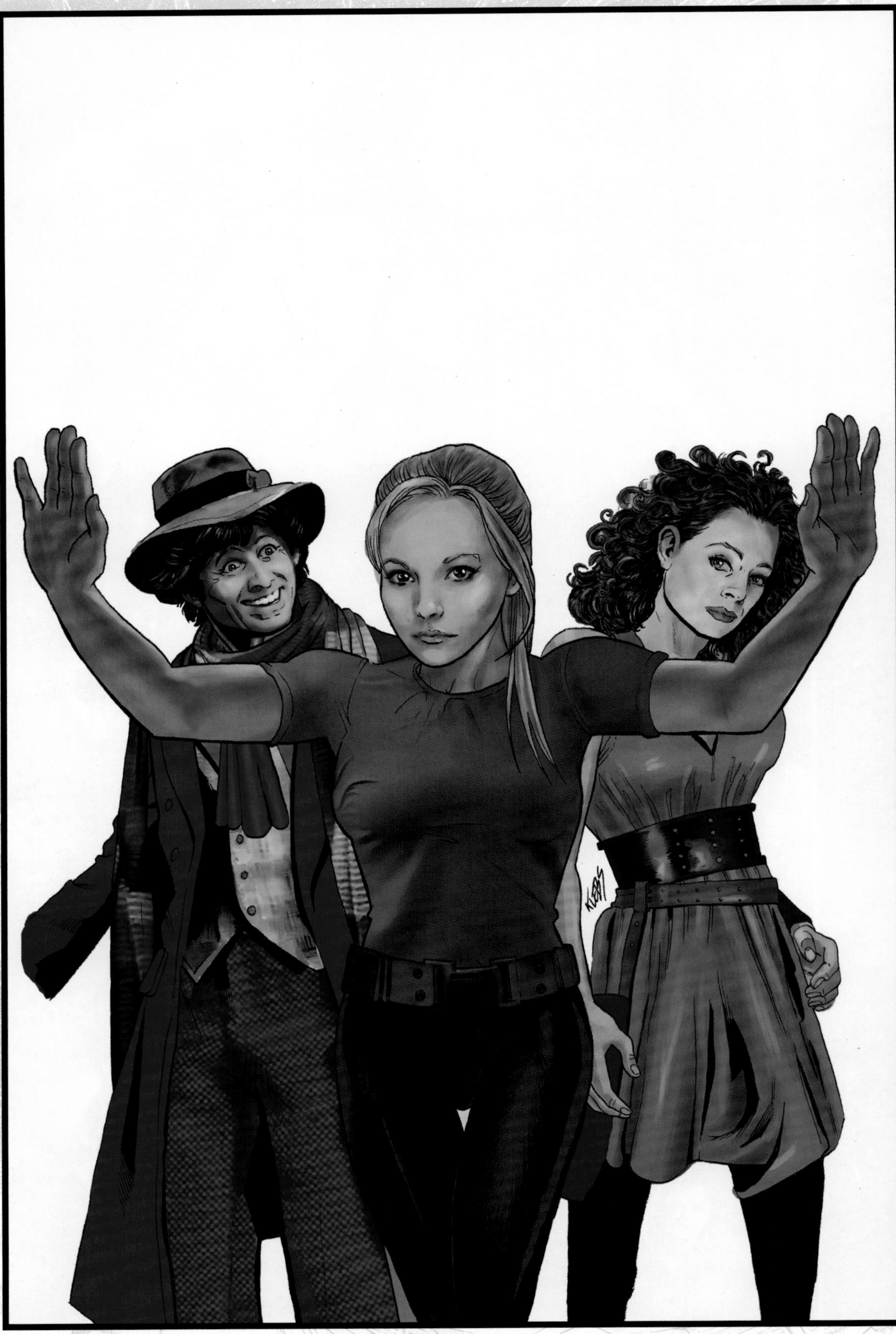

Special #2 Cover A: KLEBS JR

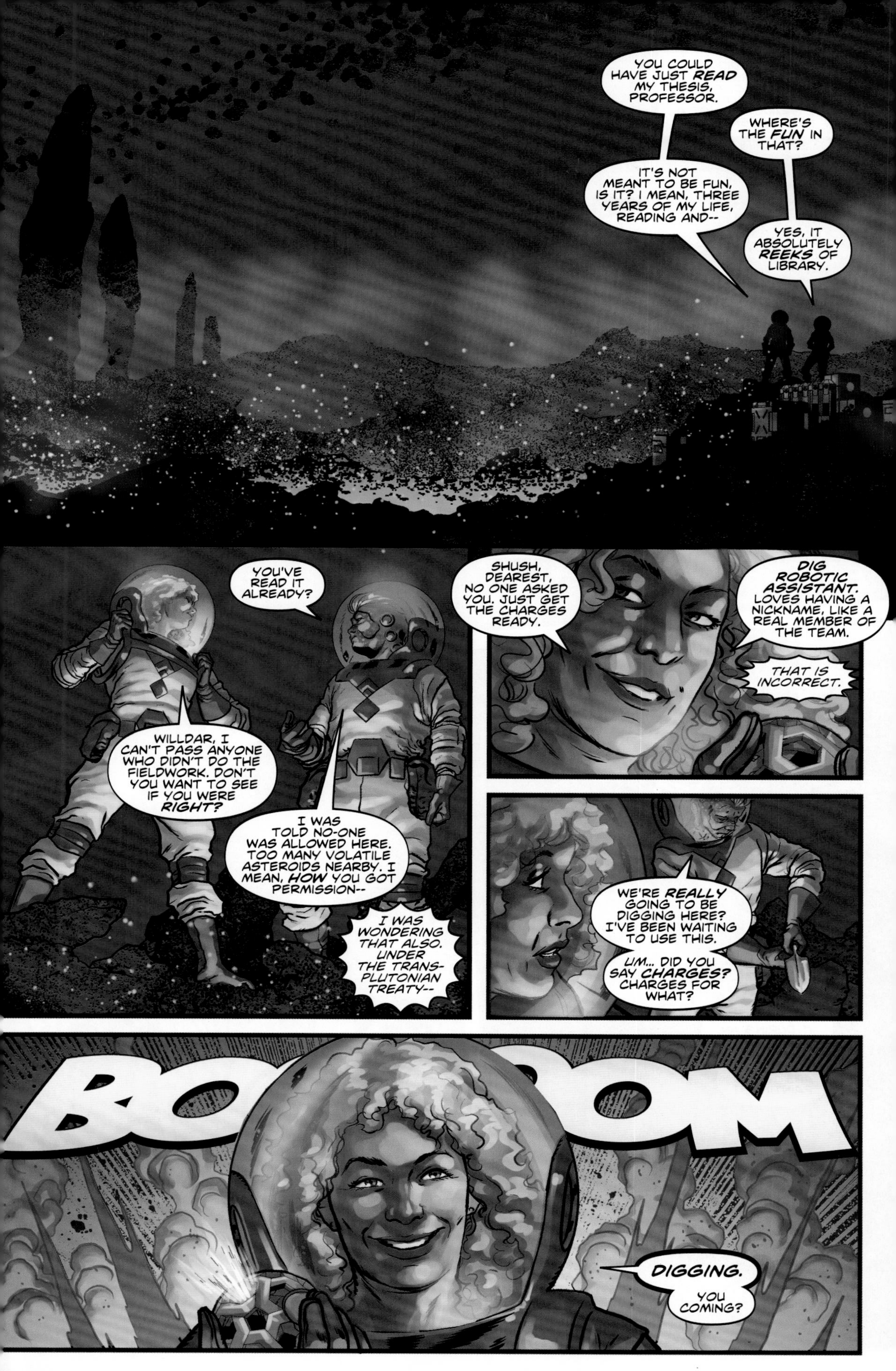
YOU COULD HAVE JUST READ MY THESIS, PROFESSOR.
WHERE'S THE FUN IN THAT?
IT'S NOT MEANT TO BE FUN, IS IT? I MEAN, THREE YEARS OF MY LIFE, READING AND--
YES, IT ABSOLUTELY REEKS OF LIBRARY.
YOU'VE READ IT ALREADY?
WILLDAR, I CAN'T PASS ANYONE WHO DIDN'T DO THE FIELDWORK. DON'T YOU WANT TO SEE IF YOU WERE RIGHT?
I WAS TOLD NO-ONE WAS ALLOWED HERE. TOO MANY VOLATILE ASTEROIDS NEARBY. I MEAN, HOW YOU GOT PERMISSION--
I WAS WONDERING THAT ALSO. UNDER THE TRANS-PLUTONIAN TREATY--
SHUSH, DEAREST, NO ONE ASKED YOU. JUST GET THE CHARGES READY.
DIG ROBOTIC ASSISTANT. LOVES HAVING A NICKNAME, LIKE A REAL MEMBER OF THE TEAM.
THAT IS INCORRECT.
WE'RE REALLY GOING TO BE DIGGING HERE? I'VE BEEN WAITING TO USE THIS.
UM... DID YOU SAY CHARGES? CHARGES FOR WHAT?
BOOOOM
DIGGING.
YOU COMING?

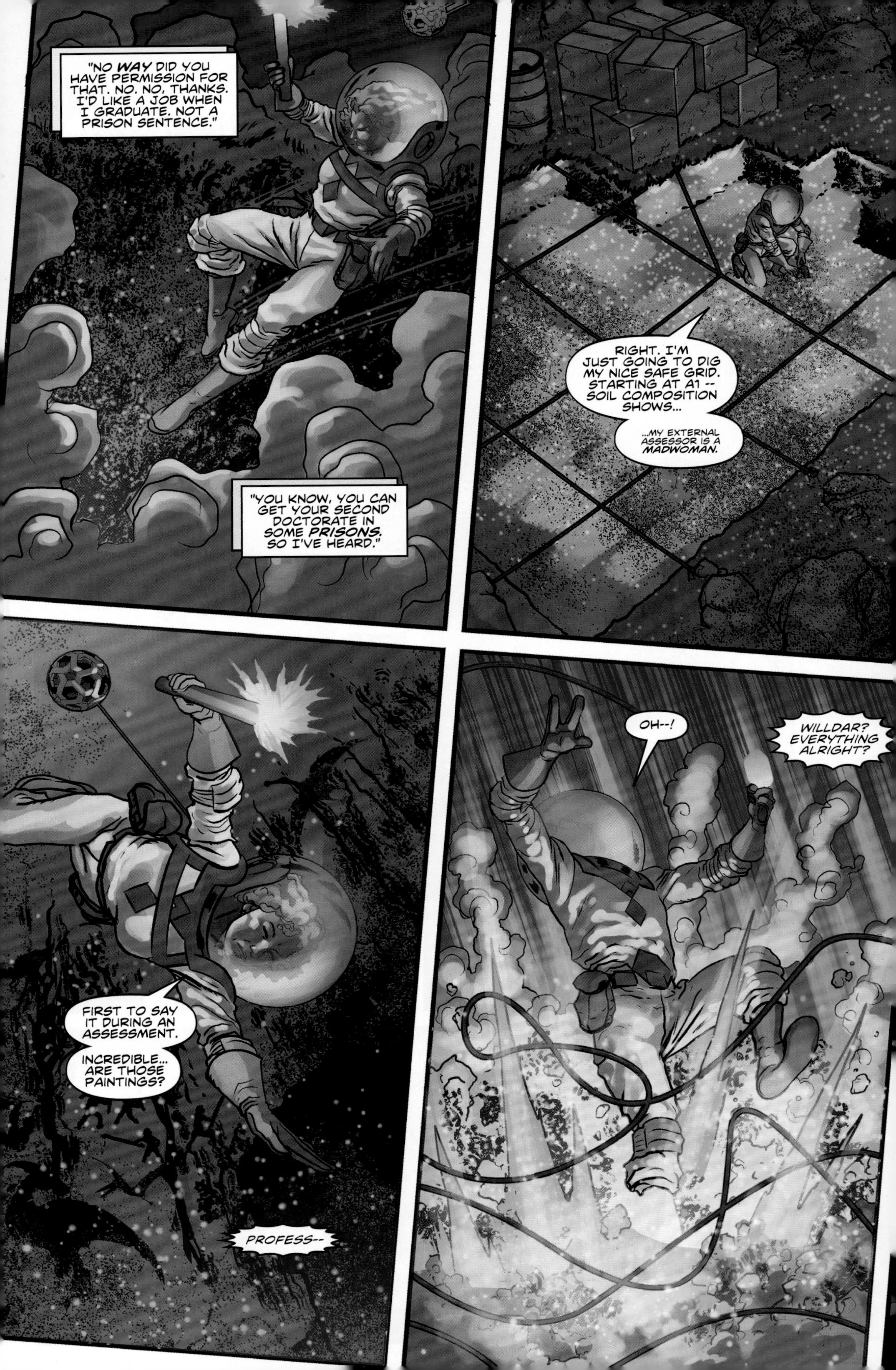
"NO WAY DID YOU HAVE PERMISSION FOR THAT. NO. NO, THANKS. I'D LIKE A JOB WHEN I GRADUATE. NOT A PRISON SENTENCE."
"YOU KNOW, YOU CAN GET YOUR SECOND DOCTORATE IN SOME PRISONS. SO I'VE HEARD."
RIGHT. I'M JUST GOING TO DIG MY NICE SAFE GRID. STARTING AT A1 -- SOIL COMPOSITION SHOWS...
...MY EXTERNAL ASSESSOR IS A MADWOMAN.
FIRST TO SAY IT DURING AN ASSESSMENT.
INCREDIBLE... ARE THOSE PAINTINGS?
PROFESS--
OH--!
WILLDAR? EVERYTHING ALRIGHT?

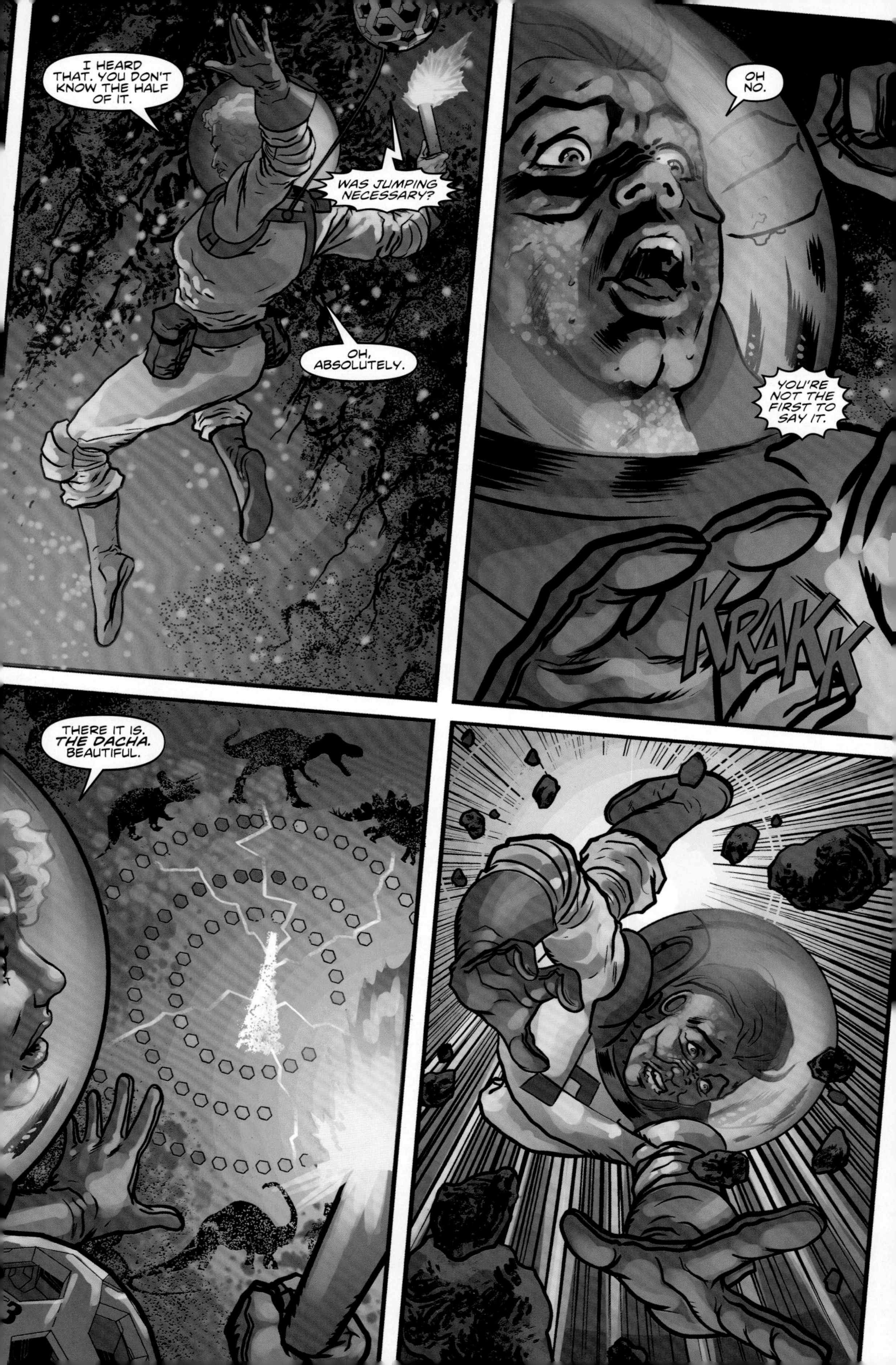
I HEARD THAT. YOU DON'T KNOW THE HALF OF IT.
WAS JUMPING NECESSARY?
OH, ABSOLUTELY.
OH NO.
YOU'RE NOT THE FIRST TO SAY IT.
KRAKK
THERE IT IS. *THE DACHA.* BEAUTIFUL.

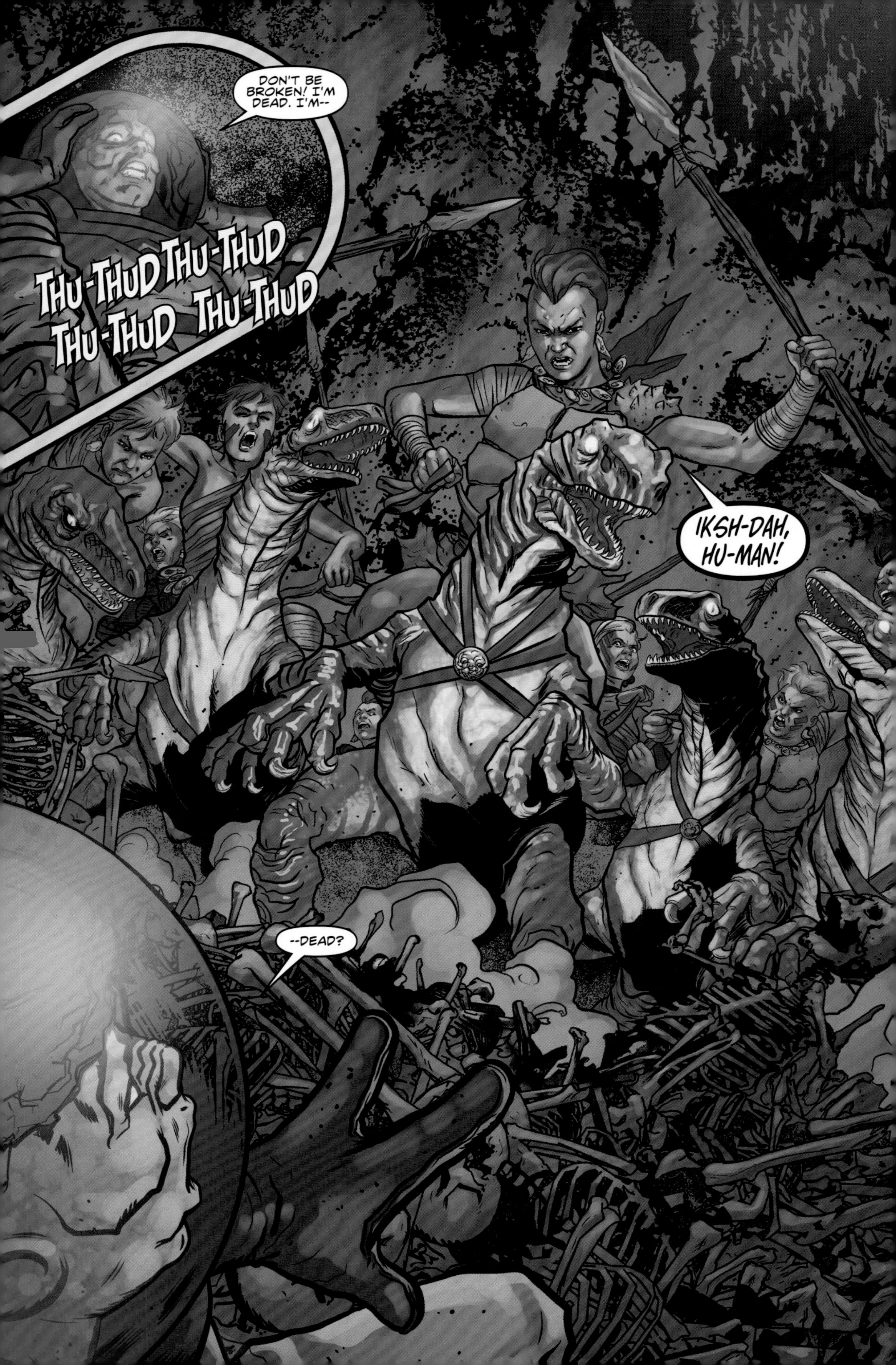
DON'T BE BROKEN! I'M DEAD. I'M--
THU-THUD THU-THUD THU-THUD THU-THUD
IKSH-DAH, HU-MAN!
--DEAD?

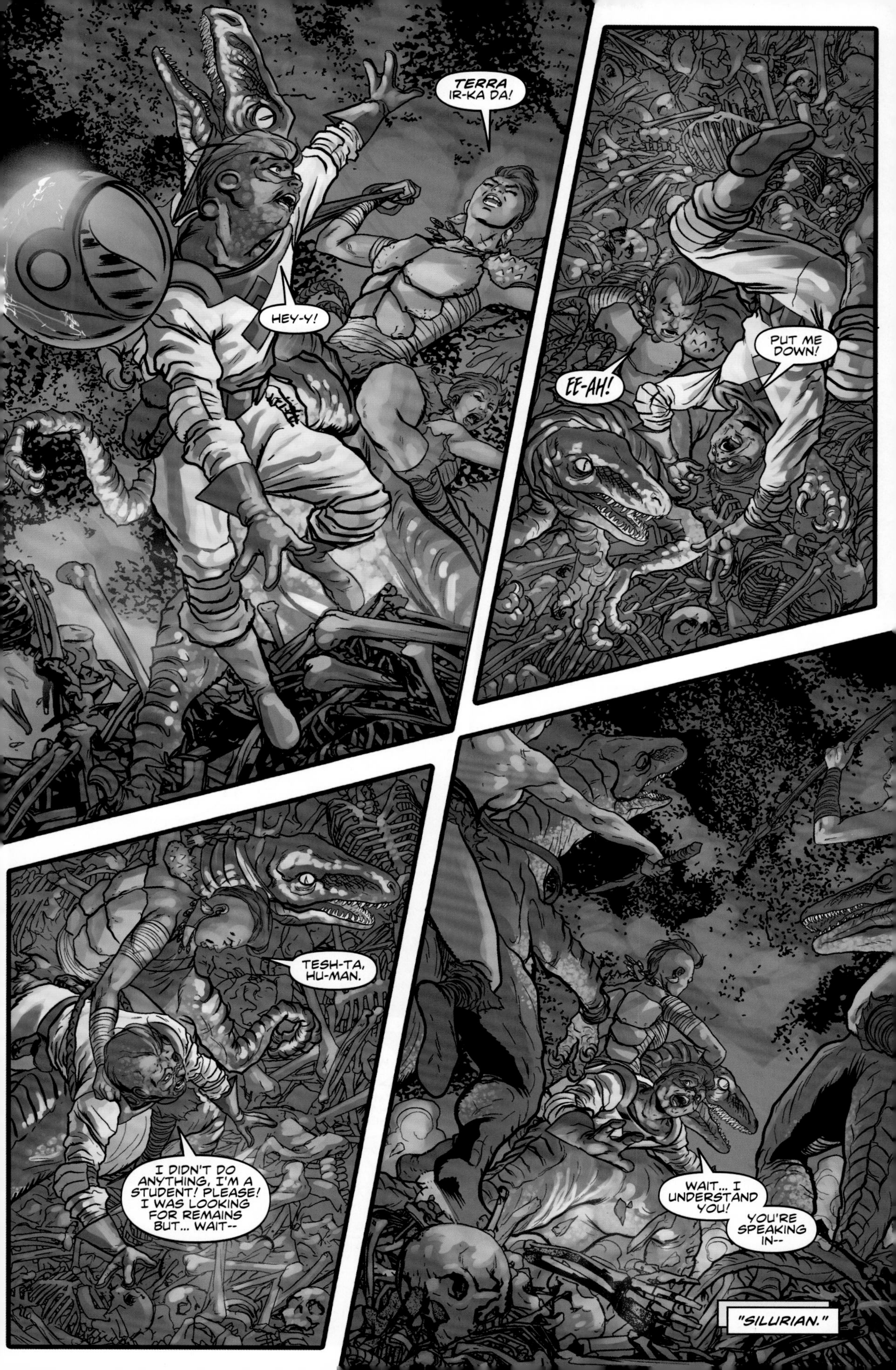
TERRA IR-KA DA!
HEY-Y!
EE-AH!
PUT ME DOWN!
TESH-TA, HU-MAN.
I DIDN'T DO ANYTHING, I'M A STUDENT! PLEASE! I WAS LOOKING FOR REMAINS BUT... WAIT--
WAIT... I UNDERSTAND YOU!
YOU'RE SPEAKING IN--
"SILURIAN."

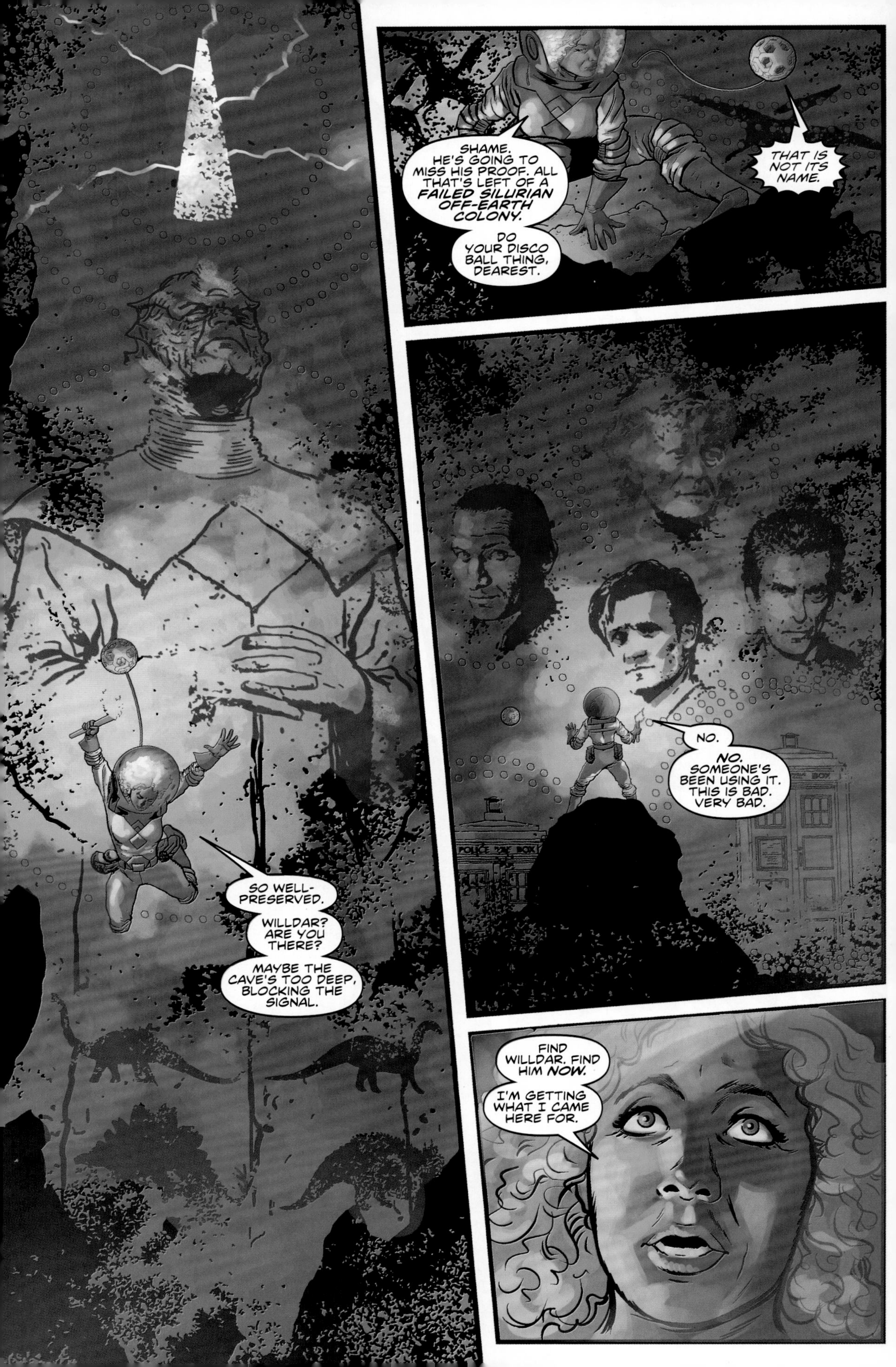
SO WELL-PRESERVED.
WILLDAR? ARE YOU THERE?
MAYBE THE CAVE'S TOO DEEP, BLOCKING THE SIGNAL.
SHAME. HE'S GOING TO MISS HIS PROOF. ALL THAT'S LEFT OF A FAILED SILURIAN OFF-EARTH COLONY.
DO YOUR DISCO BALL THING, DEAREST.
THAT IS NOT ITS NAME.
NO.
NO. SOMEONE'S BEEN USING IT. THIS IS BAD. VERY BAD.
POLICE BOX
FIND WILLDAR. FIND HIM NOW.
I'M GETTING WHAT I CAME HERE FOR.

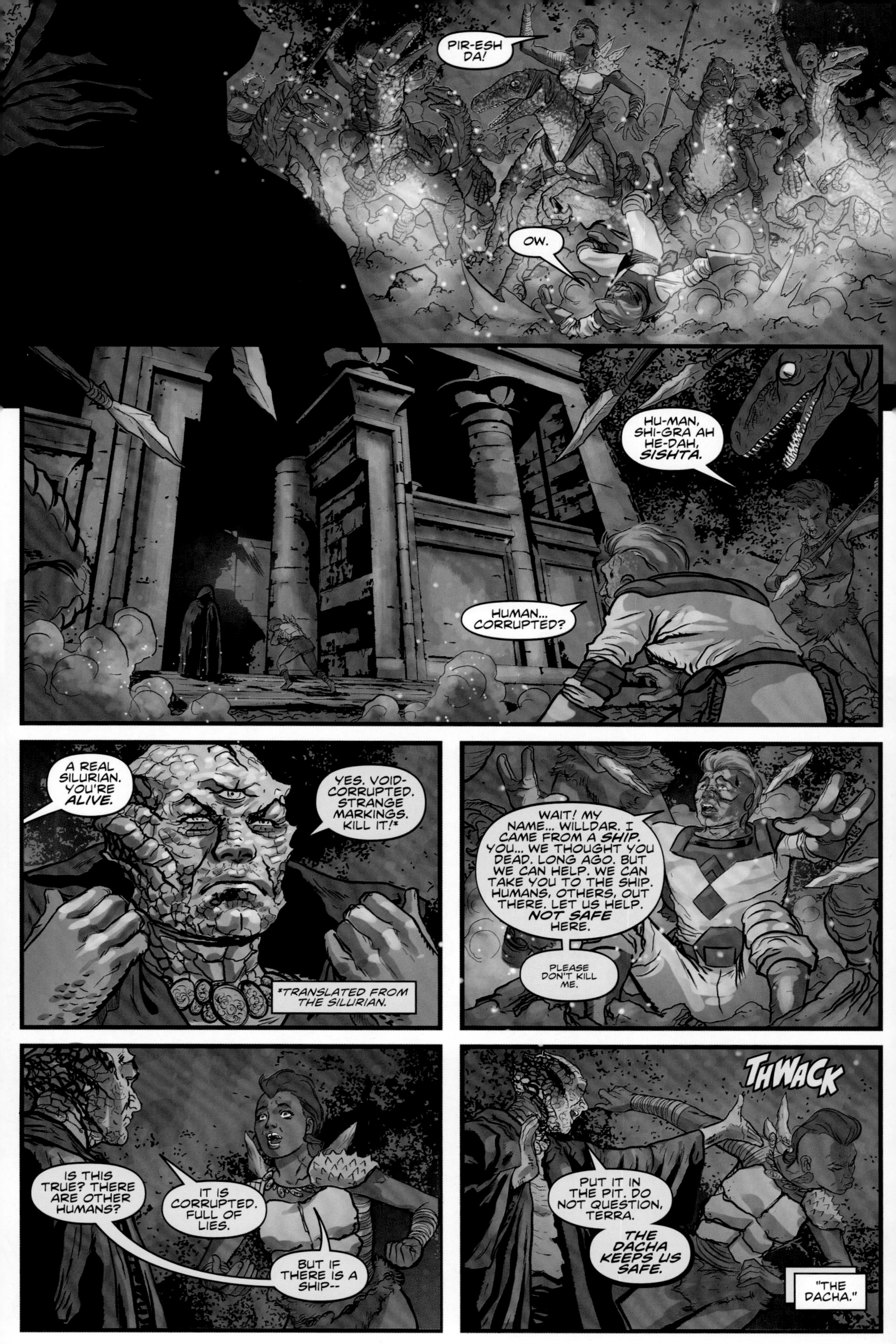
PIR-ESH DA!
OW.
HU-MAN, SHI-GRA AH HE-DAH, SISHTA.
HUMAN... CORRUPTED?
A REAL SILURIAN. YOU'RE ALIVE.
YES. VOID-CORRUPTED. STRANGE MARKINGS. KILL IT!*
*TRANSLATED FROM THE SILURIAN.
WAIT! MY NAME... WILLDAR. I CAME FROM A SHIP. YOU... WE THOUGHT YOU DEAD. LONG AGO. BUT WE CAN HELP. WE CAN TAKE YOU TO THE SHIP. HUMANS, OTHERS, OUT THERE. LET US HELP. NOT SAFE HERE.
PLEASE DON'T KILL ME.
IS THIS TRUE? THERE ARE OTHER HUMANS?
IT IS CORRUPTED. FULL OF LIES.
BUT IF THERE IS A SHIP--
THWACK
PUT IT IN THE PIT. DO NOT QUESTION, TERRA.
THE DACHA KEEPS US SAFE.
"THE DACHA."

PROFESSOR SONG, TIME TO DIG SITE ESTIMATED THREE MINUTES AND TWENTY FOUR SECONDS.

FASCINATING. UPDATE ME WHEN YOU GET THERE.

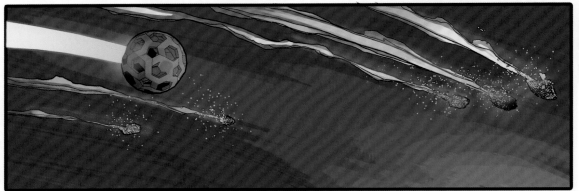

PROFESSOR SONG.

THERE HAS BEEN A DEVELOPMENT.

YOU'RE NOT THERE YET, SO -- AND I'M JUST GUESSING HERE -- AN EXPLODING ASTEROID LIKELY TO CAUSE A CHAIN REACTION AND ENDANGER THE PLANETOID?

CORRECT. WOULD YOU LIKE A DESTRUCTION TIMESCALE?

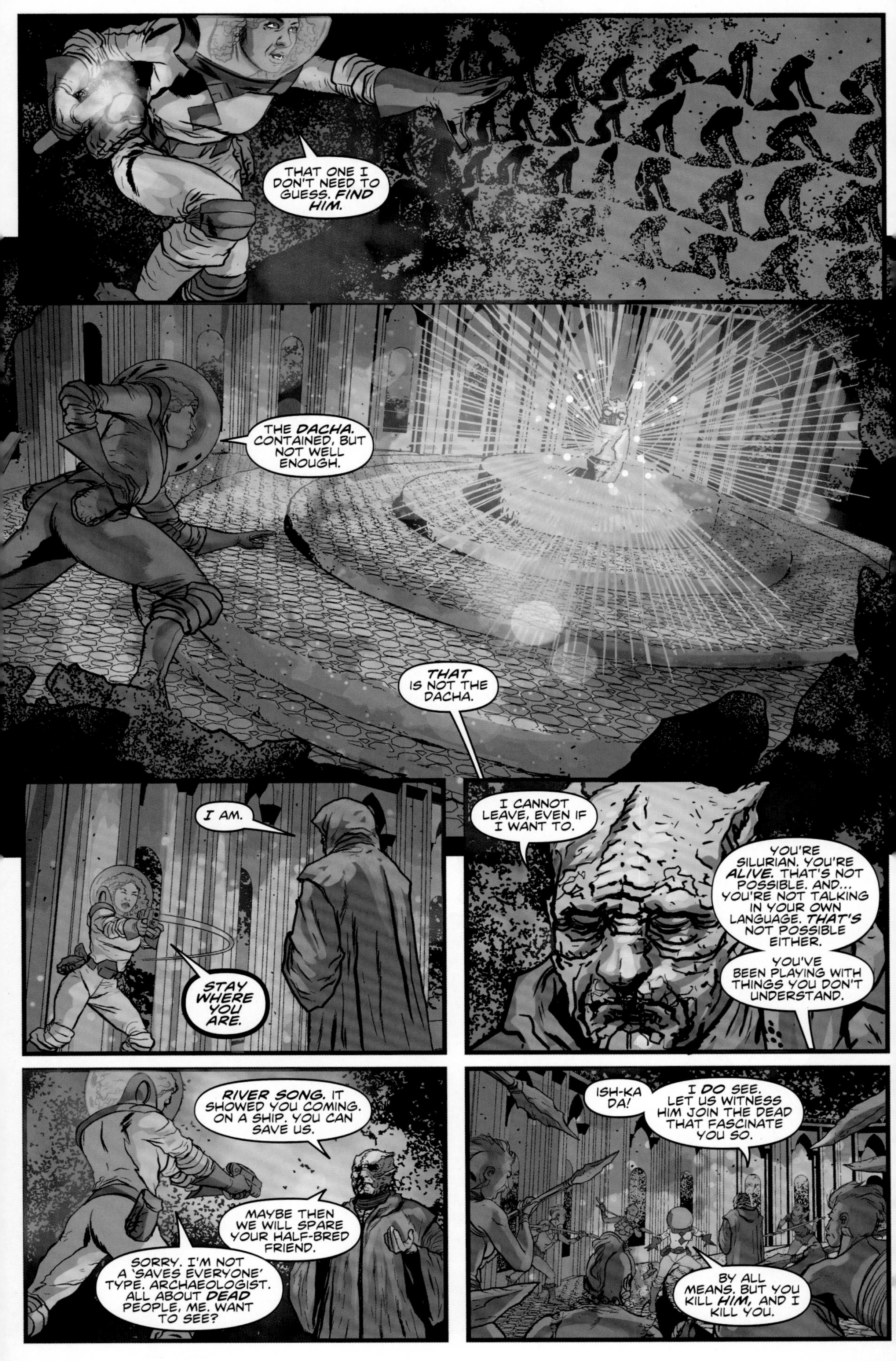

THAT ONE I DON'T NEED TO GUESS. FIND HIM.
THE DACHA. CONTAINED, BUT NOT WELL ENOUGH.
THAT IS NOT THE DACHA.
I AM.
STAY WHERE YOU ARE.
I CANNOT LEAVE, EVEN IF I WANT TO.
YOU'RE SILURIAN. YOU'RE ALIVE. THAT'S NOT POSSIBLE. AND... YOU'RE NOT TALKING IN YOUR OWN LANGUAGE. THAT'S NOT POSSIBLE EITHER.
YOU'VE BEEN PLAYING WITH THINGS YOU DON'T UNDERSTAND.
RIVER SONG. IT SHOWED YOU COMING. ON A SHIP. YOU CAN SAVE US.
MAYBE THEN WE WILL SPARE YOUR HALF-BRED FRIEND.
SORRY. I'M NOT A 'SAVES EVERYONE' TYPE. ARCHAEOLOGIST. ALL ABOUT DEAD PEOPLE, ME. WANT TO SEE?
ISH-KA DA!
I DO SEE. LET US WITNESS HIM JOIN THE DEAD THAT FASCINATE YOU SO.
BY ALL MEANS. BUT YOU KILL HIM, AND I KILL YOU.

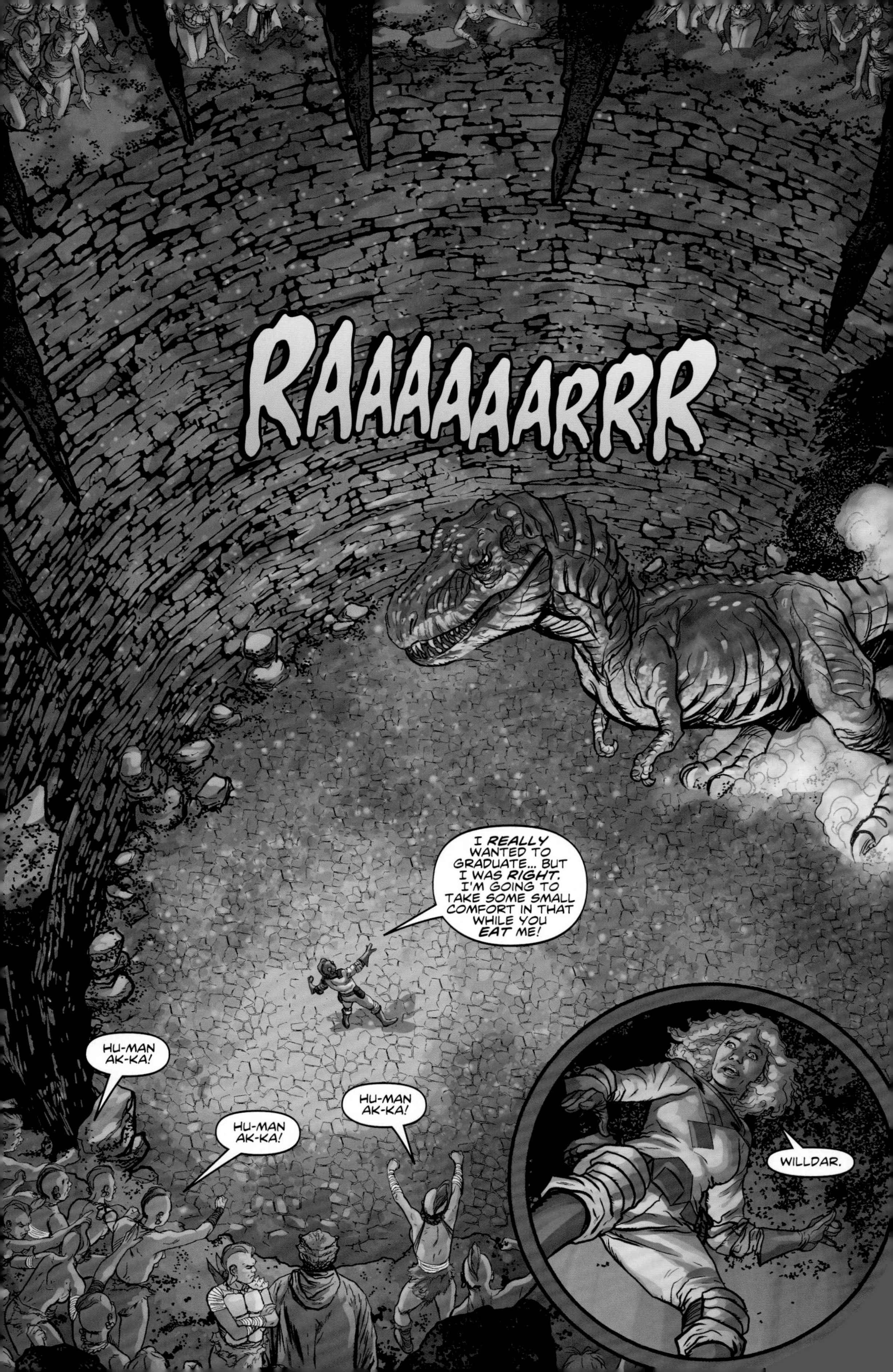
RAAAAAARRR
I REALLY WANTED TO GRADUATE... BUT I WAS RIGHT. I'M GOING TO TAKE SOME SMALL COMFORT IN THAT WHILE YOU EAT ME!
HU-MAN AK-KA!
HU-MAN AK-KA!
HU-MAN AK-KA!
WILLDAR.

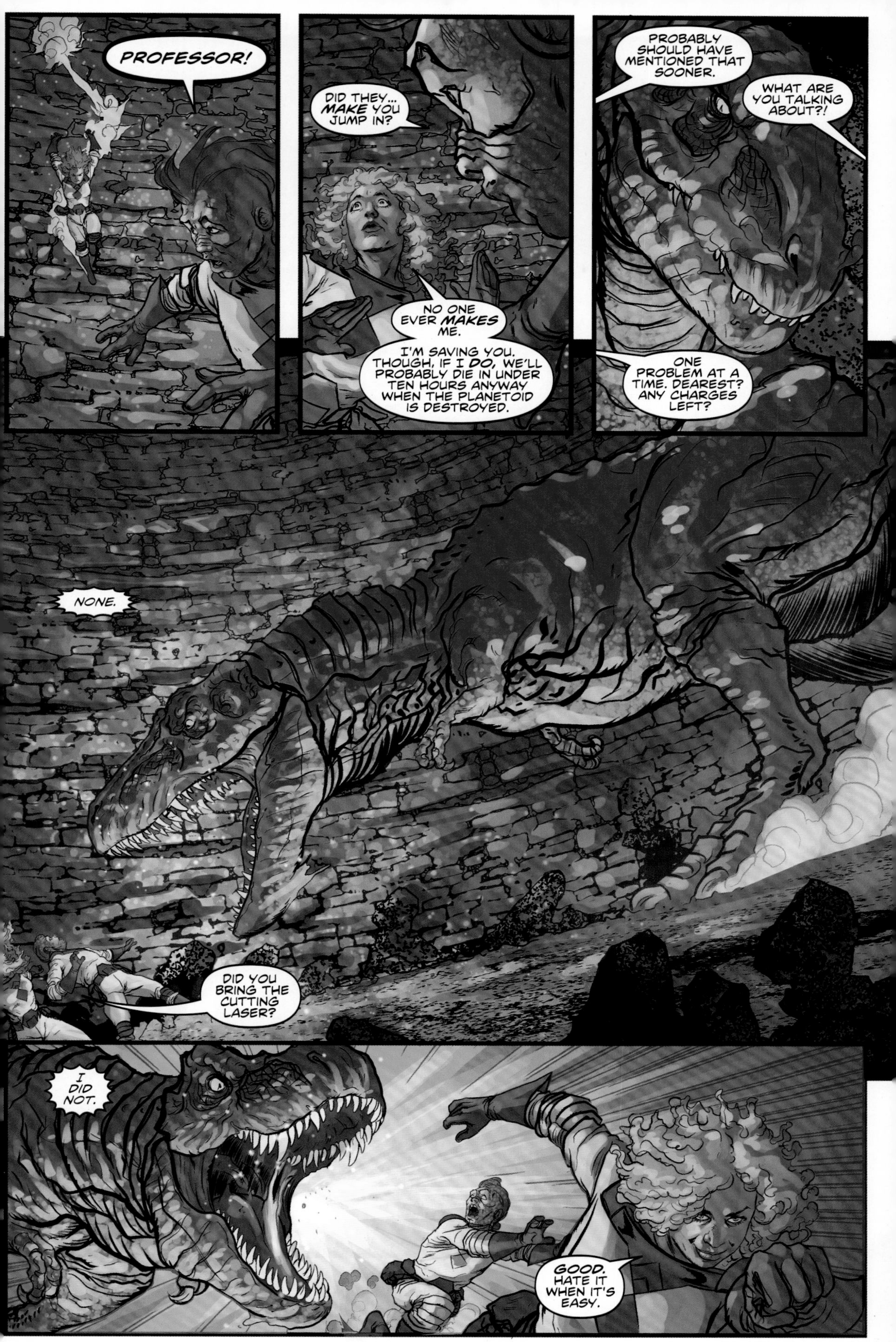
PROFESSOR!
DID THEY... MAKE YOU JUMP IN?
NO ONE EVER MAKES ME.
I'M SAVING YOU. THOUGH, IF I DO, WE'LL PROBABLY DIE IN UNDER TEN HOURS ANYWAY WHEN THE PLANETOID IS DESTROYED.
PROBABLY SHOULD HAVE MENTIONED THAT SOONER.
WHAT ARE YOU TALKING ABOUT?!
ONE PROBLEM AT A TIME. DEAREST? ANY CHARGES LEFT?
NONE.
DID YOU BRING THE CUTTING LASER?
I DID NOT.
GOOD. HATE IT WHEN IT'S EASY.

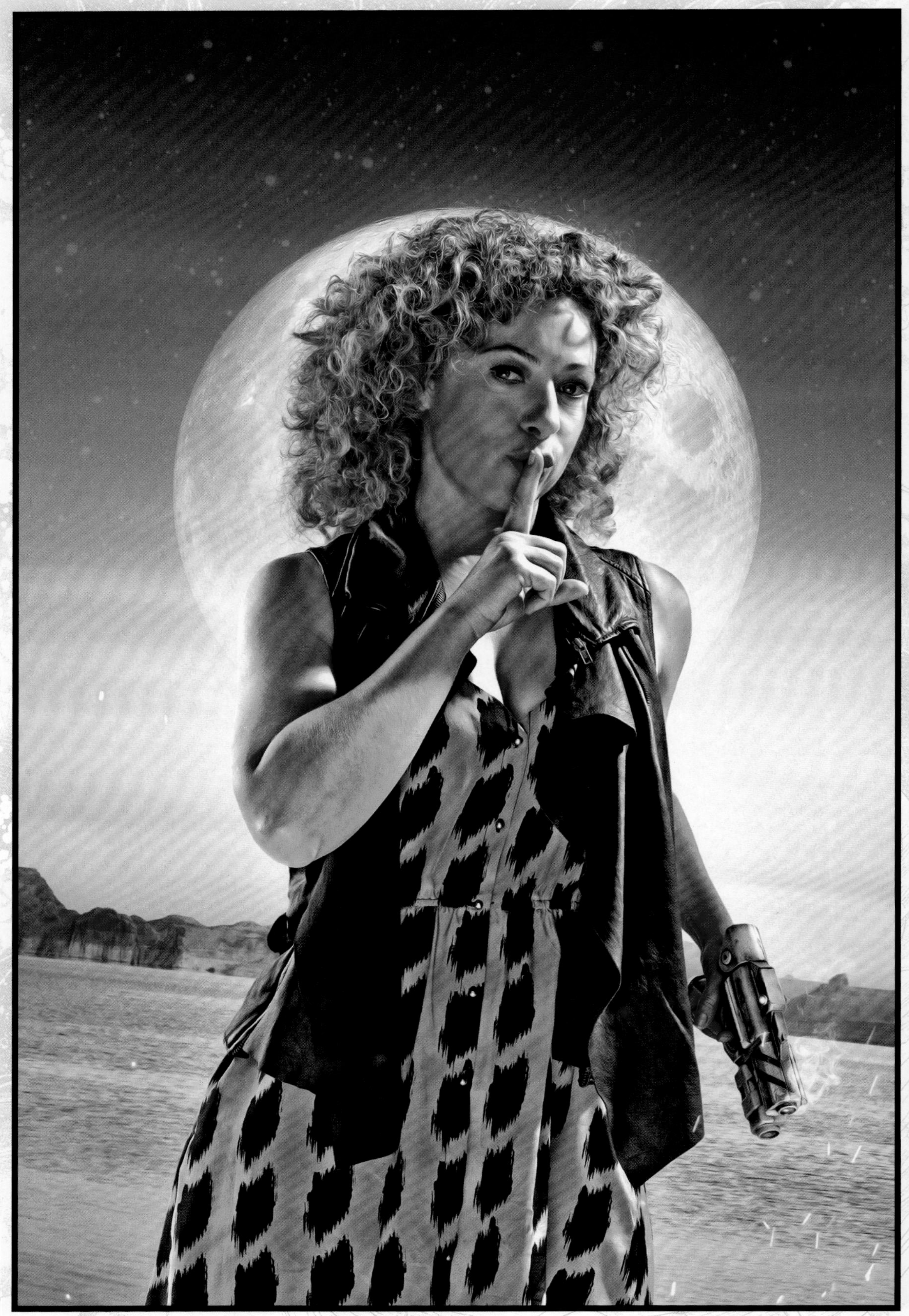

Special #2 Cover B: WILL BROOKS

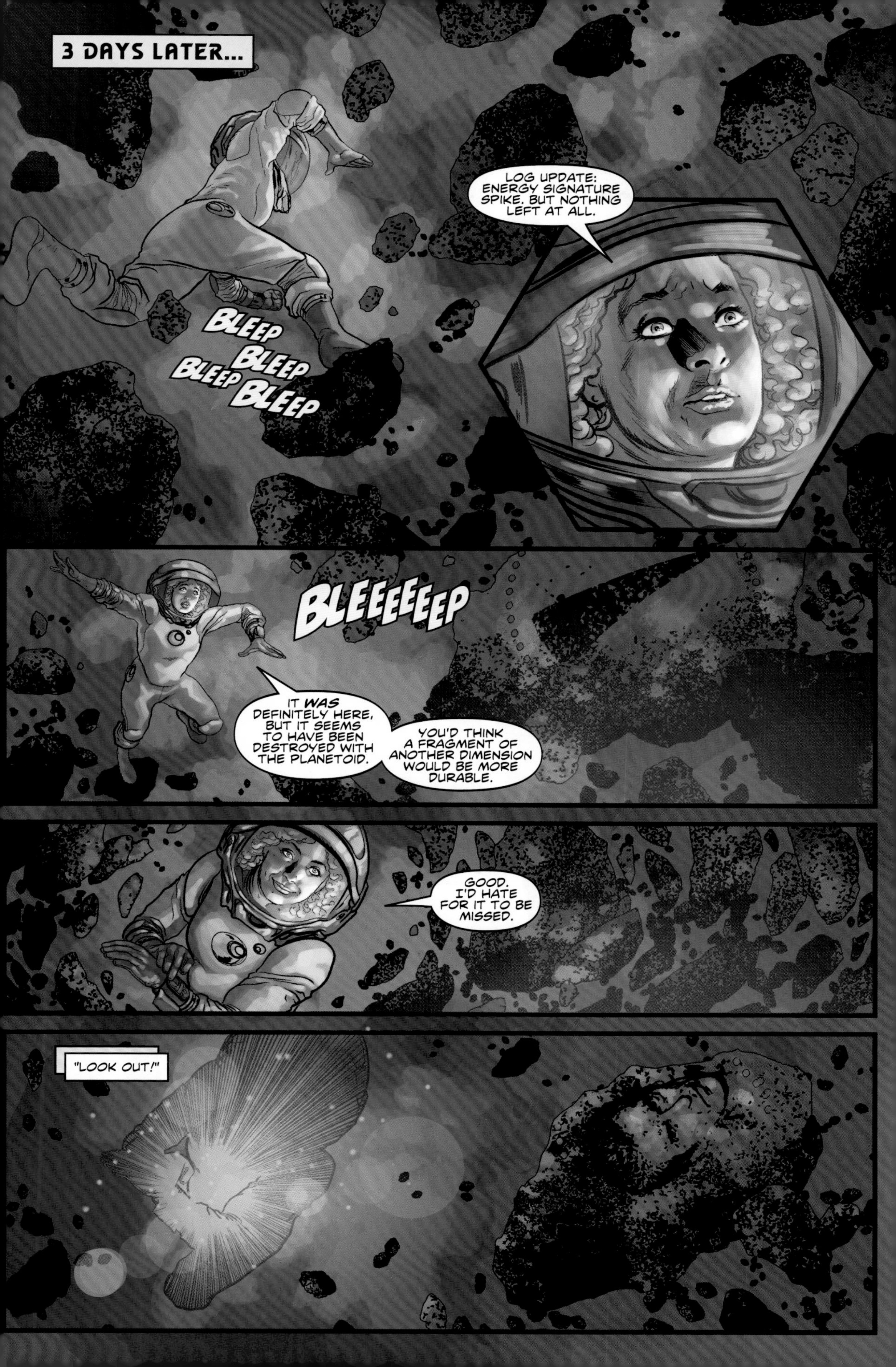
3 DAYS LATER...
BLEEP BLEEP BLEEP BLEEP
LOG UPDATE: ENERGY SIGNATURE SPIKE. BUT NOTHING LEFT AT ALL.
BLEEEEEEP
IT WAS DEFINITELY HERE, BUT IT SEEMS TO HAVE BEEN DESTROYED WITH THE PLANETOID.
YOU'D THINK A FRAGMENT OF ANOTHER DIMENSION WOULD BE MORE DURABLE.
GOOD. I'D HATE FOR IT TO BE MISSED.
"LOOK OUT!"

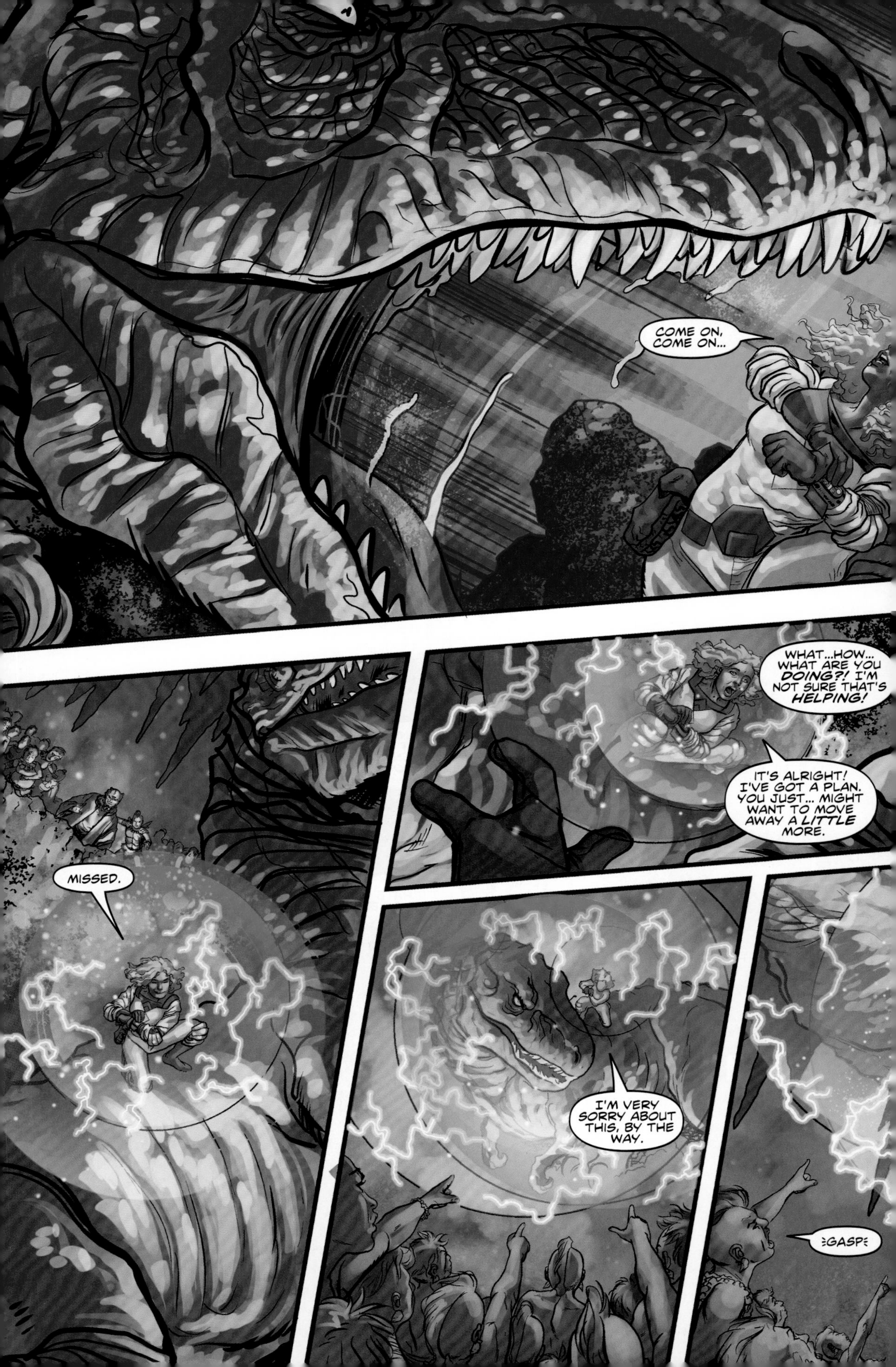
COME ON, COME ON...
MISSED.
WHAT...HOW... WHAT ARE YOU DOING?! I'M NOT SURE THAT'S HELPING!
IT'S ALRIGHT! I'VE GOT A PLAN. YOU JUST... MIGHT WANT TO MOVE AWAY A LITTLE MORE.
I'M VERY SORRY ABOUT THIS, BY THE WAY.
GASP

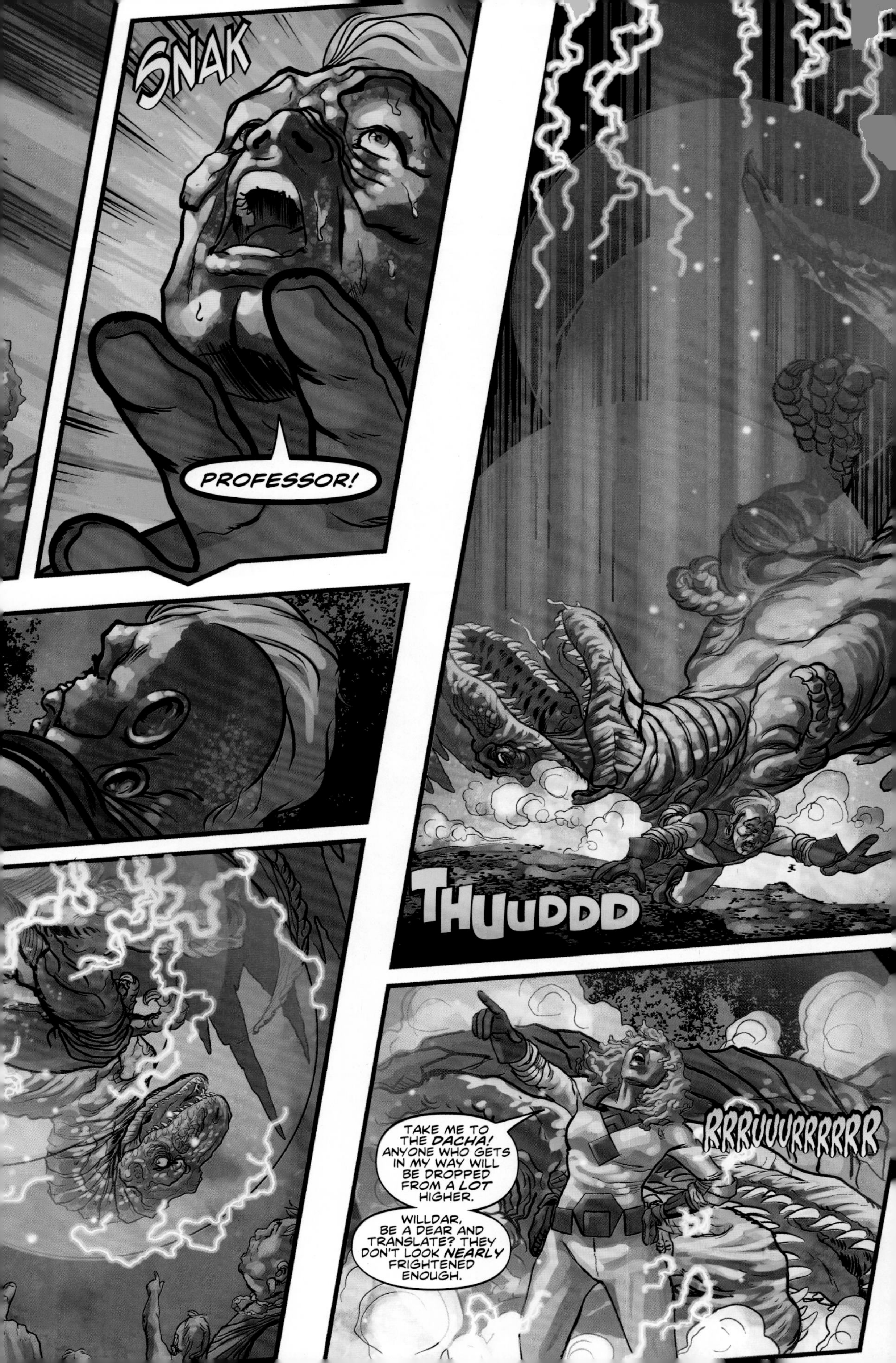
SNAK
PROFESSOR!
THUUDDD
RRRUUUURRRRRR
TAKE ME TO THE DACHA! ANYONE WHO GETS IN MY WAY WILL BE DROPPED FROM A LOT HIGHER.
WILLDAR, BE A DEAR AND TRANSLATE? THEY DON'T LOOK NEARLY FRIGHTENED ENOUGH.

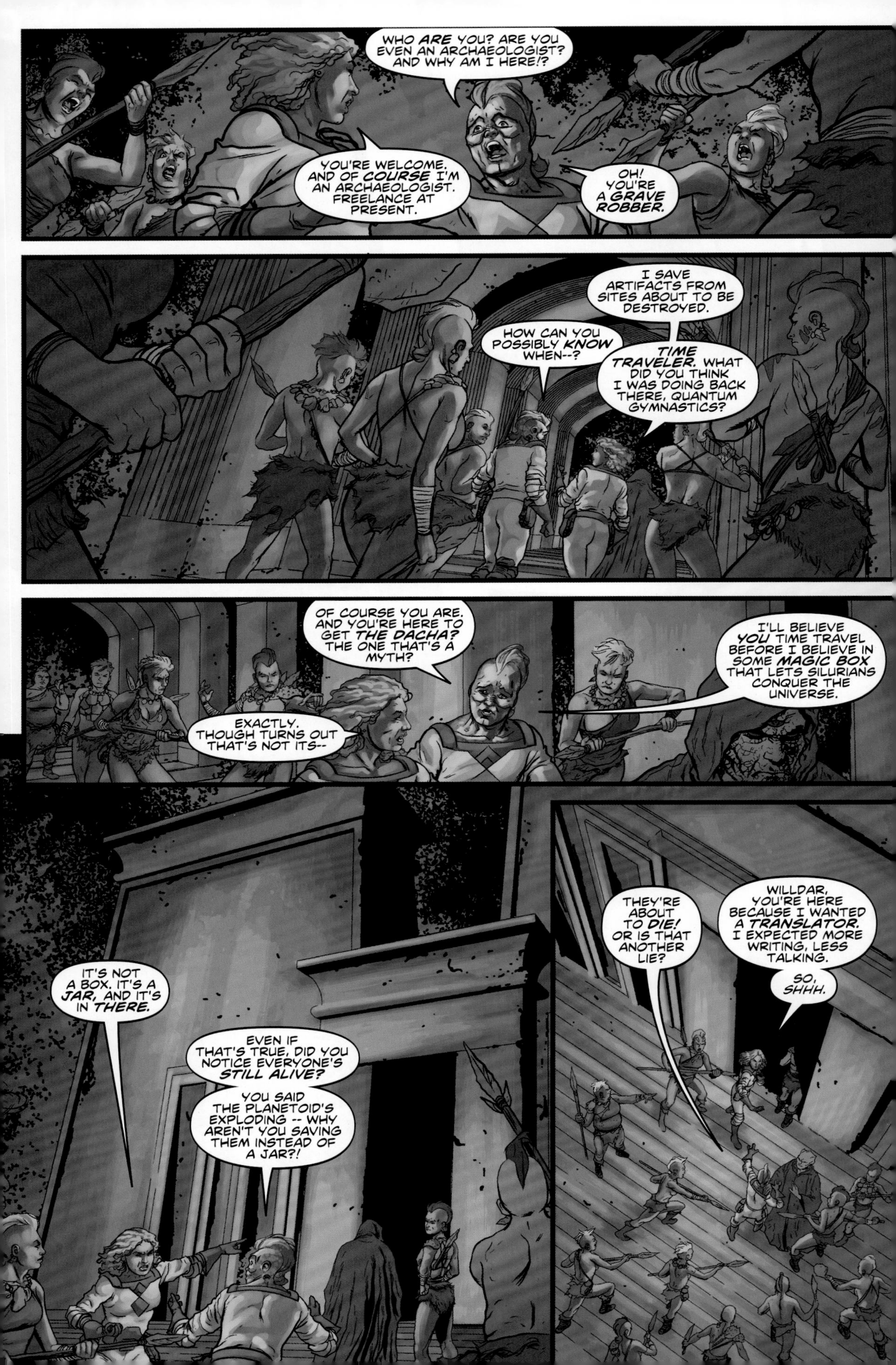
WHO ARE YOU? ARE YOU EVEN AN ARCHAEOLOGIST? AND WHY AM I HERE!?
YOU'RE WELCOME. AND OF COURSE I'M AN ARCHAEOLOGIST. FREELANCE AT PRESENT.
OH! YOU'RE A GRAVE ROBBER.
I SAVE ARTIFACTS FROM SITES ABOUT TO BE DESTROYED.
HOW CAN YOU POSSIBLY KNOW WHEN--?
TIME TRAVELER. WHAT DID YOU THINK I WAS DOING BACK THERE, QUANTUM GYMNASTICS?
OF COURSE YOU ARE. AND YOU'RE HERE TO GET THE DACHA? THE ONE THAT'S A MYTH?
EXACTLY. THOUGH TURNS OUT THAT'S NOT ITS--
I'LL BELIEVE YOU TIME TRAVEL BEFORE I BELIEVE IN SOME MAGIC BOX THAT LETS SILURIANS CONQUER THE UNIVERSE.
IT'S NOT A BOX. IT'S A JAR, AND IT'S IN THERE.
EVEN IF THAT'S TRUE, DID YOU NOTICE EVERYONE'S STILL ALIVE?
YOU SAID THE PLANETOID'S EXPLODING -- WHY AREN'T YOU SAVING THEM INSTEAD OF A JAR?!
THEY'RE ABOUT TO DIE! OR IS THAT ANOTHER LIE?
WILLDAR, YOU'RE HERE BECAUSE I WANTED A TRANSLATOR. I EXPECTED MORE WRITING, LESS TALKING.
SO, SHHH.

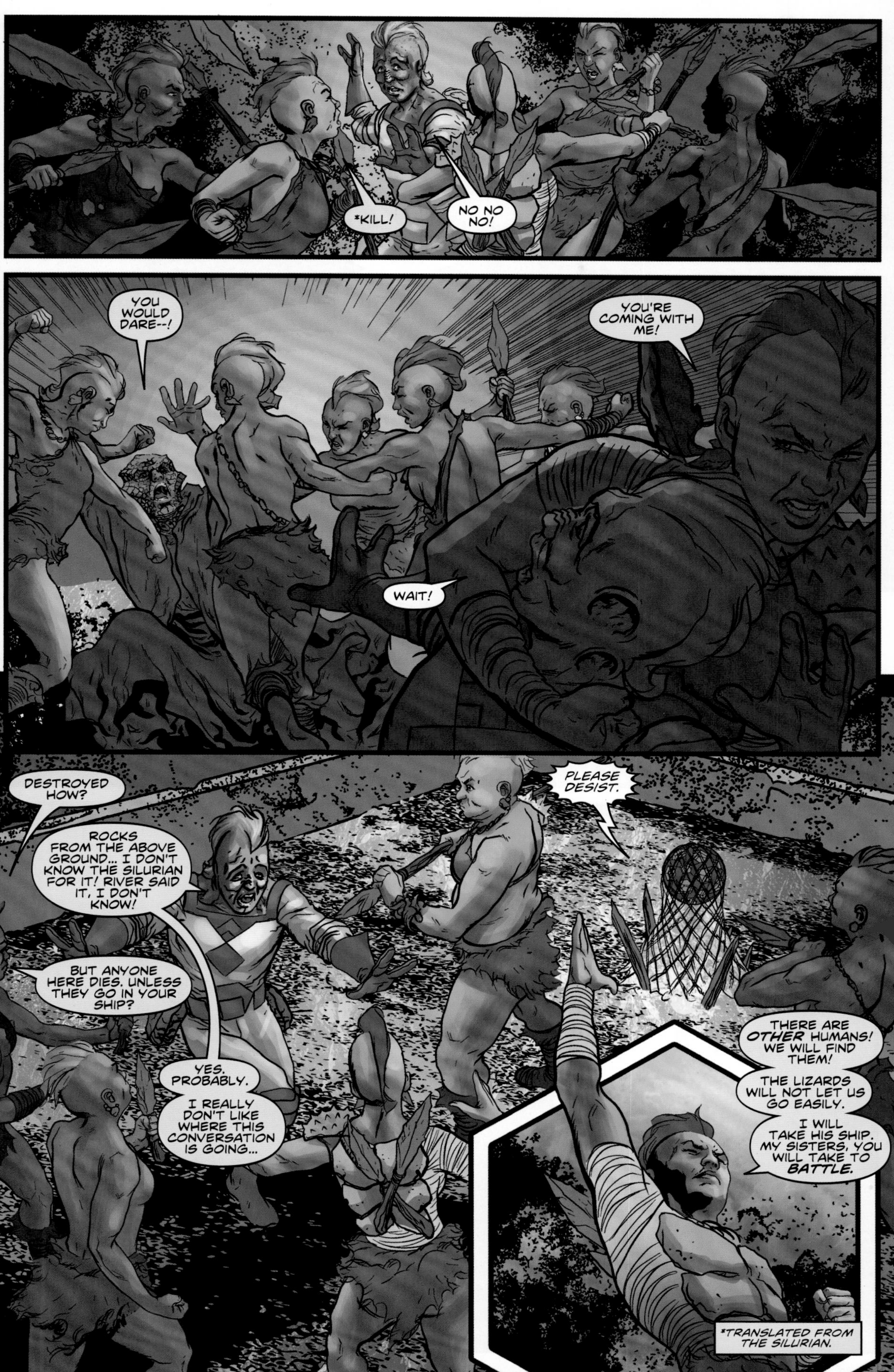
*KILL!
NO NO NO!
YOU WOULD DARE--!
YOU'RE COMING WITH ME!
WAIT!
DESTROYED HOW?
ROCKS FROM THE ABOVE GROUND... I DON'T KNOW THE SILURIAN FOR IT! RIVER SAID IT, I DON'T KNOW!
PLEASE DESIST.
BUT ANYONE HERE DIES. UNLESS THEY GO IN YOUR SHIP?
YES. PROBABLY.
I REALLY DON'T LIKE WHERE THIS CONVERSATION IS GOING...
THERE ARE *OTHER* HUMANS! WE WILL FIND THEM!
THE LIZARDS WILL NOT LET US GO EASILY.
I WILL TAKE HIS SHIP. MY SISTERS, YOU WILL TAKE TO *BATTLE*.
*TRANSLATED FROM THE SILURIAN.

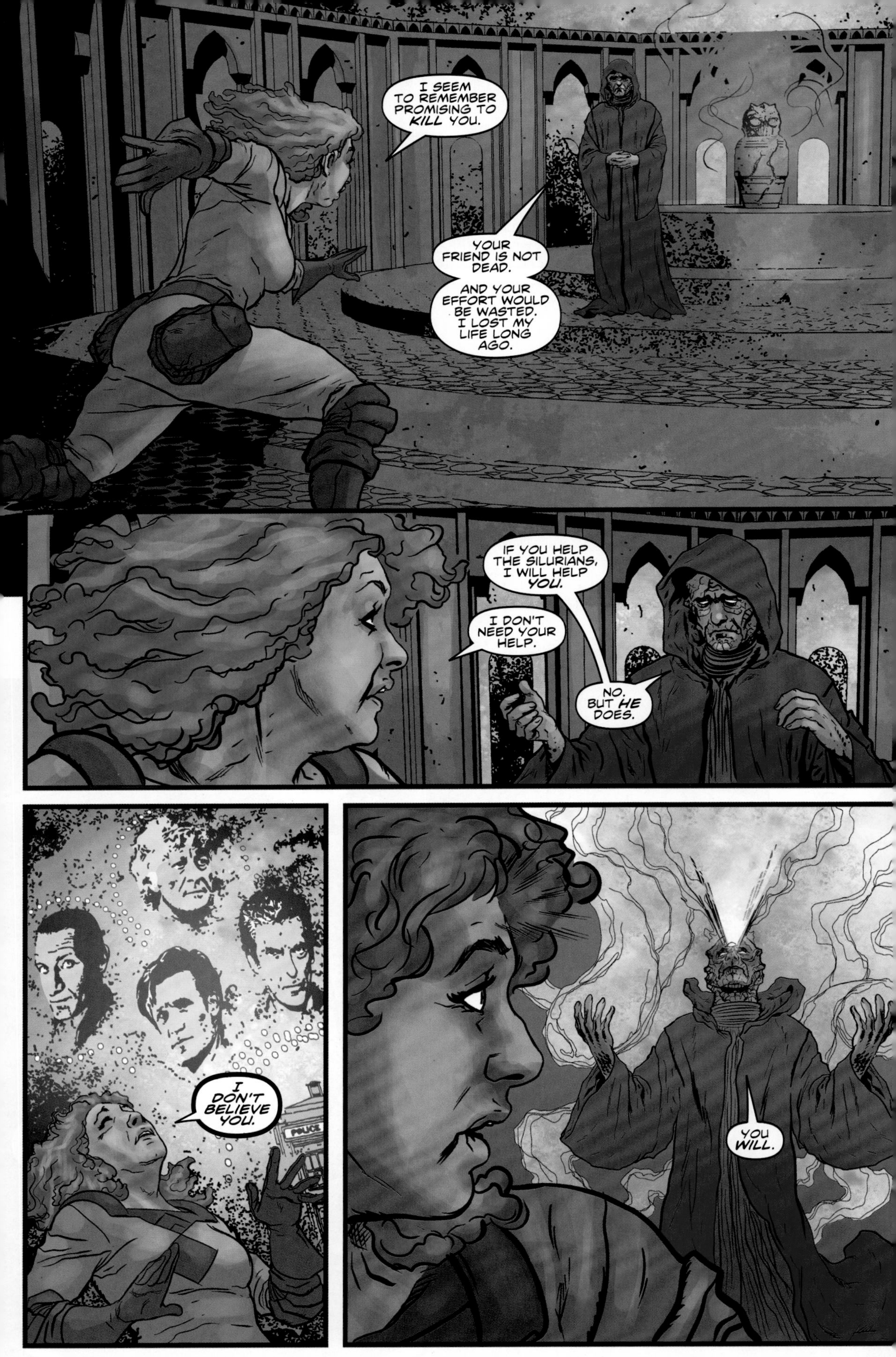
I SEEM TO REMEMBER PROMISING TO KILL YOU.
YOUR FRIEND IS NOT DEAD.
AND YOUR EFFORT WOULD BE WASTED. I LOST MY LIFE LONG AGO.
IF YOU HELP THE SILURIANS, I WILL HELP YOU.
I DON'T NEED YOUR HELP.
NO. BUT HE DOES.
I DON'T BELIEVE YOU.
POLICE
YOU WILL.

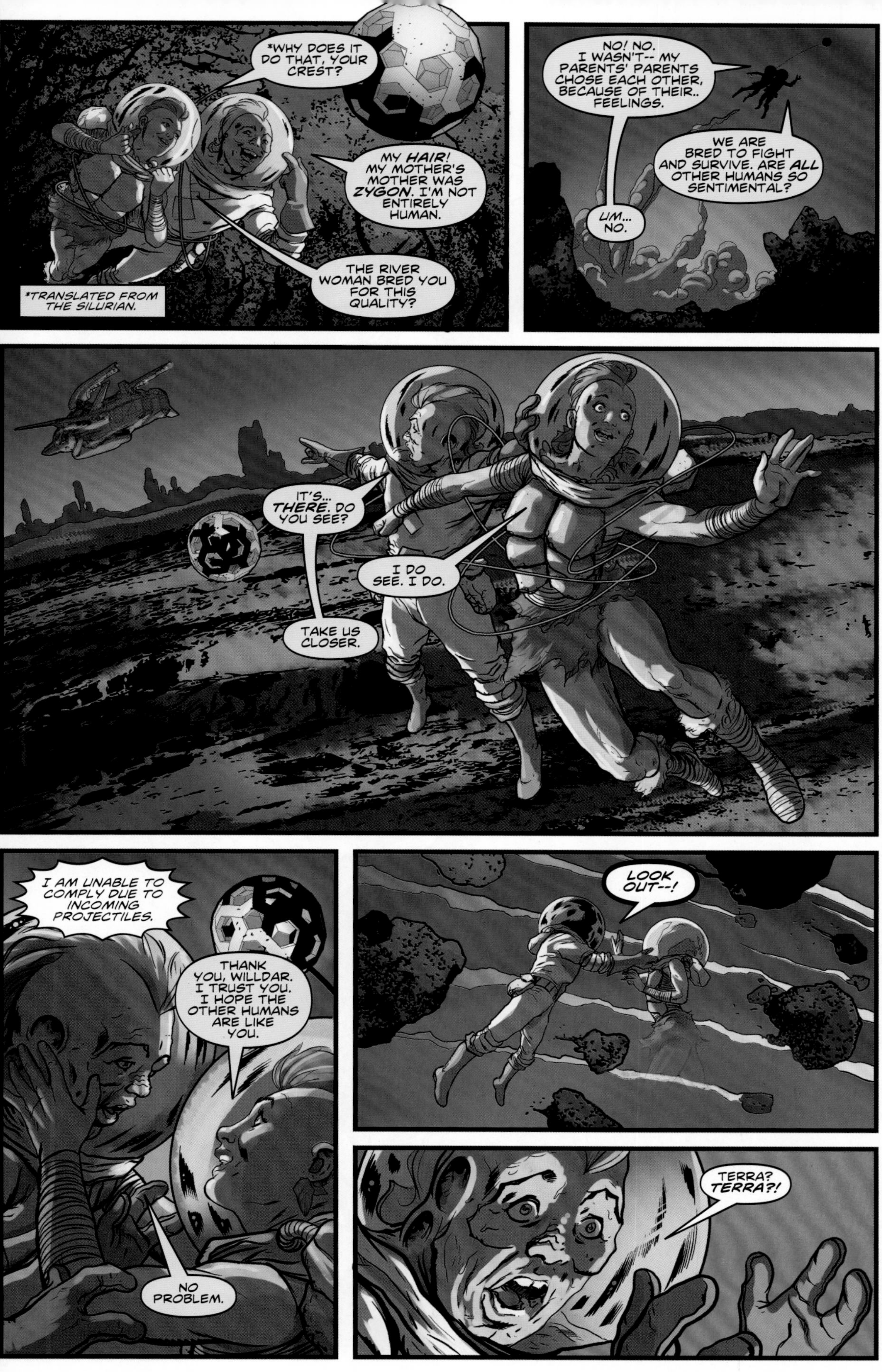
*WHY DOES IT DO THAT, YOUR CREST?
MY HAIR! MY MOTHER'S MOTHER WAS ZYGON. I'M NOT ENTIRELY HUMAN.
THE RIVER WOMAN BRED YOU FOR THIS QUALITY?
*TRANSLATED FROM THE SILURIAN.
NO! NO. I WASN'T-- MY PARENTS' PARENTS CHOSE EACH OTHER, BECAUSE OF THEIR.. FEELINGS.
WE ARE BRED TO FIGHT AND SURVIVE. ARE ALL OTHER HUMANS SO SENTIMENTAL?
UM... NO.
IT'S... THERE. DO YOU SEE?
I DO SEE. I DO.
TAKE US CLOSER.
I AM UNABLE TO COMPLY DUE TO INCOMING PROJECTILES.
THANK YOU, WILLDAR. I TRUST YOU. I HOPE THE OTHER HUMANS ARE LIKE YOU.
NO PROBLEM.
LOOK OUT--!
TERRA? TERRA?!

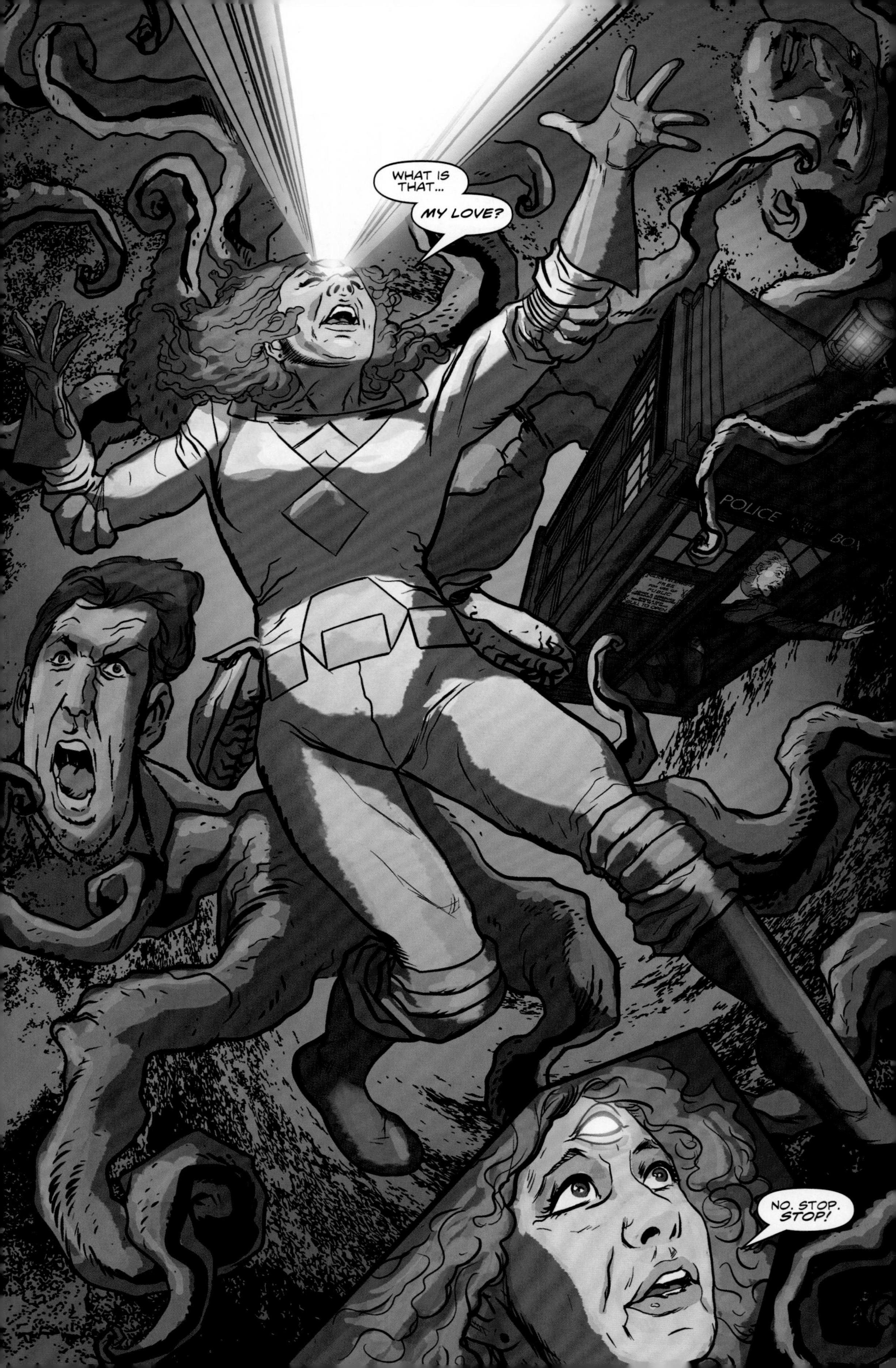
WHAT IS THAT...
MY LOVE?
POLICE
NO. STOP. STOP!

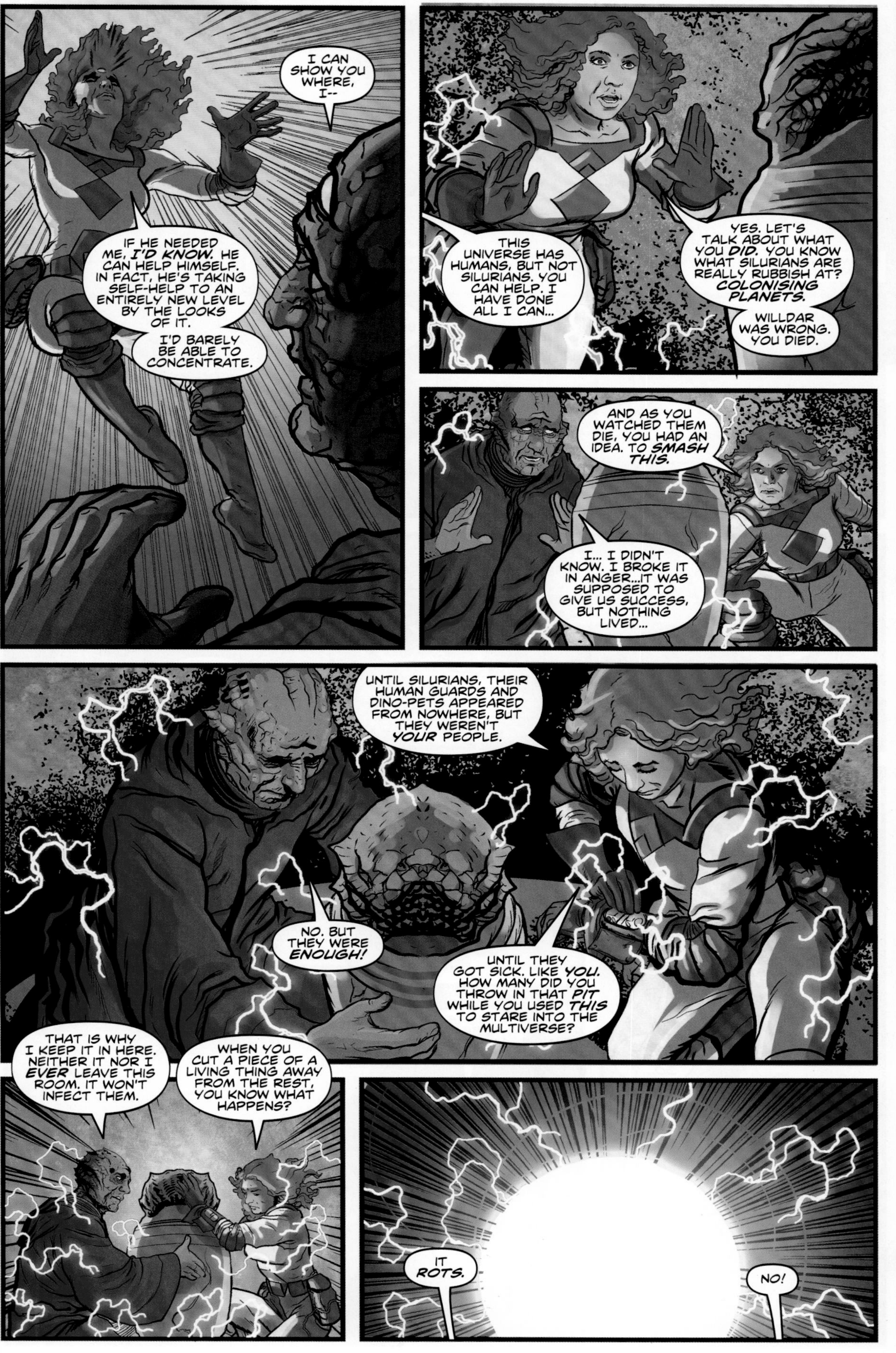
I CAN SHOW YOU WHERE, I--
IF HE NEEDED ME, I'D KNOW. HE CAN HELP HIMSELF. IN FACT, HE'S TAKING SELF-HELP TO AN ENTIRELY NEW LEVEL BY THE LOOKS OF IT.
I'D BARELY BE ABLE TO CONCENTRATE.
THIS UNIVERSE HAS HUMANS, BUT NOT SILURIANS. YOU CAN HELP. I HAVE DONE ALL I CAN...
YES. LET'S TALK ABOUT WHAT YOU DID. YOU KNOW WHAT SILURIANS ARE REALLY RUBBISH AT? COLONISING PLANETS.
WILLDAR WAS WRONG. YOU DIED.
AND AS YOU WATCHED THEM DIE, YOU HAD AN IDEA. TO SMASH THIS.
I... I DIDN'T KNOW. I BROKE IT IN ANGER...IT WAS SUPPOSED TO GIVE US SUCCESS, BUT NOTHING LIVED...
UNTIL SILURIANS, THEIR HUMAN GUARDS AND DINO-PETS APPEARED FROM NOWHERE, BUT THEY WEREN'T YOUR PEOPLE.
NO. BUT THEY WERE ENOUGH!
UNTIL THEY GOT SICK. LIKE YOU. HOW MANY DID YOU THROW IN THAT PIT WHILE YOU USED THIS TO STARE INTO THE MULTIVERSE?
THAT IS WHY I KEEP IT IN HERE. NEITHER IT NOR I EVER LEAVE THIS ROOM. IT WON'T INFECT THEM.
WHEN YOU CUT A PIECE OF A LIVING THING AWAY FROM THE REST, YOU KNOW WHAT HAPPENS?
IT ROTS.
NO!

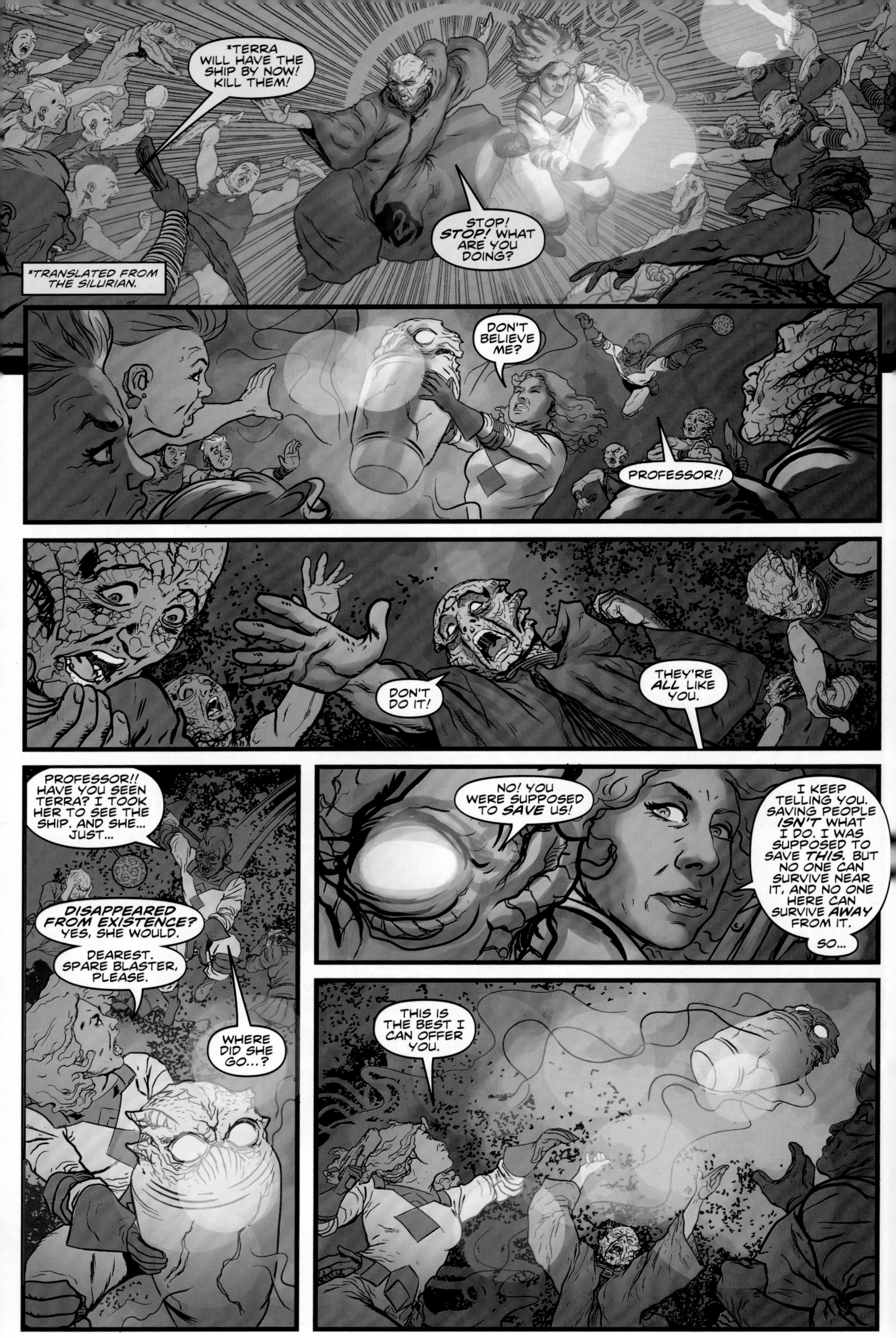
*TERRA WILL HAVE THE SHIP BY NOW! KILL THEM!
STOP! STOP! WHAT ARE YOU DOING?
*TRANSLATED FROM THE SILURIAN.
DON'T BELIEVE ME?
PROFESSOR!!
DON'T DO IT!
THEY'RE ALL LIKE YOU.
PROFESSOR!! HAVE YOU SEEN TERRA? I TOOK HER TO SEE THE SHIP. AND SHE... JUST...
DISAPPEARED FROM EXISTENCE? YES, SHE WOULD.
DEAREST. SPARE BLASTER, PLEASE.
WHERE DID SHE GO...?
NO! YOU WERE SUPPOSED TO SAVE US!
I KEEP TELLING YOU. SAVING PEOPLE ISN'T WHAT I DO. I WAS SUPPOSED TO SAVE THIS. BUT NO ONE CAN SURVIVE NEAR IT, AND NO ONE HERE CAN SURVIVE AWAY FROM IT.
SO...
THIS IS THE BEST I CAN OFFER YOU.

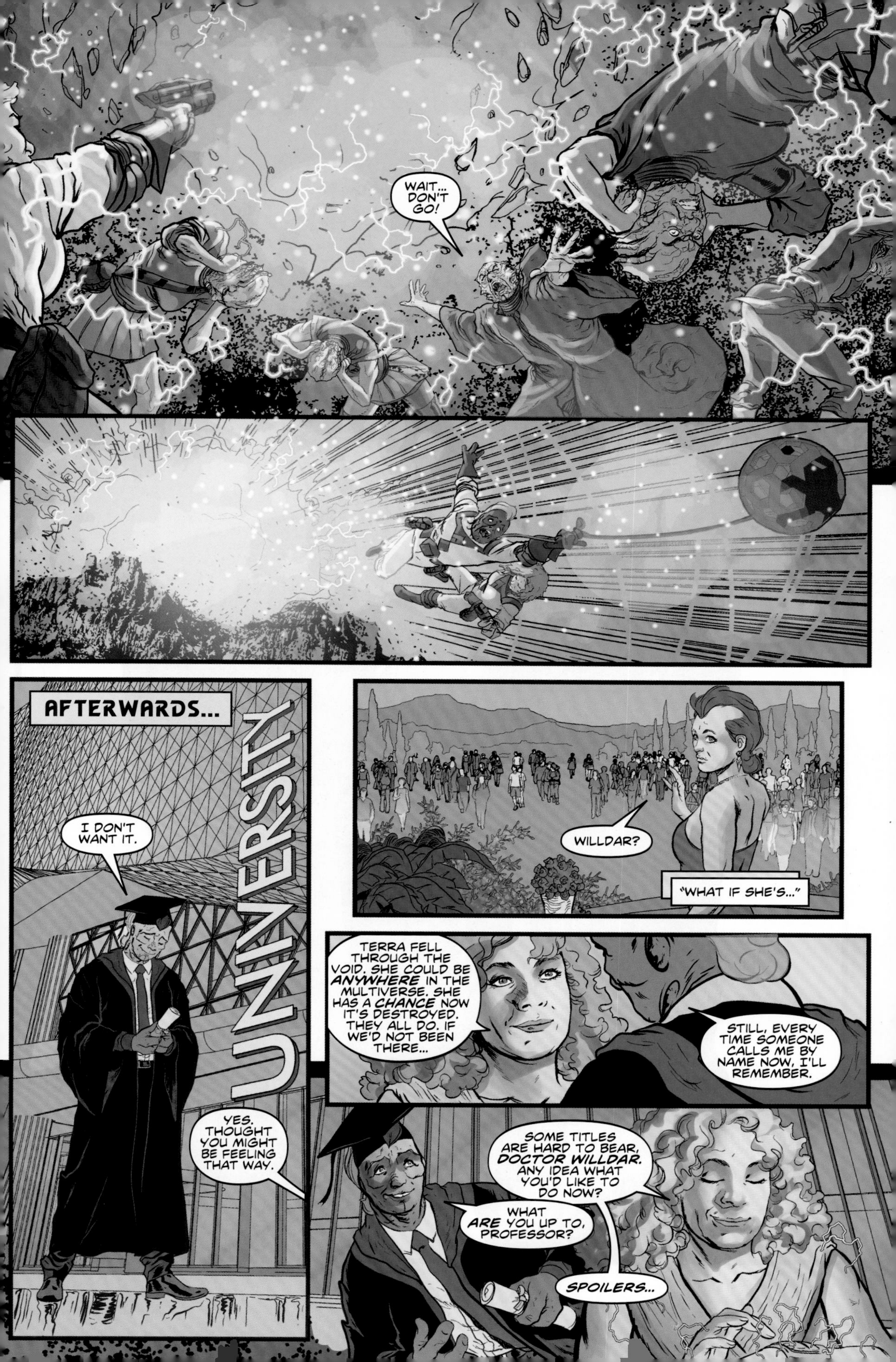
WAIT... DON'T GO!
AFTERWARDS...
UNIVERSITY
I DON'T WANT IT.
WILLDAR?
"WHAT IF SHE'S..."
TERRA FELL THROUGH THE VOID. SHE COULD BE ANYWHERE IN THE MULTIVERSE. SHE HAS A CHANCE NOW IT'S DESTROYED. THEY ALL DO. IF WE'D NOT BEEN THERE...
STILL, EVERY TIME SOMEONE CALLS ME BY NAME NOW, I'LL REMEMBER.
YES. THOUGHT YOU MIGHT BE FEELING THAT WAY.
SOME TITLES ARE HARD TO BEAR, DOCTOR WILLDAR. ANY IDEA WHAT YOU'D LIKE TO DO NOW?
WHAT ARE YOU UP TO, PROFESSOR?
SPOILERS...

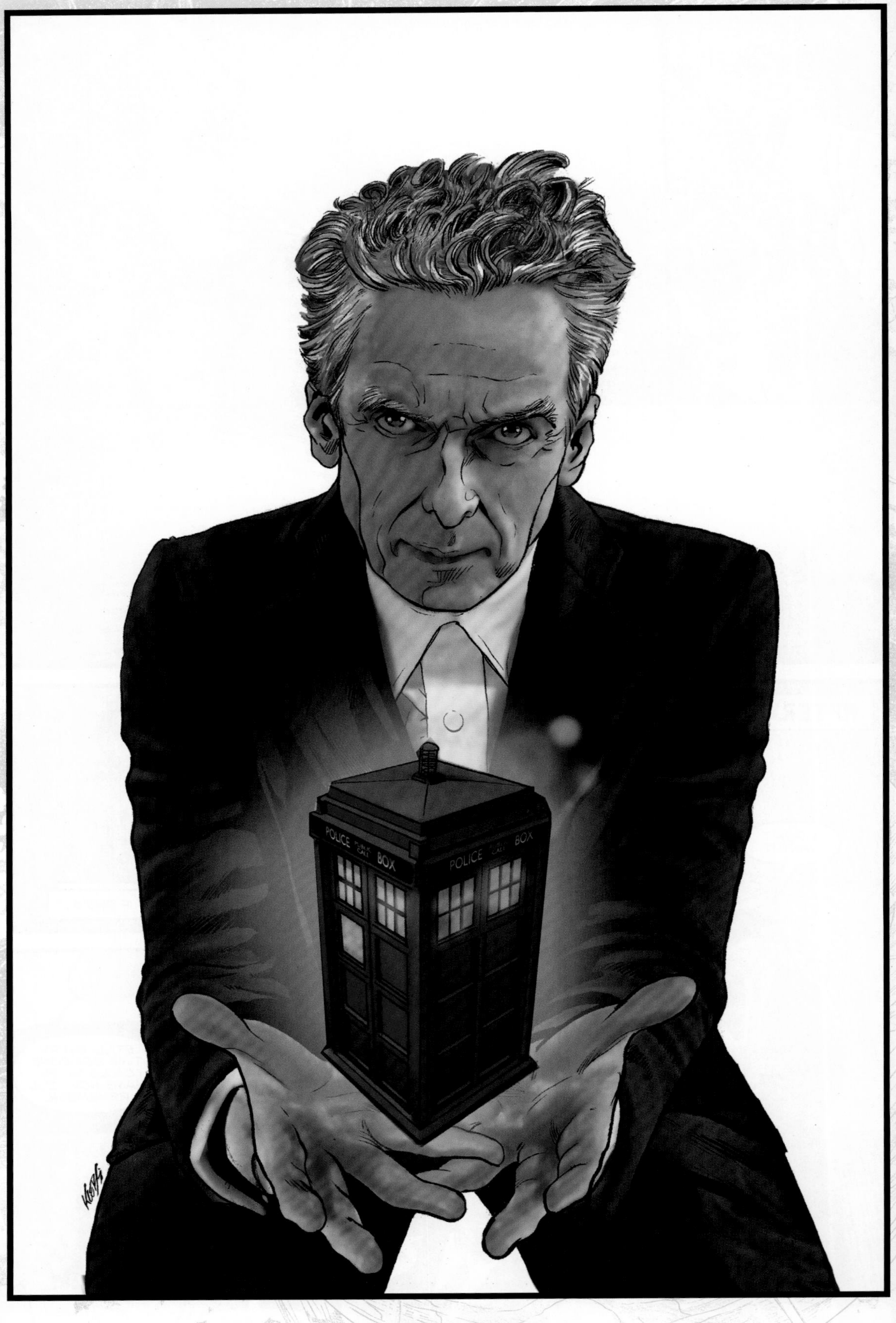
POLICE PUBLIC CALL BOX
POLICE PUBLIC CALL BOX

12D #3.8 Cover A: KLEBS JR

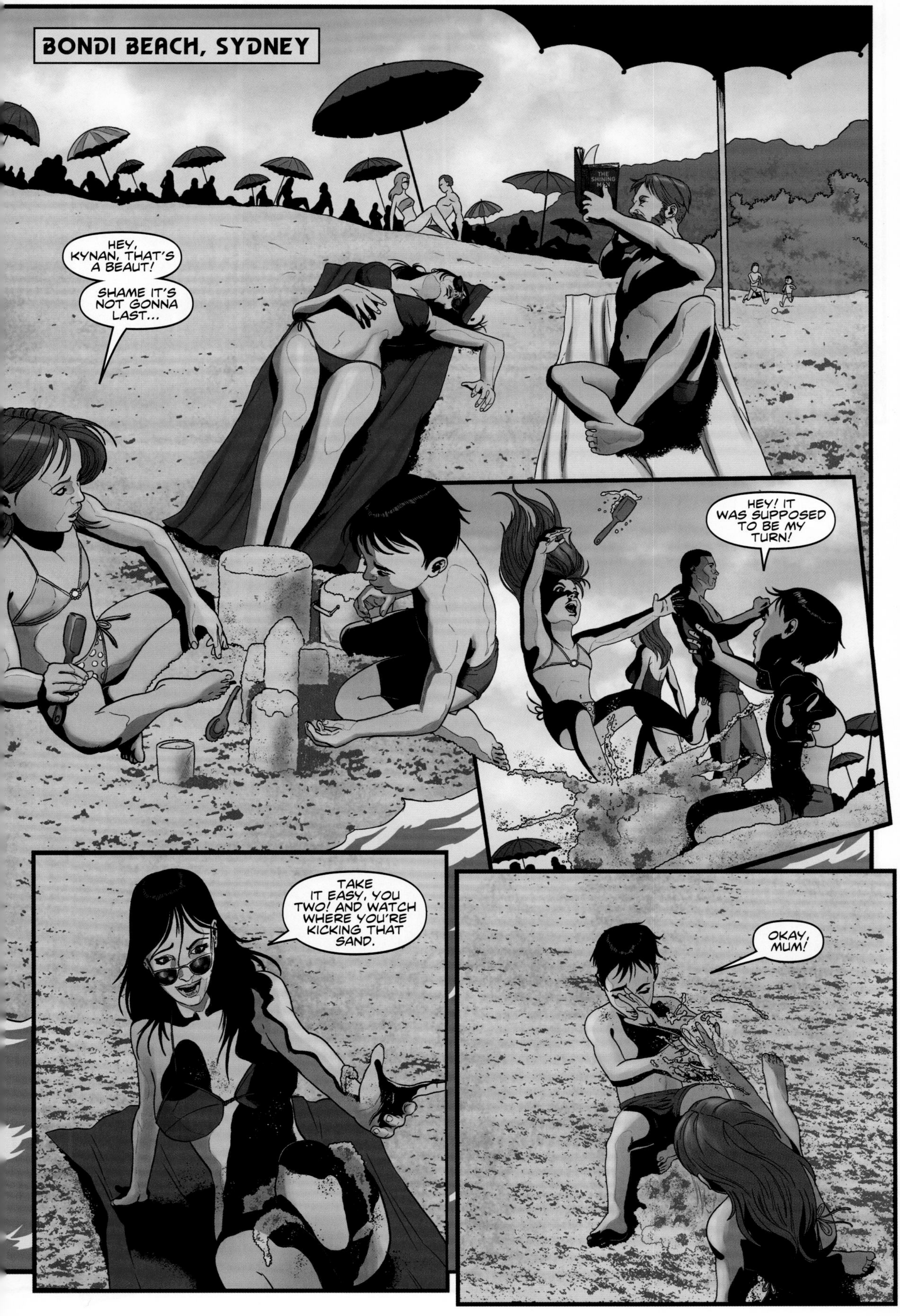
BONDI BEACH, SYDNEY
THE SHINING MAN
HEY, KYNAN, THAT'S A BEAUT!
SHAME IT'S NOT GONNA LAST...
HEY! IT WAS SUPPOSED TO BE MY TURN!
TAKE IT EASY, YOU TWO! AND WATCH WHERE YOU'RE KICKING THAT SAND.
OKAY, MUM!

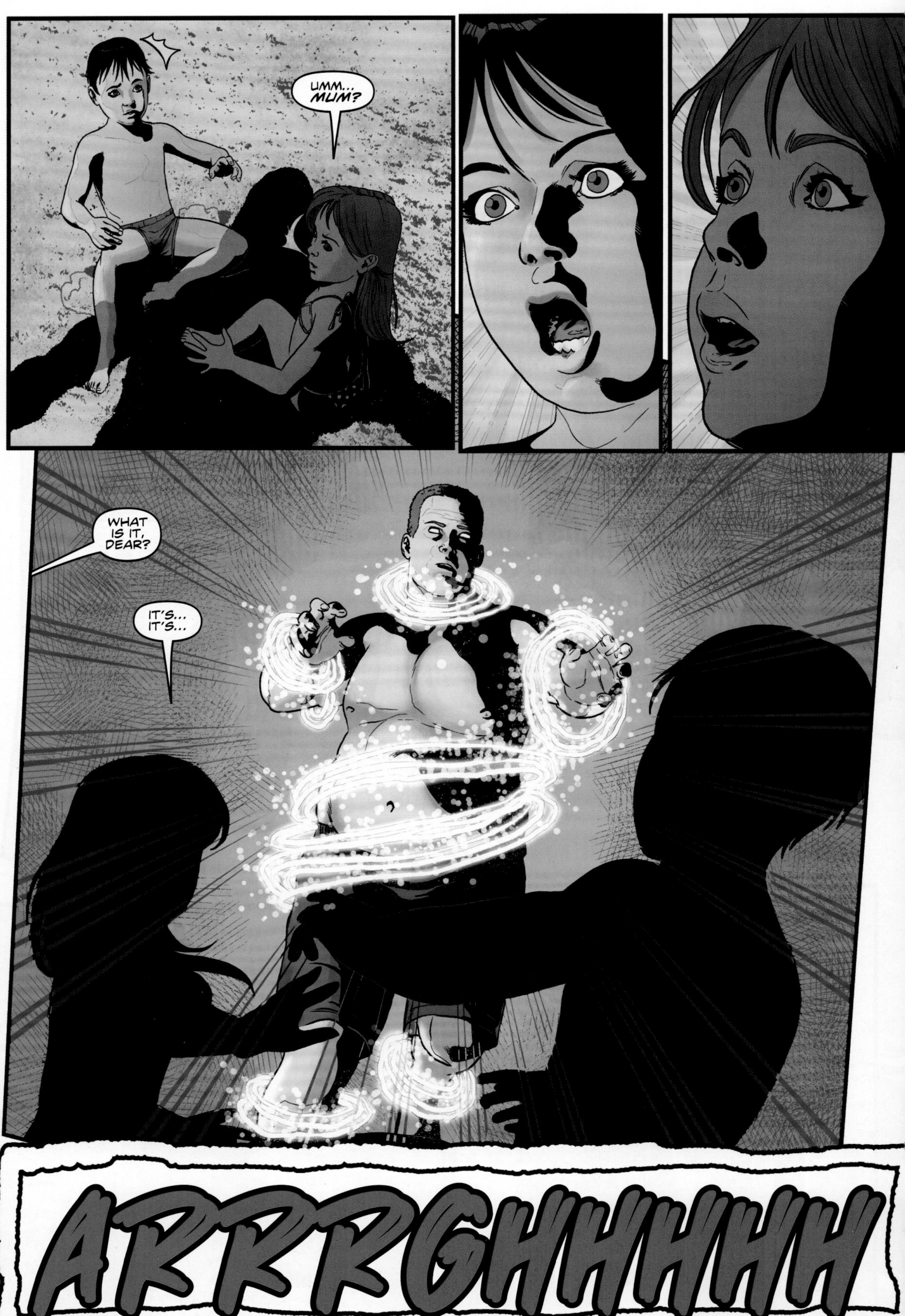
UMM... MUM?
WHAT IS IT, DEAR?
IT'S... IT'S...
ARRRGHHHHH

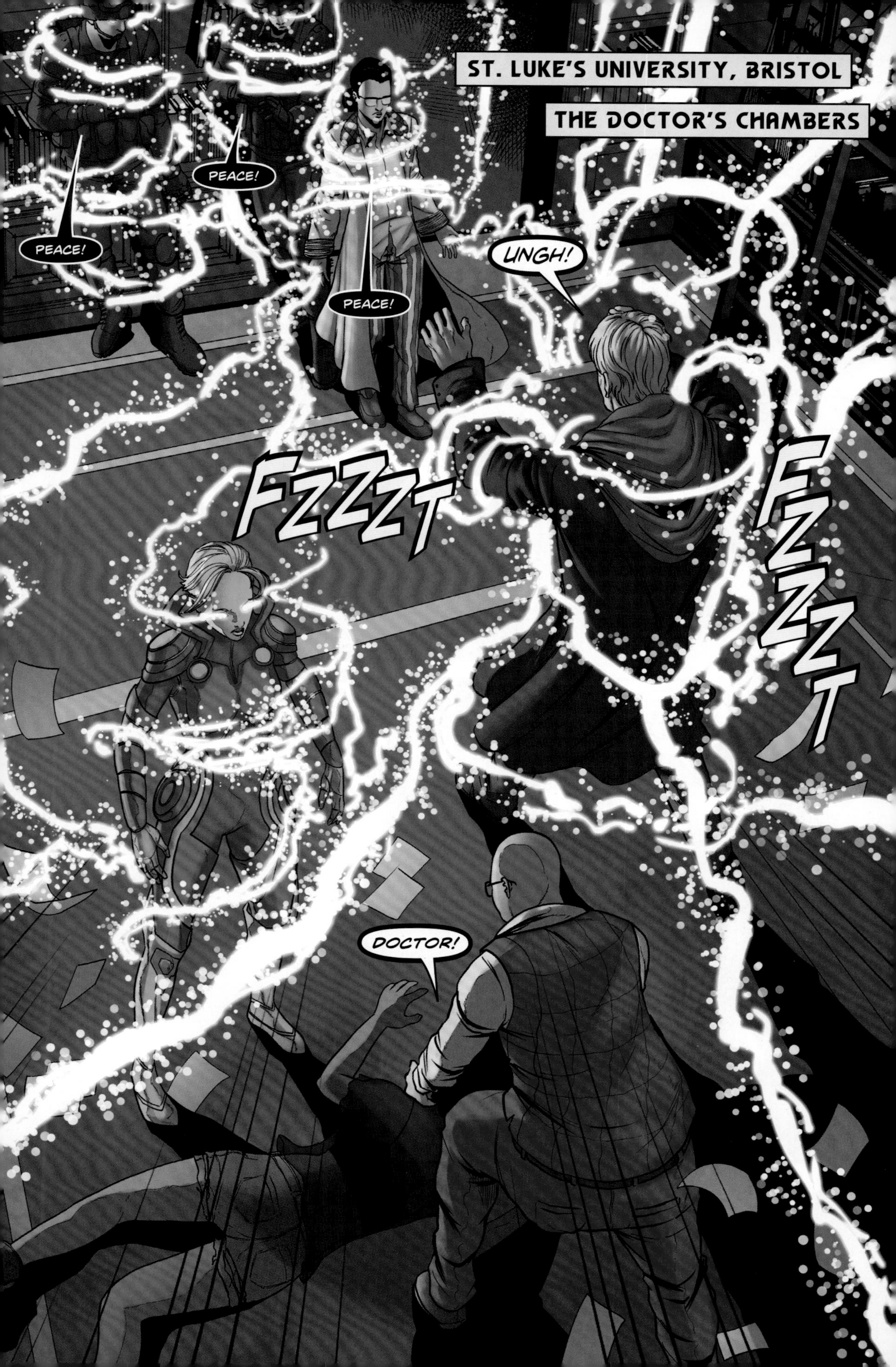
ST. LUKE'S UNIVERSITY, BRISTOL
THE DOCTOR'S CHAMBERS
PEACE!
PEACE!
PEACE!
UNGH!
FZZZT
FZZZT
DOCTOR!

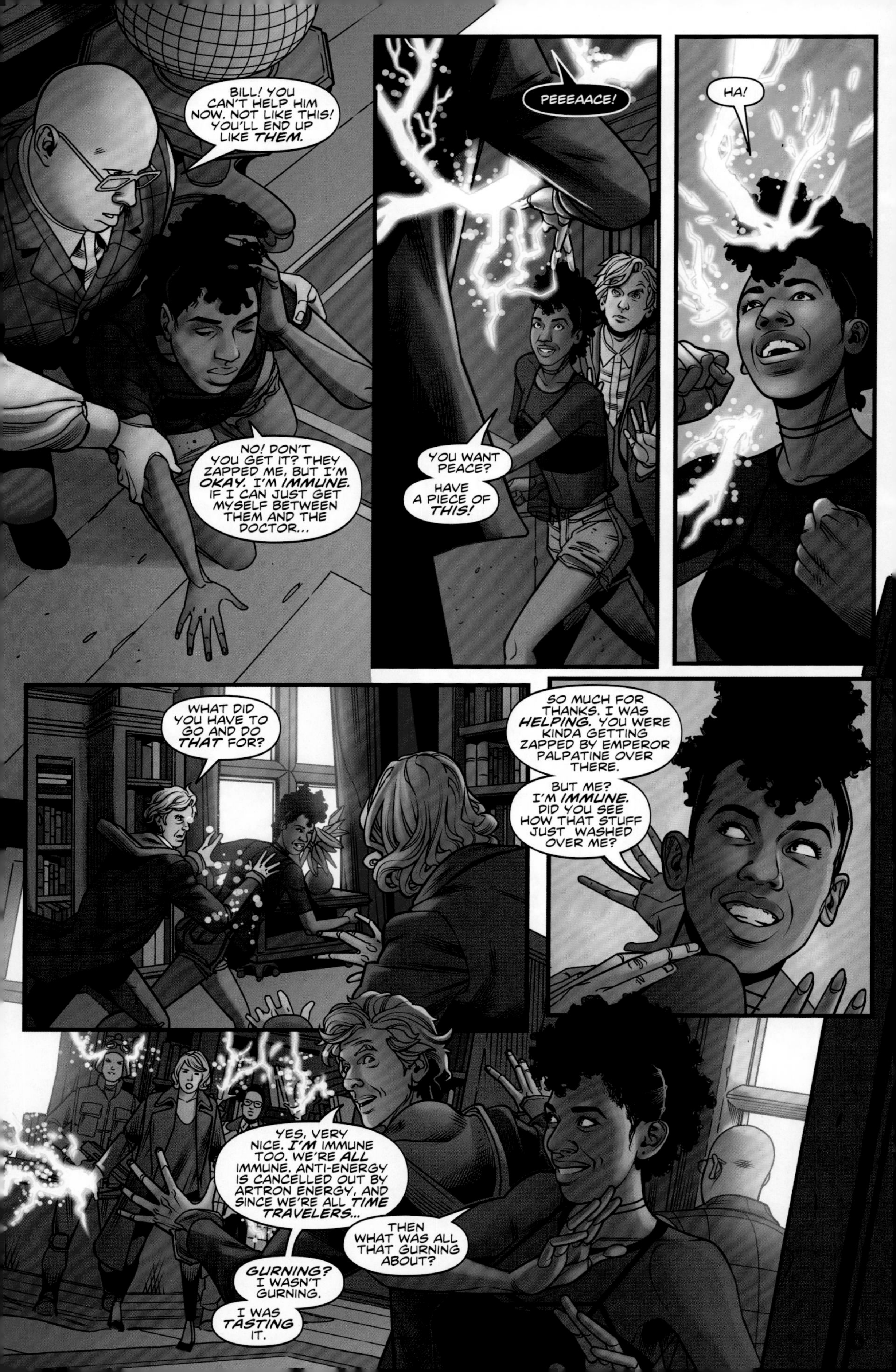
BILL! YOU CAN'T HELP HIM NOW. NOT LIKE THIS! YOU'LL END UP LIKE THEM.
NO! DON'T YOU GET IT? THEY ZAPPED ME, BUT I'M OKAY. I'M IMMUNE. IF I CAN JUST GET MYSELF BETWEEN THEM AND THE DOCTOR...
PEEEAAACE!
YOU WANT PEACE?
HAVE A PIECE OF THIS!
HA!
WHAT DID YOU HAVE TO GO AND DO THAT FOR?
SO MUCH FOR THANKS. I WAS HELPING. YOU WERE KINDA GETTING ZAPPED BY EMPEROR PALPATINE OVER THERE.
BUT ME? I'M IMMUNE. DID YOU SEE HOW THAT STUFF JUST WASHED OVER ME?
YES, VERY NICE. I'M IMMUNE TOO. WE'RE ALL IMMUNE. ANTI-ENERGY IS CANCELLED OUT BY ARTRON ENERGY, AND SINCE WE'RE ALL TIME TRAVELERS...
THEN WHAT WAS ALL THAT GURNING ABOUT?
GURNING? I WASN'T GURNING.
I WAS TASTING IT.

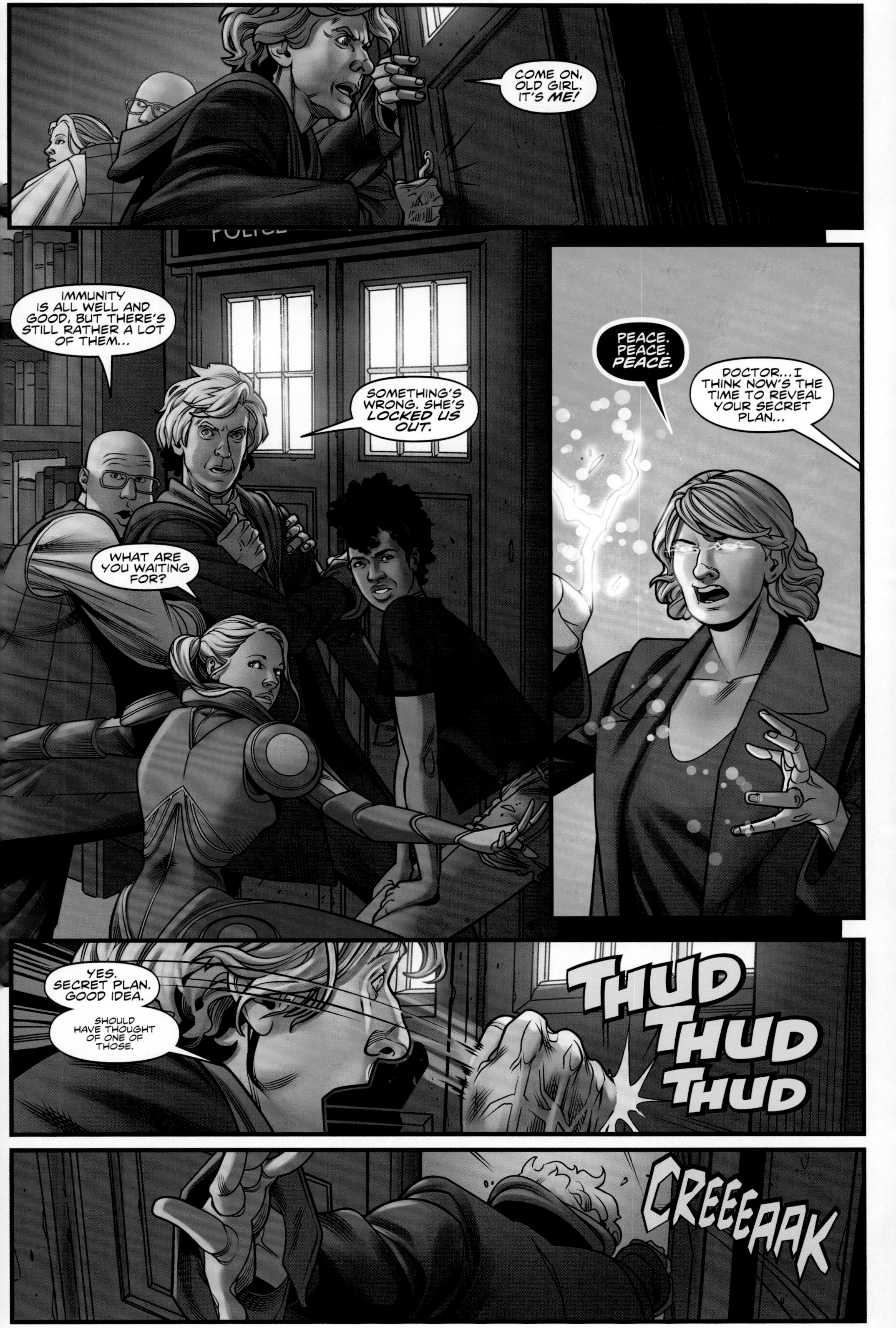
COME ON, OLD GIRL. IT'S *ME!*
POLICE
IMMUNITY IS ALL WELL AND GOOD, BUT THERE'S STILL RATHER A LOT OF THEM...
SOMETHING'S WRONG. SHE'S *LOCKED US OUT.*
WHAT ARE YOU WAITING FOR?
PEACE. PEACE. *PEACE.*
DOCTOR... I THINK NOW'S THE TIME TO REVEAL YOUR SECRET PLAN...
YES. SECRET PLAN. GOOD IDEA.
SHOULD HAVE THOUGHT OF ONE OF THOSE.
THUD THUD THUD
CREEEAAK

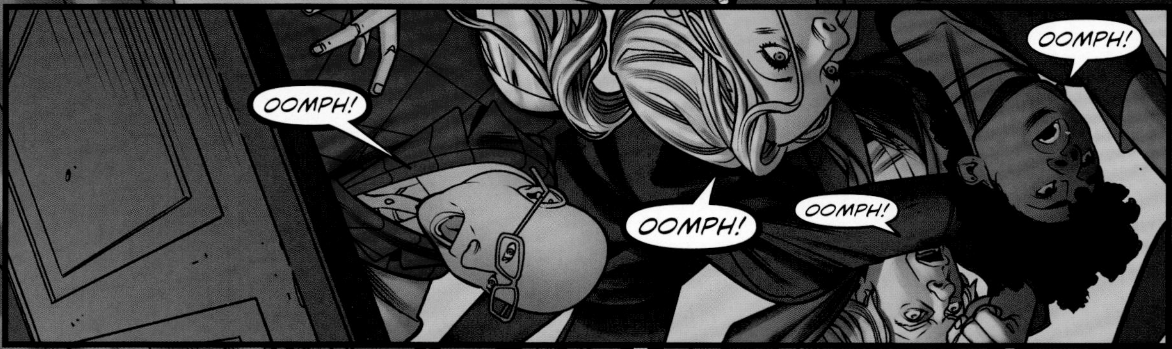
OOMPH!
OOMPH!
OOMPH!
OOMPH!

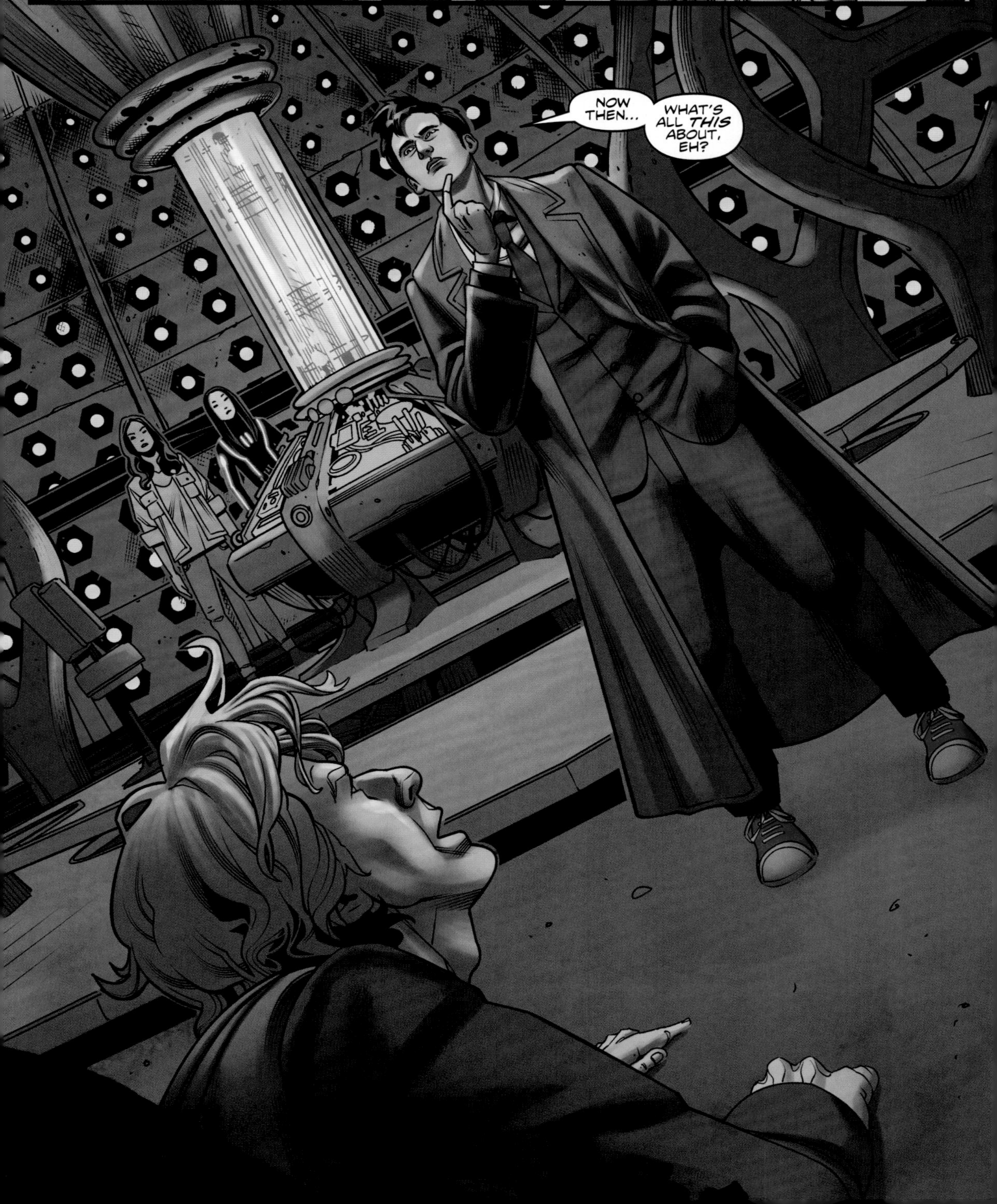
NOW THEN...
WHAT'S ALL THIS ABOUT, EH?

PEACE. PEACE. **PEACE.**

PEACE. PEACE. **PEACE.**

TELEPHONE

REE

USE OF

BLIC

& ASSISTAN
IMMEDIA LY

ER & CARS
D TO ALL

TOO

OH, NO. NOT *YOU*. IT HAD TO BE *YOU*.

I'LL TELL YOU NOW -- I'VE NO TIME FOR THE EXCITED PUPPY ROUTINE. AND ALL THAT *GRINNING*. WHY DID I EVER THINK THAT WAS A GOOD IDEA?

YOU!

AH, SO YOU'VE COTTONED ON AT LAST.

COME HERE!

I THOUGHT YOU WERE *DEAD.*

...

I KNOW. BUT TURNS OUT: DEFYING DEATH KINDA RUNS IN THE FAMILY.

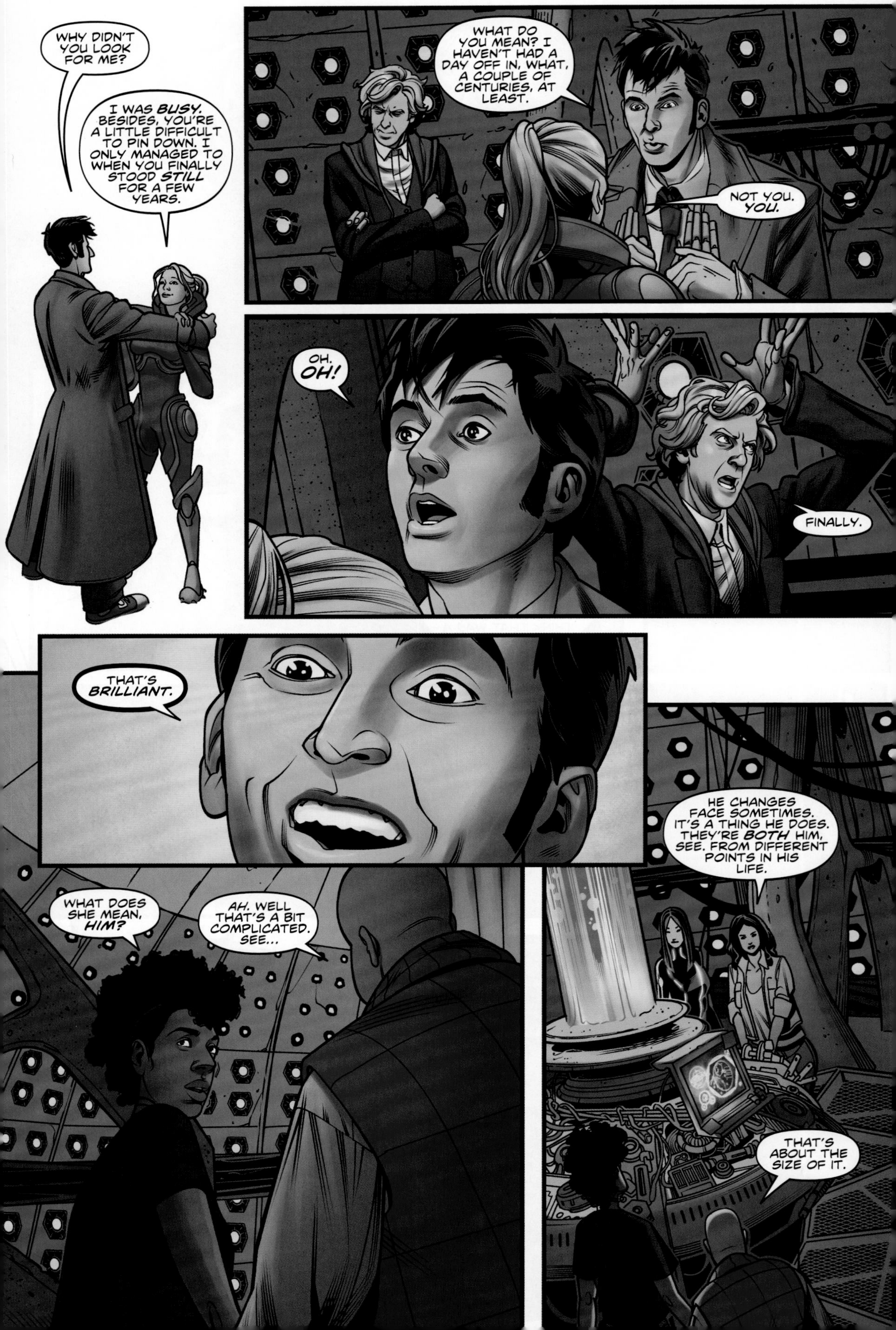
WHY DIDN'T YOU LOOK FOR ME?
I WAS BUSY. BESIDES, YOU'RE A LITTLE DIFFICULT TO PIN DOWN. I ONLY MANAGED TO WHEN YOU FINALLY STOOD STILL FOR A FEW YEARS.
WHAT DO YOU MEAN? I HAVEN'T HAD A DAY OFF IN, WHAT, A COUPLE OF CENTURIES, AT LEAST.
NOT YOU. YOU.
OH. OH!
FINALLY.
THAT'S BRILLIANT.
WHAT DOES SHE MEAN, HIM?
AH. WELL THAT'S A BIT COMPLICATED. SEE...
HE CHANGES FACE SOMETIMES. IT'S A THING HE DOES. THEY'RE BOTH HIM, SEE. FROM DIFFERENT POINTS IN HIS LIFE.
THAT'S ABOUT THE SIZE OF IT.

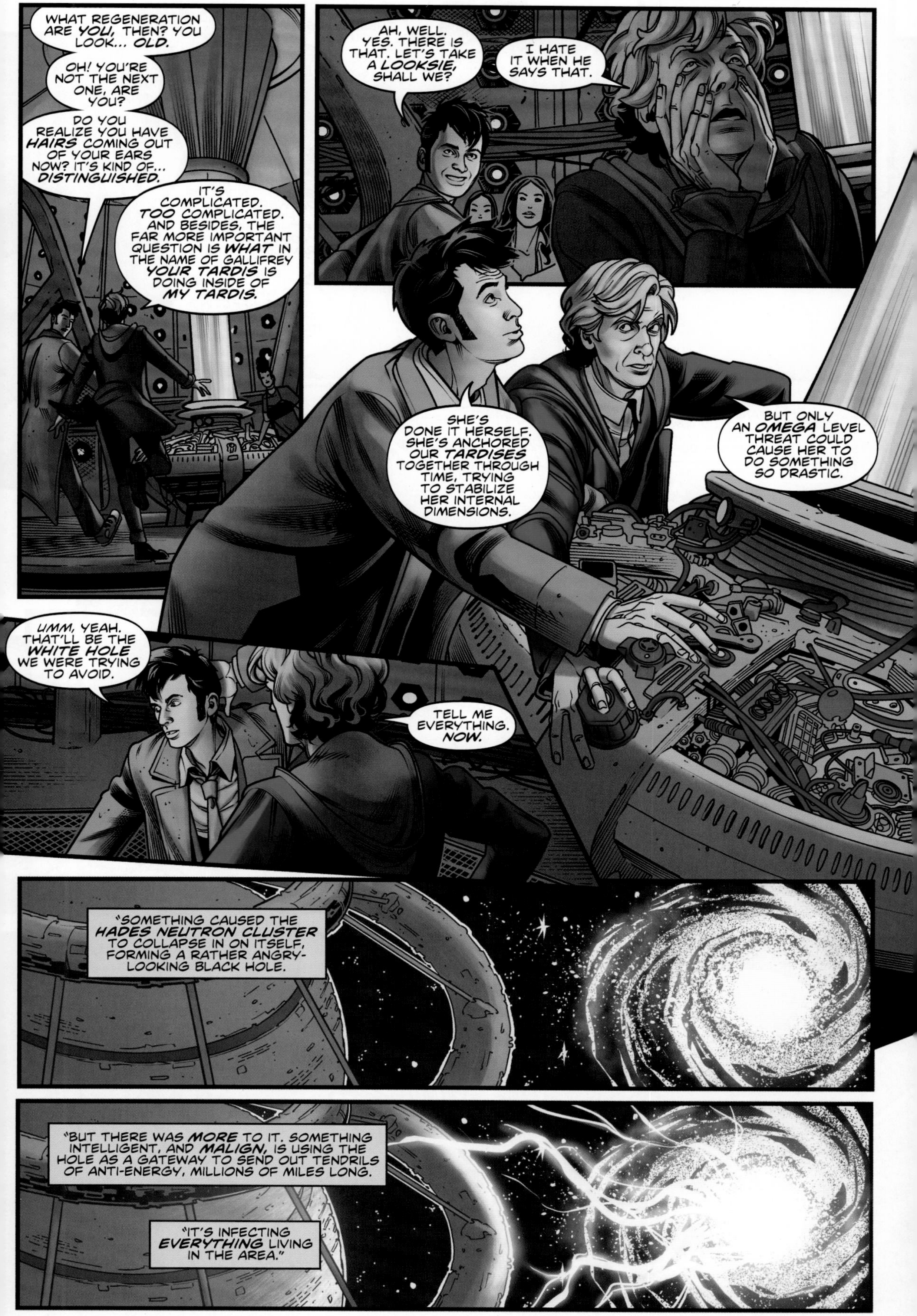
WHAT REGENERATION ARE YOU, THEN? YOU LOOK... OLD.
OH! YOU'RE NOT THE NEXT ONE, ARE YOU?
DO YOU REALIZE YOU HAVE HAIRS COMING OUT OF YOUR EARS NOW? IT'S KIND OF... DISTINGUISHED.
IT'S COMPLICATED. TOO COMPLICATED. AND BESIDES, THE FAR MORE IMPORTANT QUESTION IS WHAT IN THE NAME OF GALLIFREY YOUR TARDIS IS DOING INSIDE OF MY TARDIS.
AH, WELL. YES. THERE IS THAT. LET'S TAKE A LOOKSIE, SHALL WE?
I HATE IT WHEN HE SAYS THAT.
SHE'S DONE IT HERSELF. SHE'S ANCHORED OUR TARDISES TOGETHER THROUGH TIME, TRYING TO STABILIZE HER INTERNAL DIMENSIONS.
BUT ONLY AN OMEGA LEVEL THREAT COULD CAUSE HER TO DO SOMETHING SO DRASTIC.
UMM, YEAH. THAT'LL BE THE WHITE HOLE WE WERE TRYING TO AVOID.
TELL ME EVERYTHING. NOW.
"SOMETHING CAUSED THE HADES NEUTRON CLUSTER TO COLLAPSE IN ON ITSELF, FORMING A RATHER ANGRY-LOOKING BLACK HOLE.
"BUT THERE WAS MORE TO IT. SOMETHING INTELLIGENT, AND MALIGN, IS USING THE HOLE AS A GATEWAY TO SEND OUT TENDRILS OF ANTI-ENERGY, MILLIONS OF MILES LONG.
"IT'S INFECTING EVERYTHING LIVING IN THE AREA."

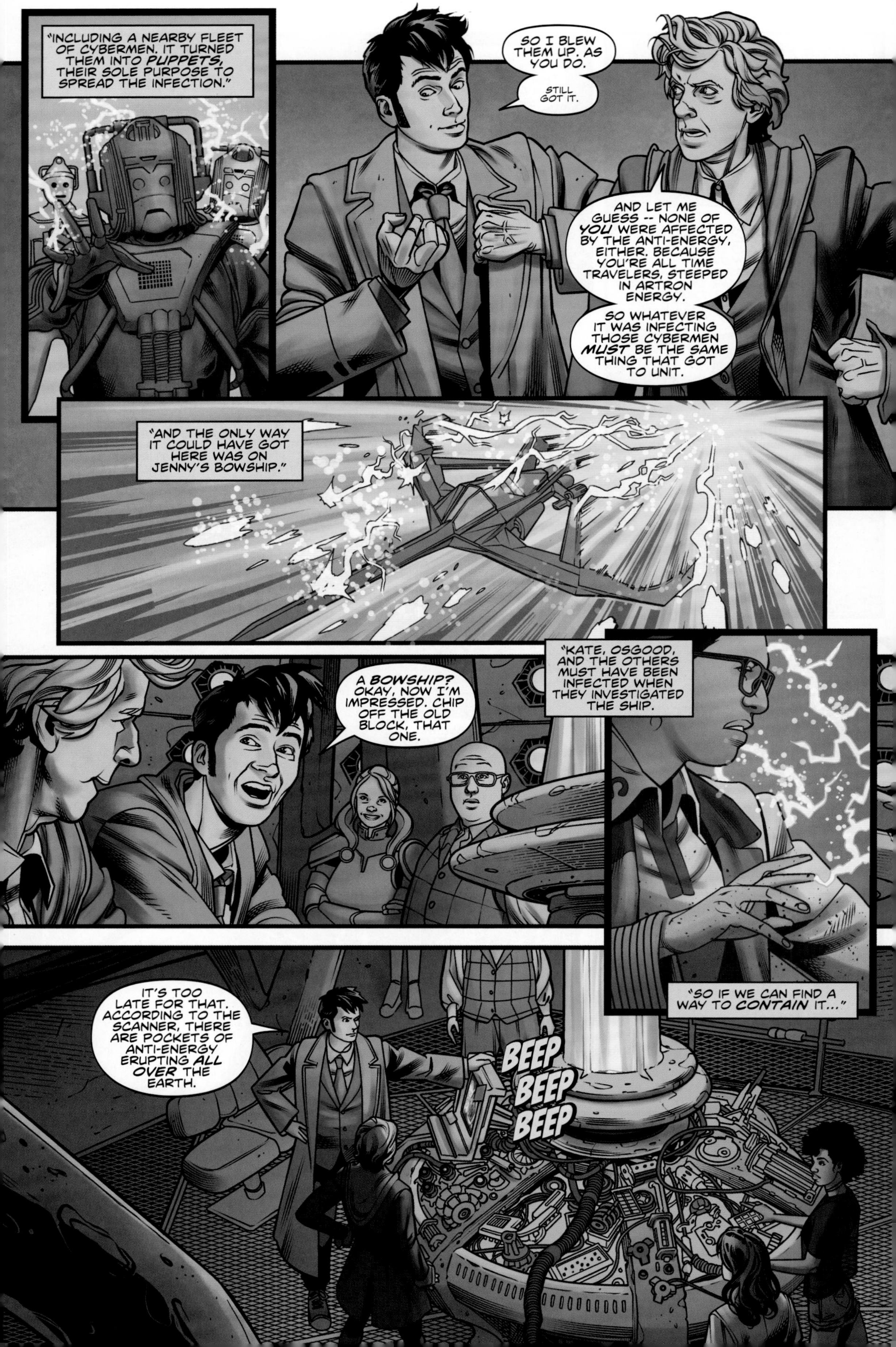

"INCLUDING A NEARBY FLEET OF CYBERMEN. IT TURNED THEM INTO *PUPPETS*, THEIR SOLE PURPOSE TO SPREAD THE INFECTION."
SO I BLEW THEM UP. AS YOU DO.
STILL GOT IT.
AND LET ME GUESS -- NONE OF *YOU* WERE AFFECTED BY THE ANTI-ENERGY, EITHER. BECAUSE YOU'RE ALL TIME TRAVELERS, STEEPED IN ARTRON ENERGY.
SO WHATEVER IT WAS INFECTING THOSE CYBERMEN *MUST* BE THE SAME THING THAT GOT TO UNIT.
"AND THE ONLY WAY IT COULD HAVE GOT HERE WAS ON JENNY'S BOWSHIP."
A *BOWSHIP*? OKAY, NOW I'M IMPRESSED. CHIP OFF THE OLD BLOCK, THAT ONE.
"KATE, OSGOOD, AND THE OTHERS MUST HAVE BEEN INFECTED WHEN THEY INVESTIGATED THE SHIP.
"SO IF WE CAN FIND A WAY TO *CONTAIN* IT..."
IT'S TOO LATE FOR THAT. ACCORDING TO THE SCANNER, THERE ARE POCKETS OF ANTI-ENERGY ERUPTING *ALL OVER* THE EARTH.
BEEP BEEP BEEP

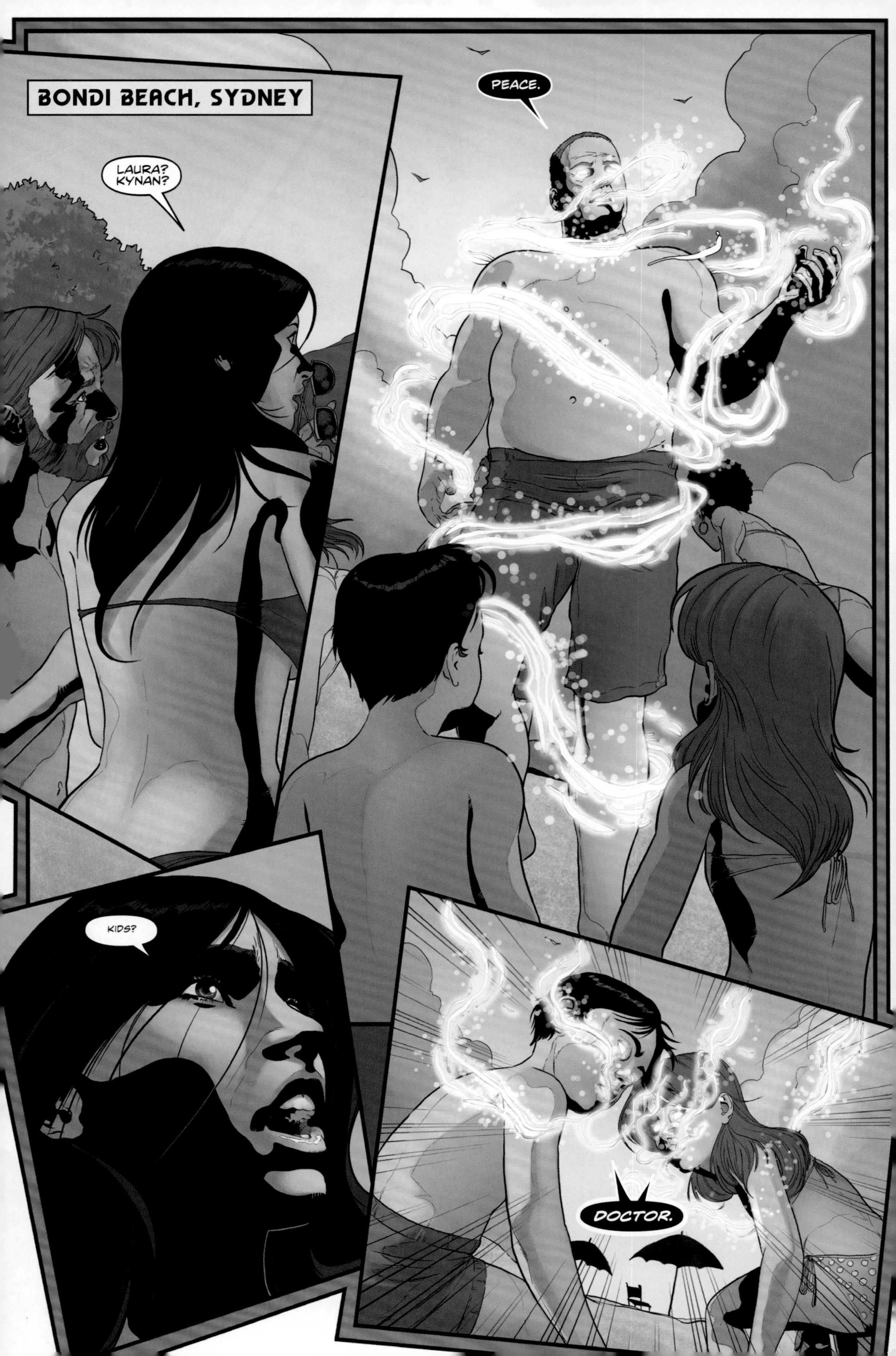
BONDI BEACH, SYDNEY
LAURA? KYNAN?
PEACE.
KIDS?
DOCTOR.

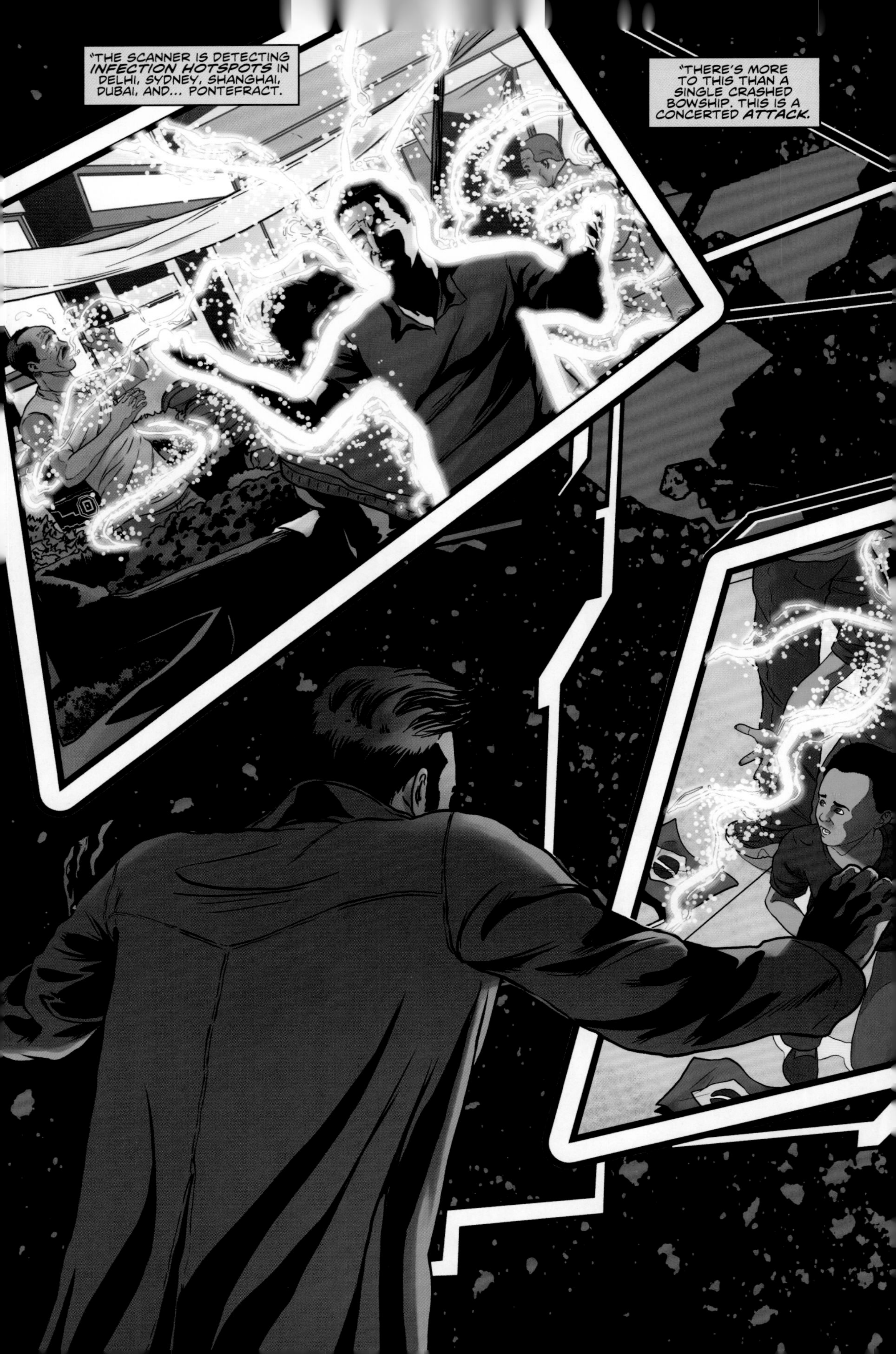
"THE SCANNER IS DETECTING INFECTION HOTSPOTS IN DELHI, SYDNEY, SHANGHAI, DUBAI, AND... PONTEFRACT.
"THERE'S MORE TO THIS THAN A SINGLE CRASHED BOWSHIP. THIS IS A CONCERTED ATTACK.

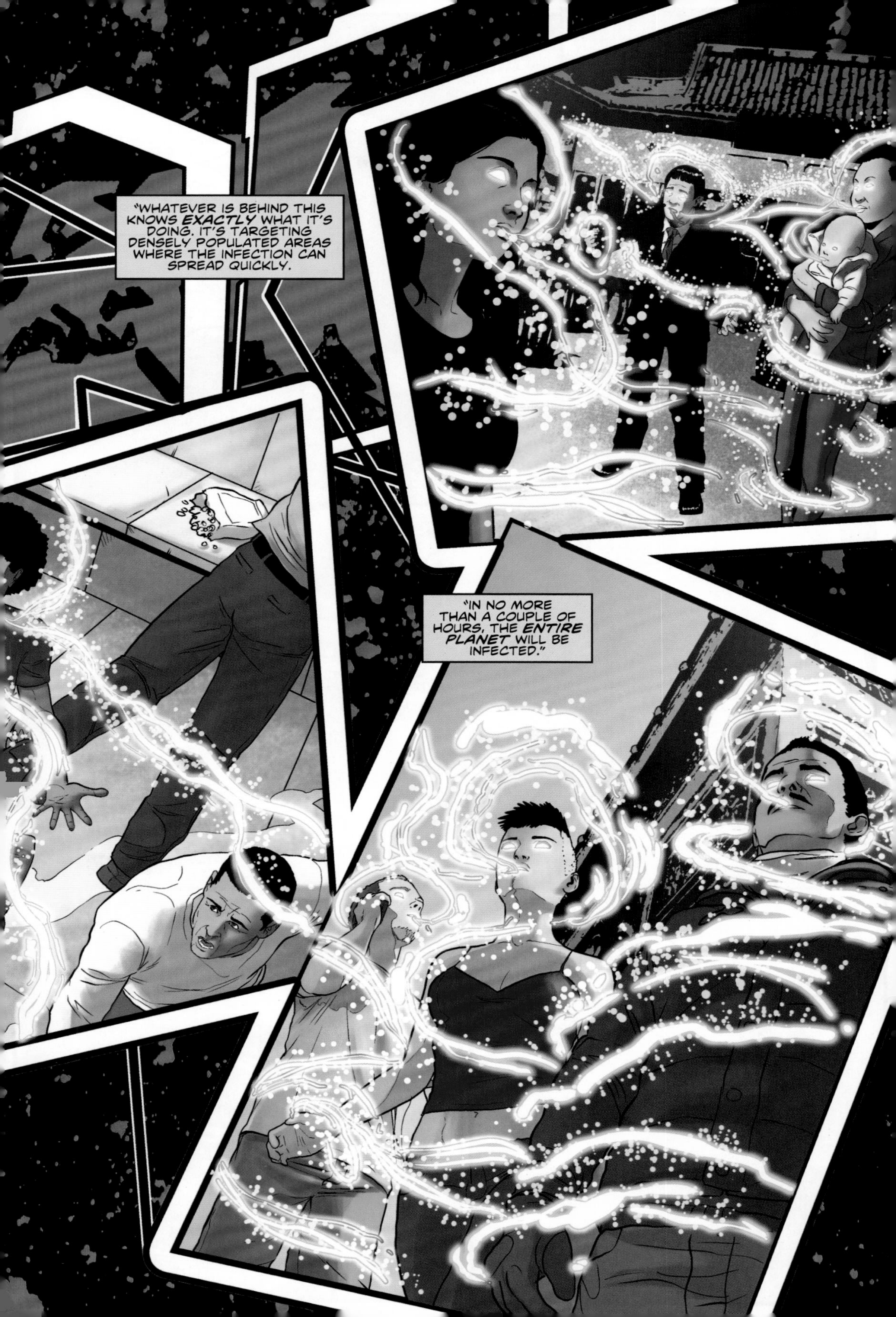
"WHATEVER IS BEHIND THIS KNOWS EXACTLY WHAT IT'S DOING. IT'S TARGETING DENSELY POPULATED AREAS WHERE THE INFECTION CAN SPREAD QUICKLY.
"IN NO MORE THAN A COUPLE OF HOURS, THE ENTIRE PLANET WILL BE INFECTED."

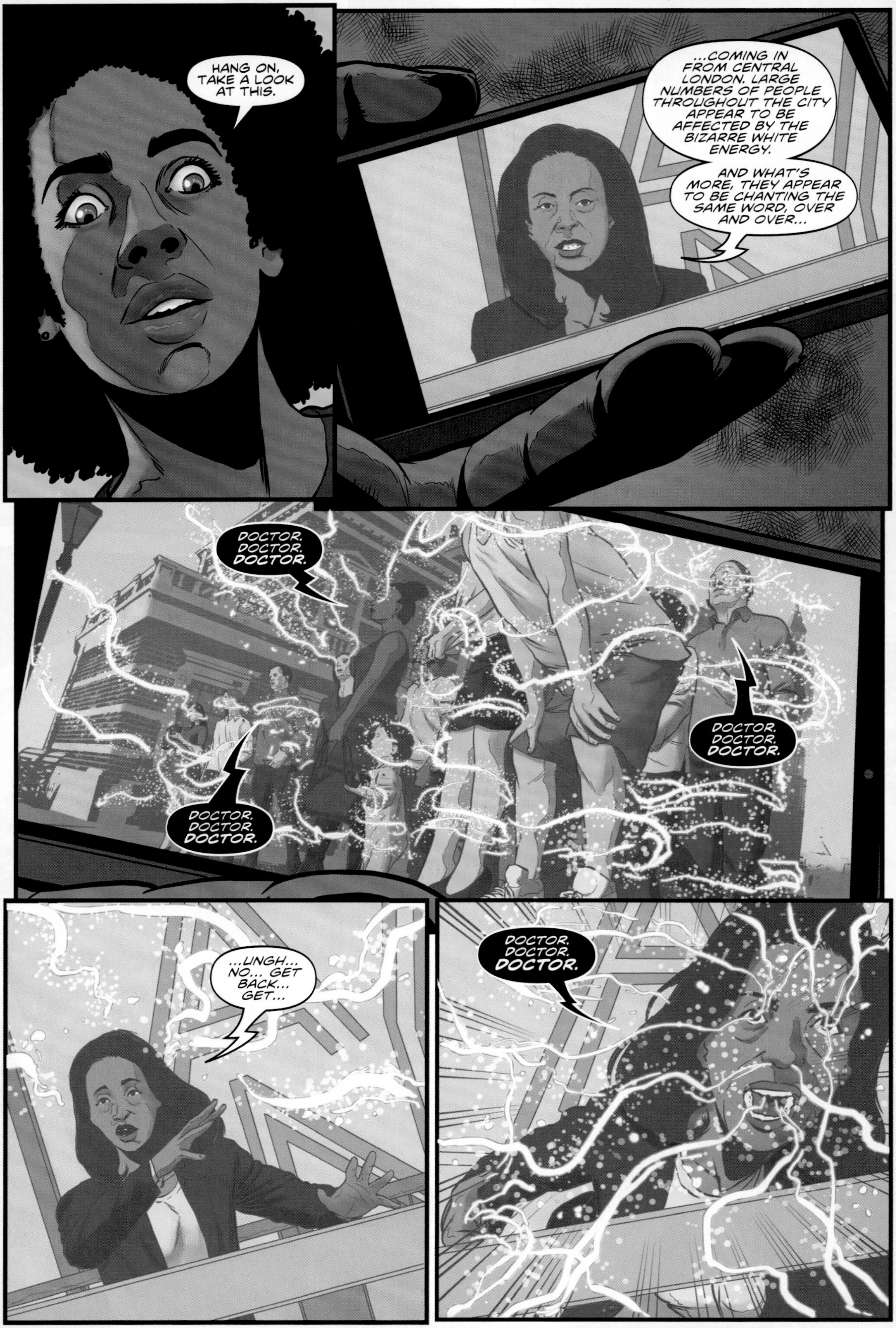
HANG ON, TAKE A LOOK AT THIS.
...COMING IN FROM CENTRAL LONDON. LARGE NUMBERS OF PEOPLE THROUGHOUT THE CITY APPEAR TO BE AFFECTED BY THE BIZARRE WHITE ENERGY.
AND WHAT'S MORE, THEY APPEAR TO BE CHANTING THE SAME WORD, OVER AND OVER...
DOCTOR. DOCTOR. DOCTOR.
DOCTOR. DOCTOR. DOCTOR.
DOCTOR. DOCTOR. DOCTOR.
...UNGH... NO... GET BACK... GET...
DOCTOR. DOCTOR. DOCTOR.

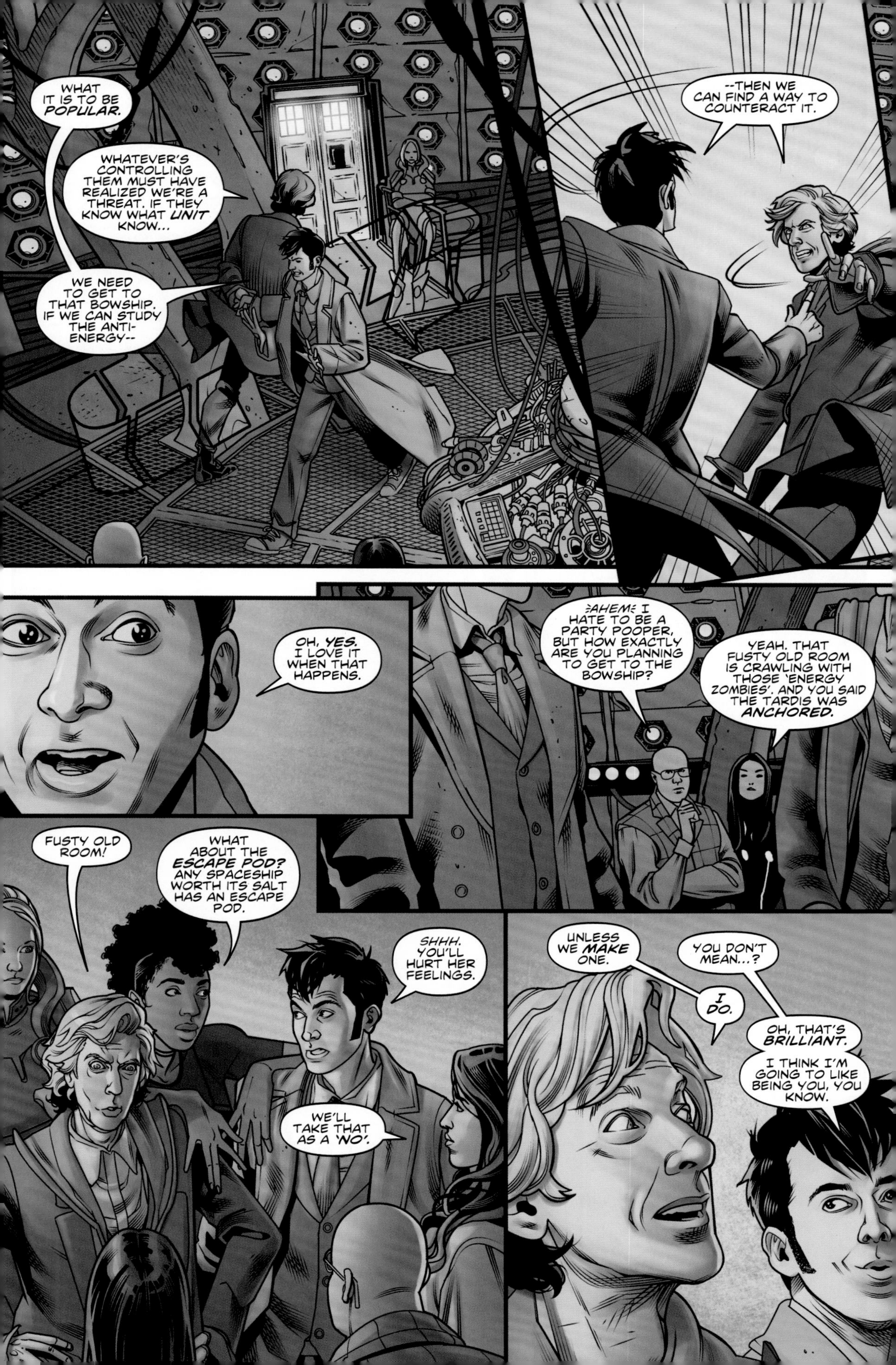
WHAT IT IS TO BE POPULAR.
WHATEVER'S CONTROLLING THEM MUST HAVE REALIZED WE'RE A THREAT. IF THEY KNOW WHAT UNIT KNOW...
WE NEED TO GET TO THAT BOWSHIP. IF WE CAN STUDY THE ANTI-ENERGY--
--THEN WE CAN FIND A WAY TO COUNTERACT IT.
OH, YES. I LOVE IT WHEN THAT HAPPENS.
AHEM I HATE TO BE A PARTY POOPER, BUT HOW EXACTLY ARE YOU PLANNING TO GET TO THE BOWSHIP?
YEAH. THAT FUSTY OLD ROOM IS CRAWLING WITH THOSE 'ENERGY ZOMBIES'. AND YOU SAID THE TARDIS WAS ANCHORED.
FUSTY OLD ROOM!
WHAT ABOUT THE ESCAPE POD? ANY SPACESHIP WORTH ITS SALT HAS AN ESCAPE POD.
SHHH. YOU'LL HURT HER FEELINGS.
WE'LL TAKE THAT AS A 'NO'.
UNLESS WE MAKE ONE.
YOU DON'T MEAN...?
I DO.
OH, THAT'S BRILLIANT.
I THINK I'M GOING TO LIKE BEING YOU, YOU KNOW.

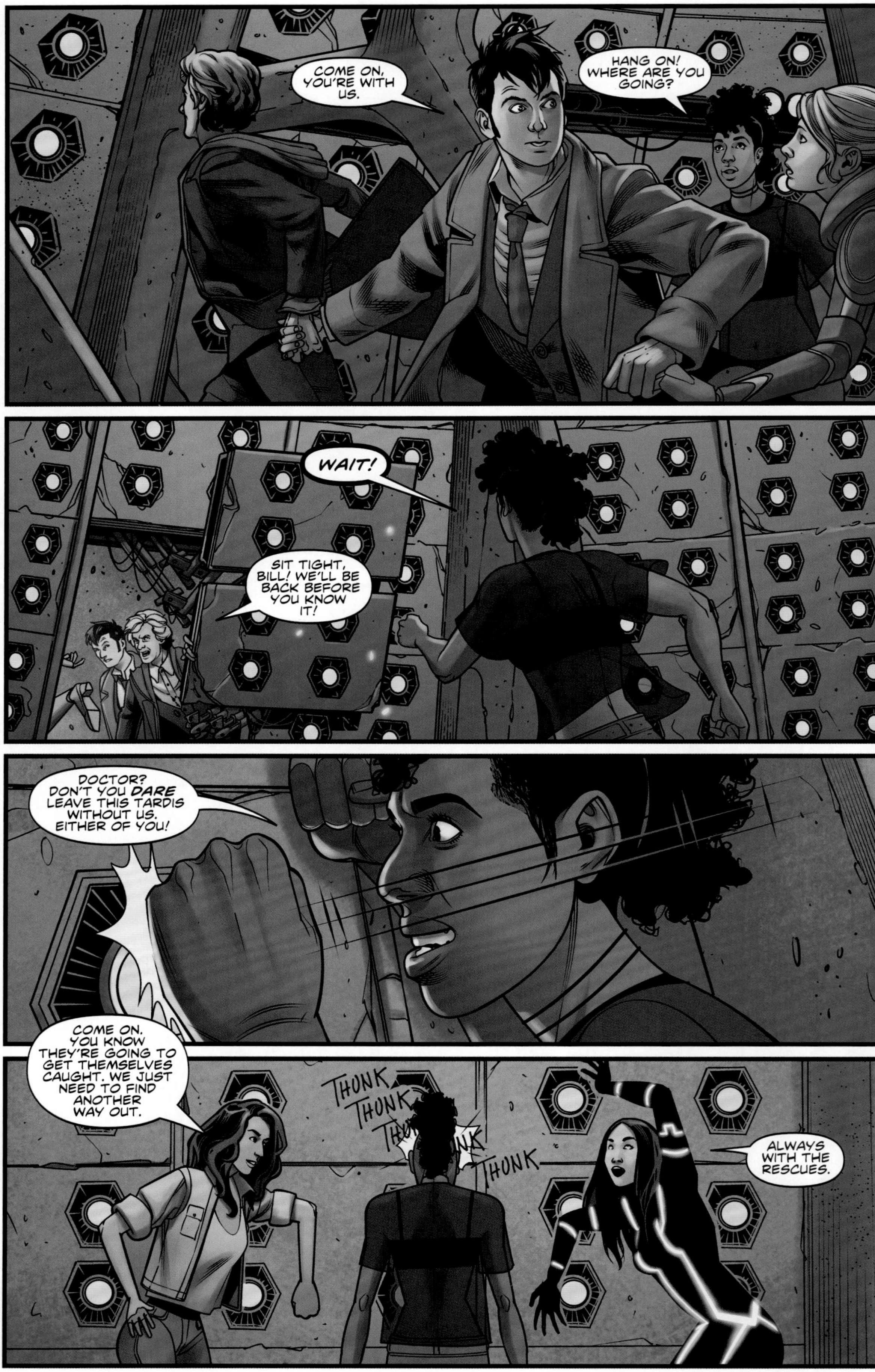
COME ON, YOU'RE WITH US.
HANG ON! WHERE ARE YOU GOING?
WAIT!
SIT TIGHT, BILL! WE'LL BE BACK BEFORE YOU KNOW IT!
DOCTOR? DON'T YOU DARE LEAVE THIS TARDIS WITHOUT US. EITHER OF YOU!
COME ON. YOU KNOW THEY'RE GOING TO GET THEMSELVES CAUGHT. WE JUST NEED TO FIND ANOTHER WAY OUT.
THUNK THUNK THUNK THUNK THUNK
ALWAYS WITH THE RESCUES.

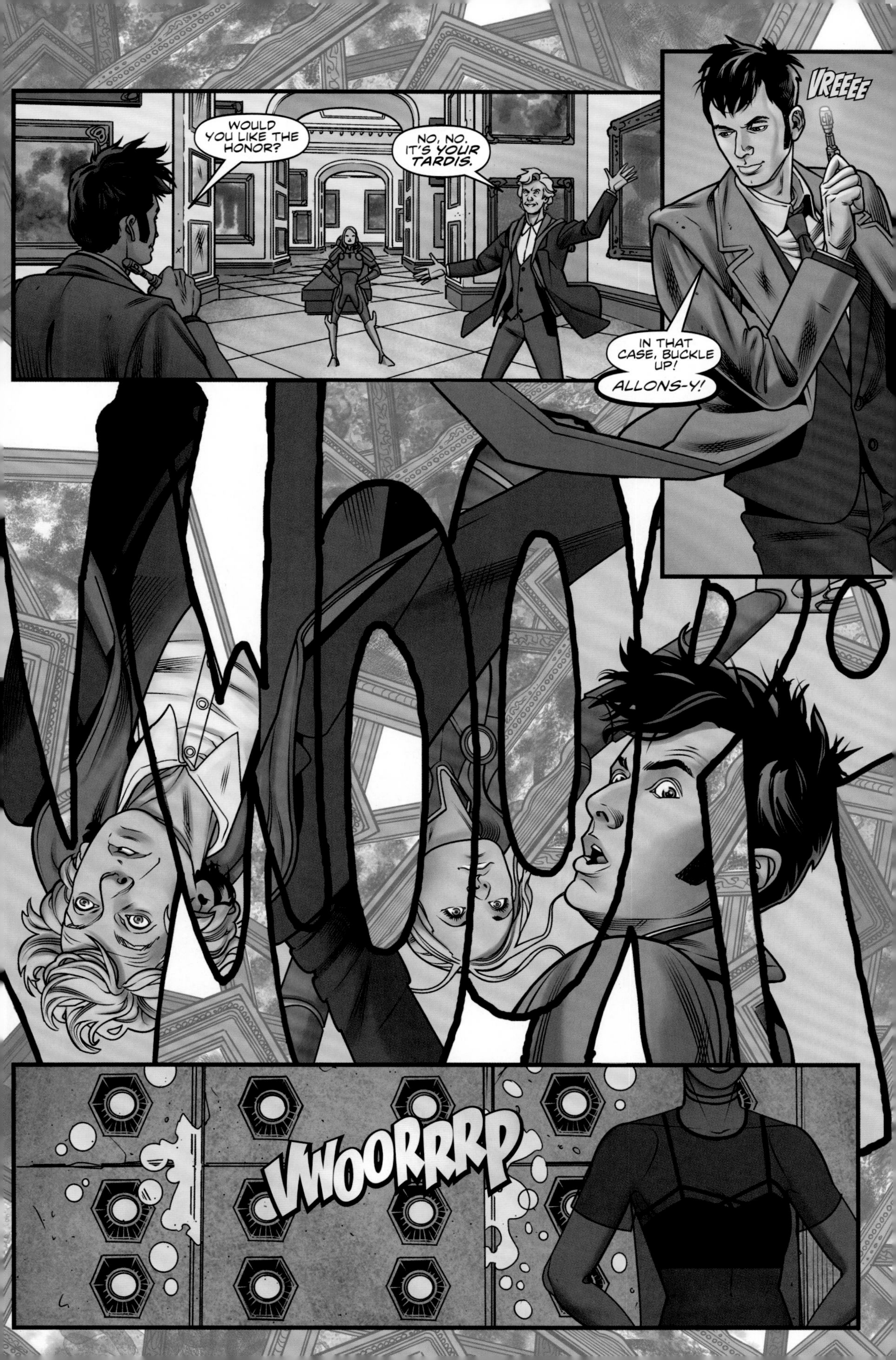
WOULD YOU LIKE THE HONOR?
NO, NO. IT'S YOUR TARDIS.
VREEEE
IN THAT CASE, BUCKLE UP!
ALLONS-Y!
VWOORRRP

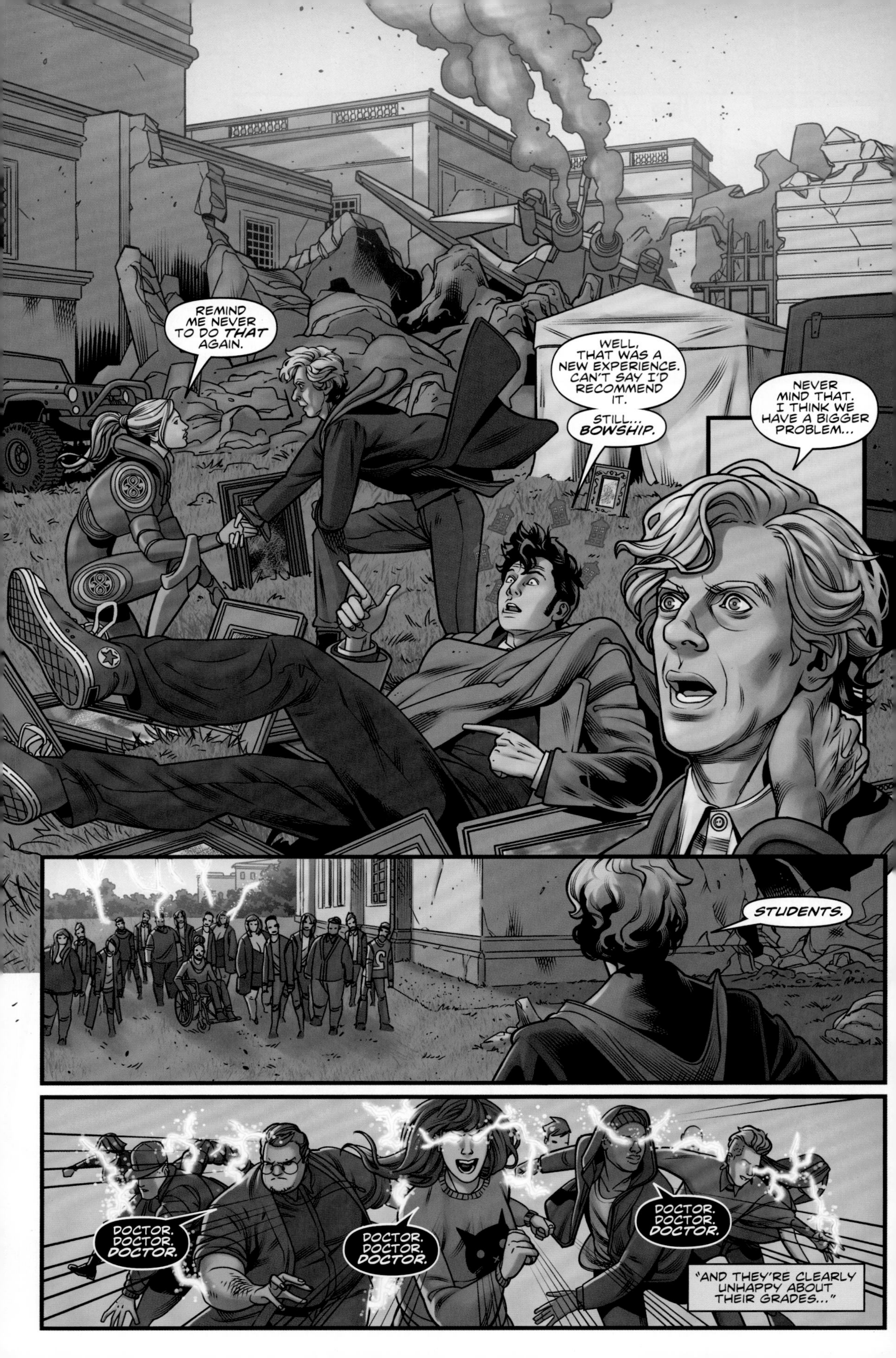
REMIND ME NEVER TO DO *THAT* AGAIN.
WELL, THAT WAS A NEW EXPERIENCE. CAN'T SAY I'D RECOMMEND IT.
STILL... ***BOWSHIP.***
NEVER MIND THAT. I THINK WE HAVE A BIGGER PROBLEM...
STUDENTS.
DOCTOR. DOCTOR. ***DOCTOR.***
DOCTOR. DOCTOR. ***DOCTOR.***
DOCTOR. DOCTOR. ***DOCTOR.***
"AND THEY'RE CLEARLY UNHAPPY ABOUT THEIR GRADES..."

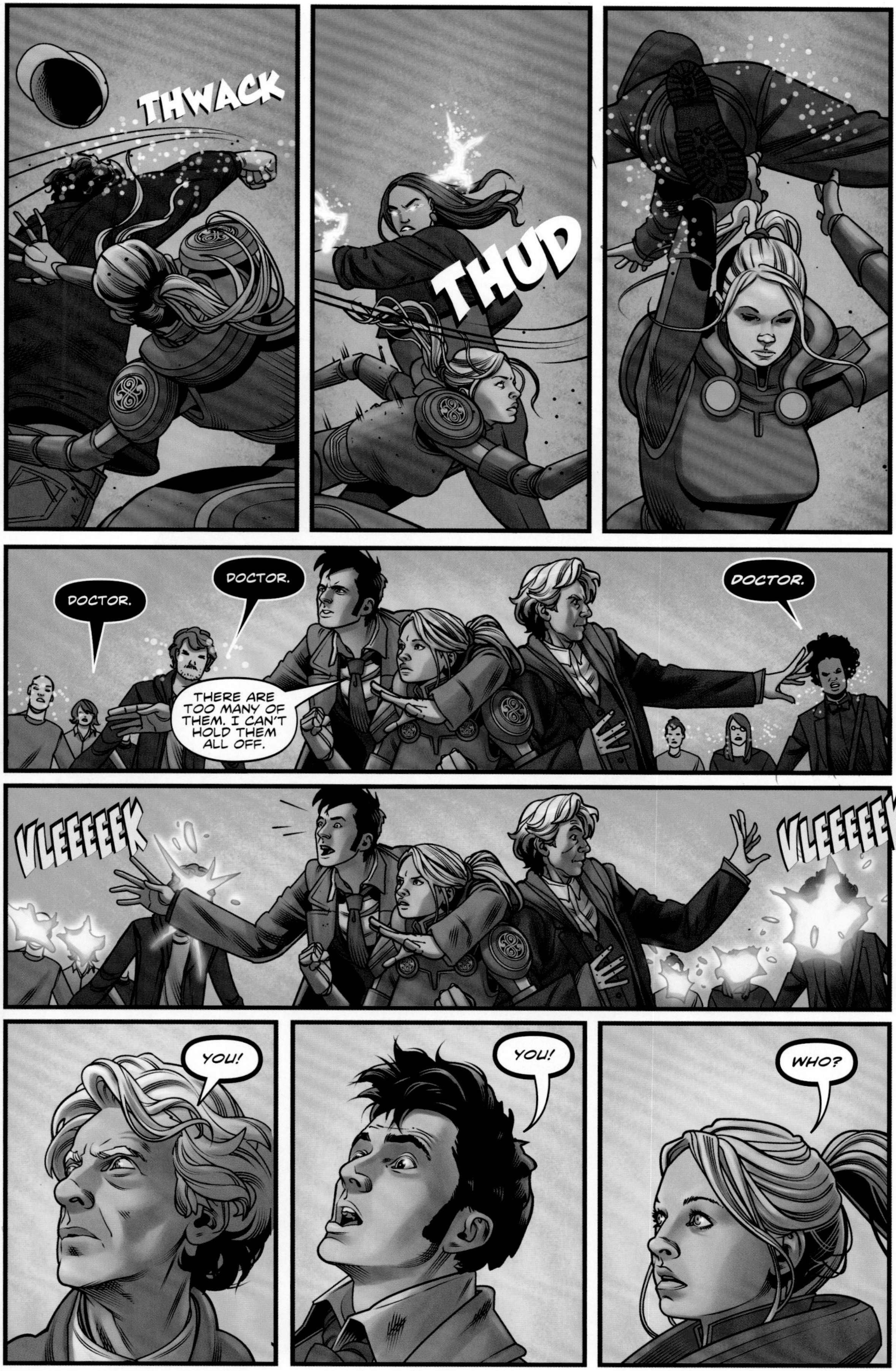
THWACK
THUD
DOCTOR.
DOCTOR.
DOCTOR.
THERE ARE TOO MANY OF THEM. I CAN'T HOLD THEM ALL OFF.
VLEEEEEK
VLEEEEEK
YOU!
YOU!
WHO?

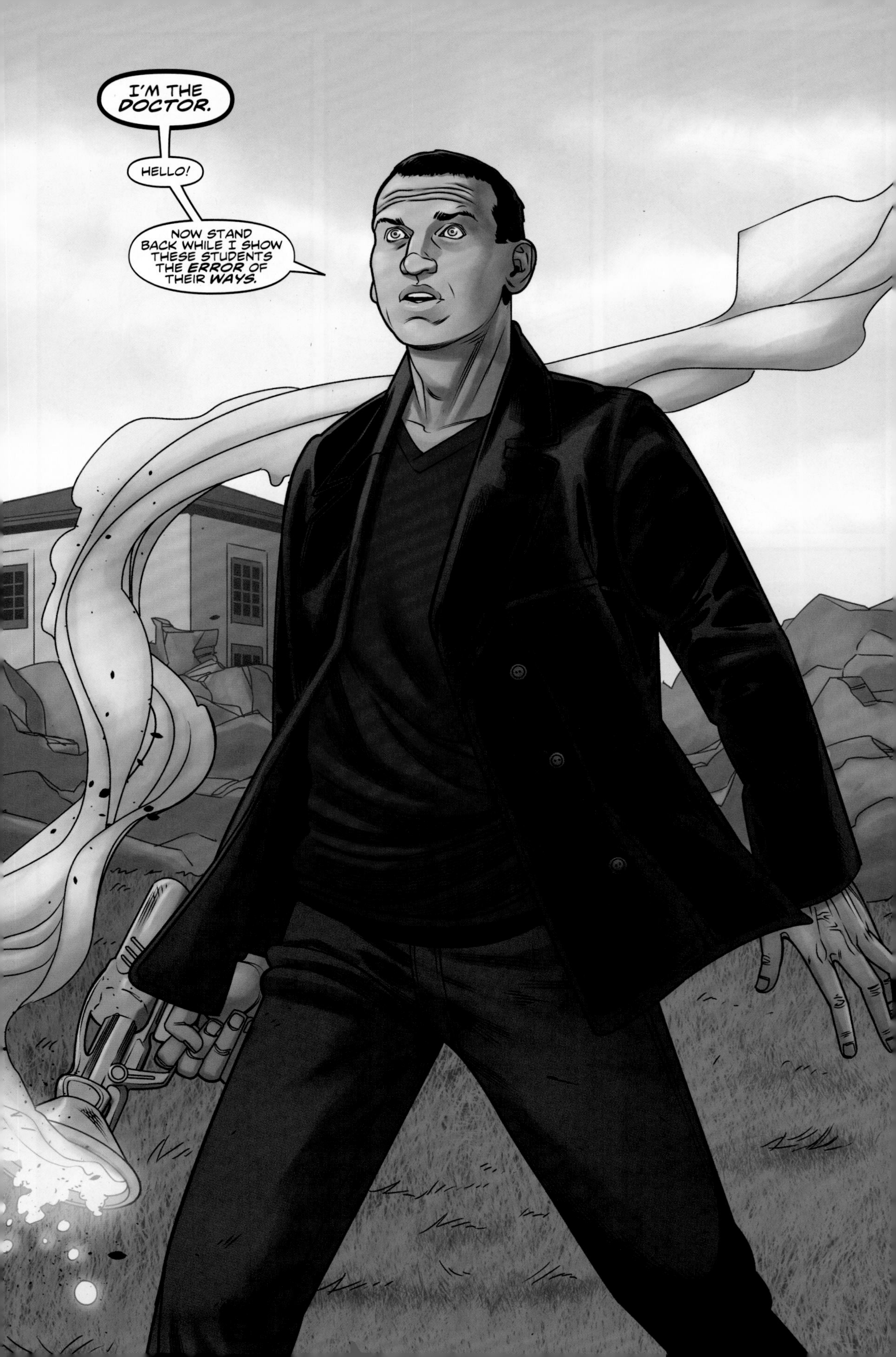
I'M THE *DOCTOR.*
HELLO!
NOW STAND BACK WHILE I SHOW THESE STUDENTS THE *ERROR* OF THEIR *WAYS.*

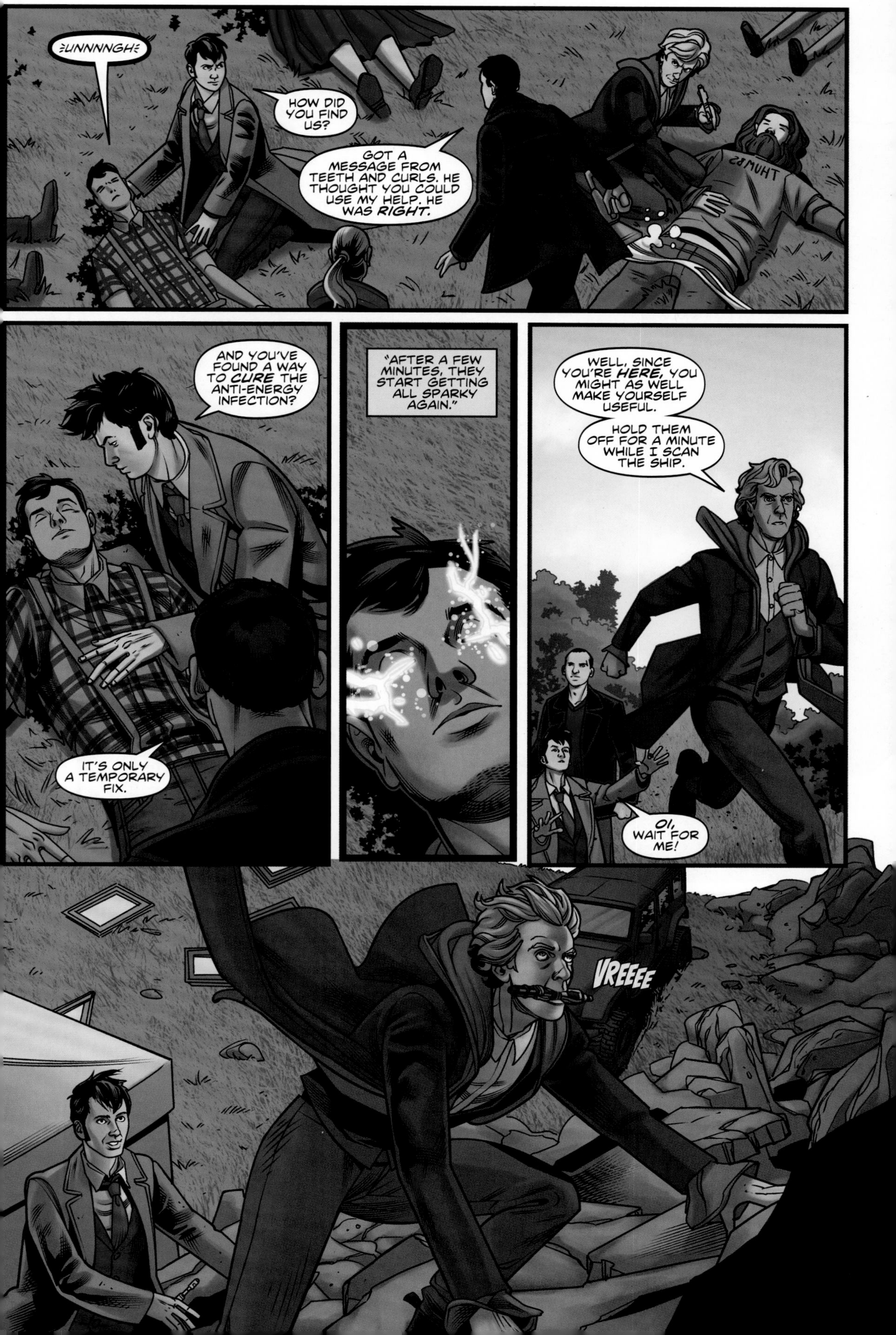
UNNNNGH
HOW DID YOU FIND US?
GOT A MESSAGE FROM TEETH AND CURLS. HE THOUGHT YOU COULD USE MY HELP. HE WAS *RIGHT.*
AND YOU'VE FOUND A WAY TO *CURE* THE ANTI-ENERGY INFECTION?
IT'S ONLY A TEMPORARY FIX.
"AFTER A FEW MINUTES, THEY START GETTING ALL SPARKY AGAIN."
WELL, SINCE YOU'RE *HERE*, YOU MIGHT AS WELL MAKE YOURSELF USEFUL.
HOLD THEM OFF FOR A MINUTE WHILE I SCAN THE SHIP.
OI, WAIT FOR ME!
VREEEE

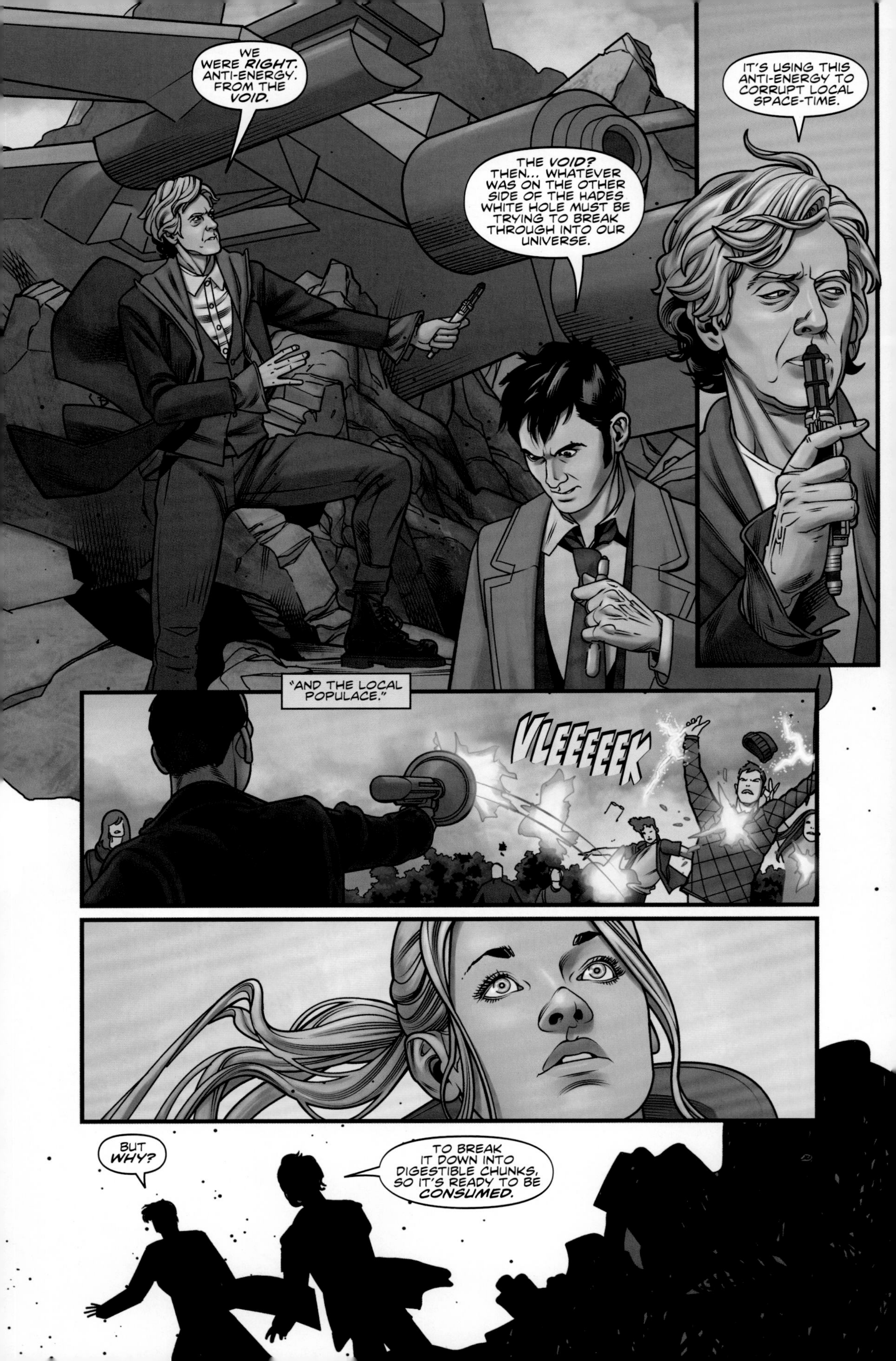
WE WERE RIGHT. ANTI-ENERGY. FROM THE VOID.
THE VOID? THEN... WHATEVER WAS ON THE OTHER SIDE OF THE HADES WHITE HOLE MUST BE TRYING TO BREAK THROUGH INTO OUR UNIVERSE.
IT'S USING THIS ANTI-ENERGY TO CORRUPT LOCAL SPACE-TIME.
"AND THE LOCAL POPULACE."
VLEEEEEK
BUT WHY?
TO BREAK IT DOWN INTO DIGESTIBLE CHUNKS, SO IT'S READY TO BE CONSUMED.

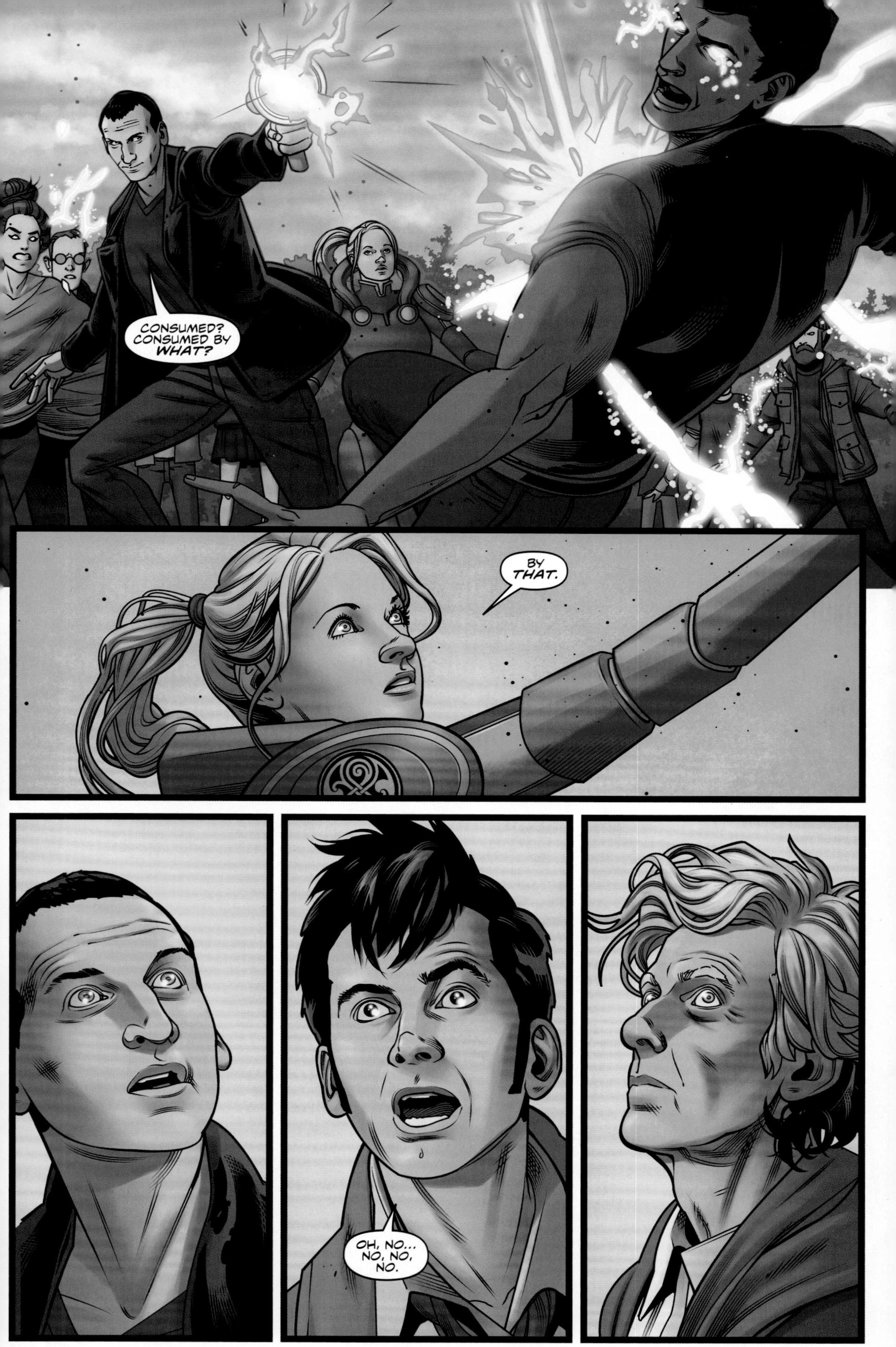
CONSUMED? CONSUMED BY WHAT?
BY THAT.
OH, NO... NO, NO, NO.

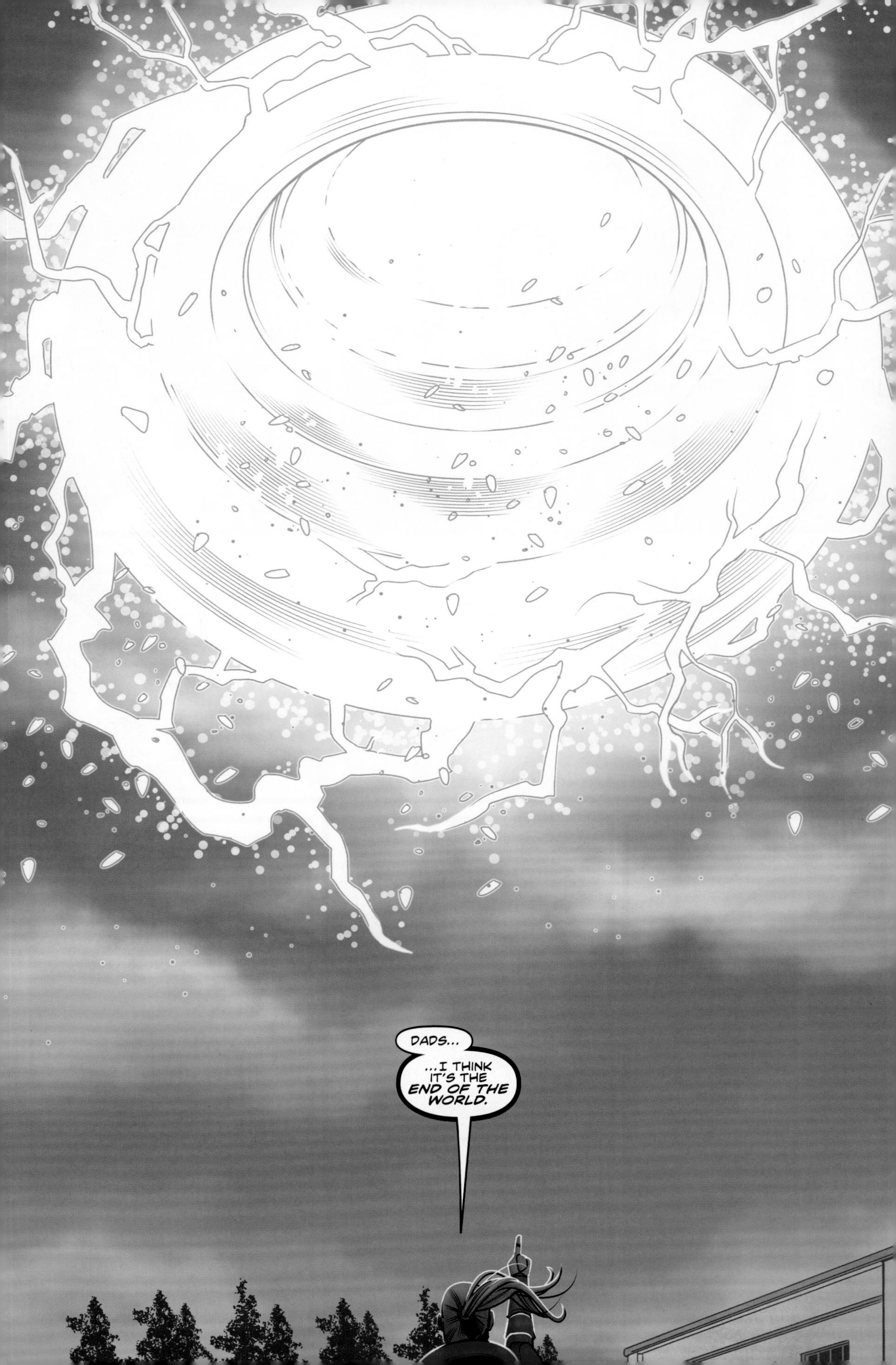
DADS...
...I THINK IT'S THE END OF THE WORLD.

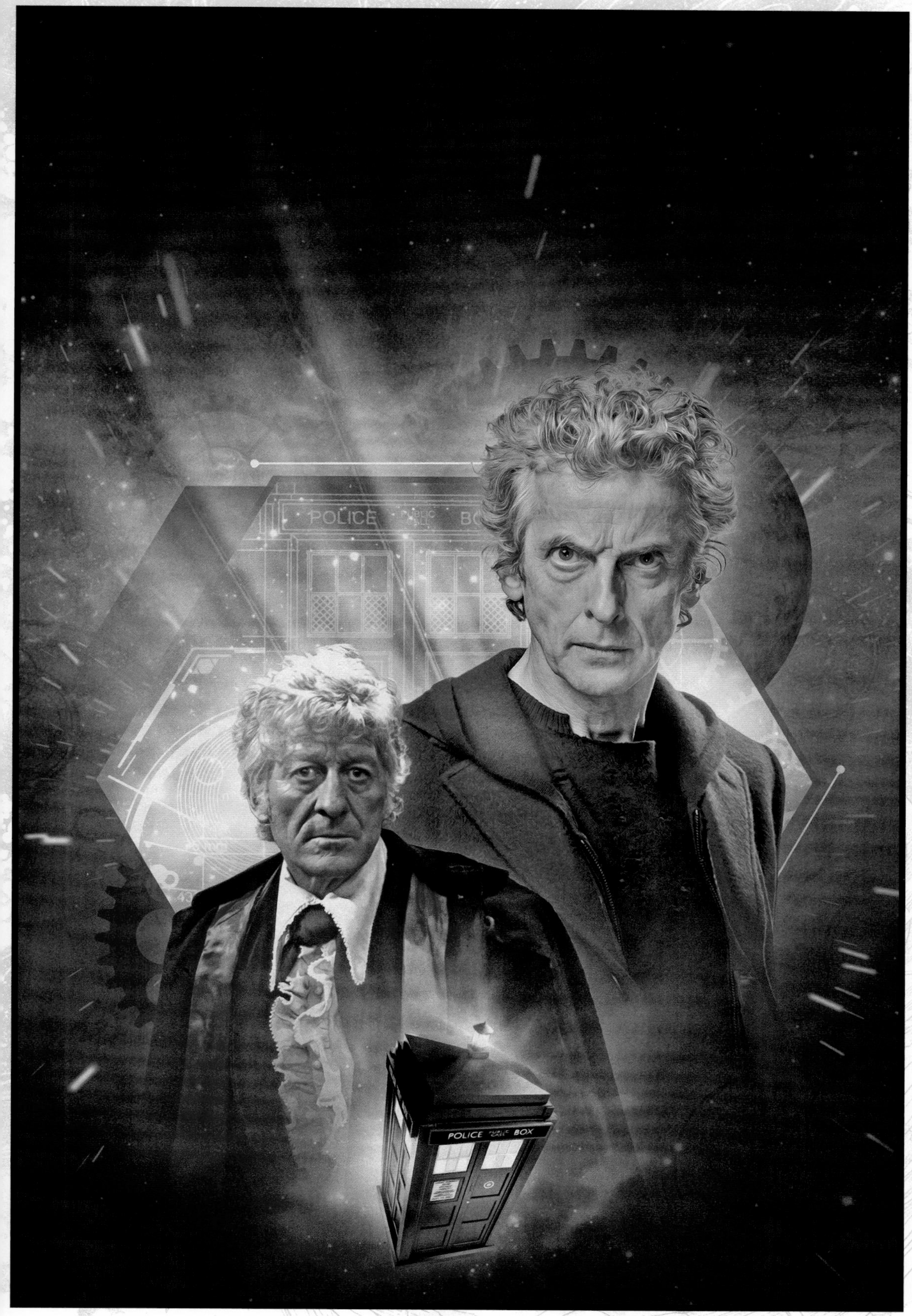
POLICE PUBLIC CALL BOX
POLICE PUBLIC CALL BOX

12D #3.8 Cover B: WILL BROOKS

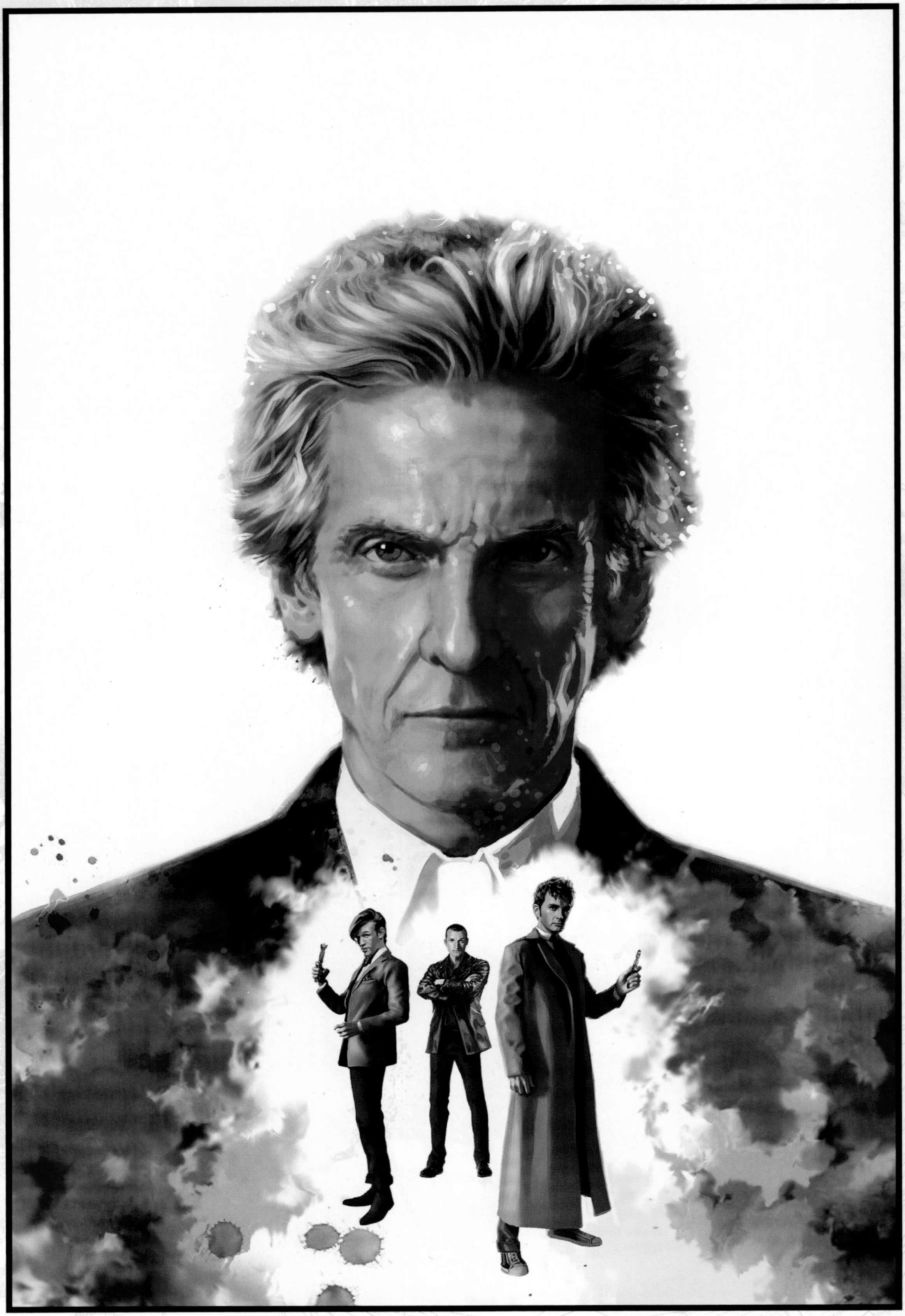

Omega Cover A: ALEX RONALD

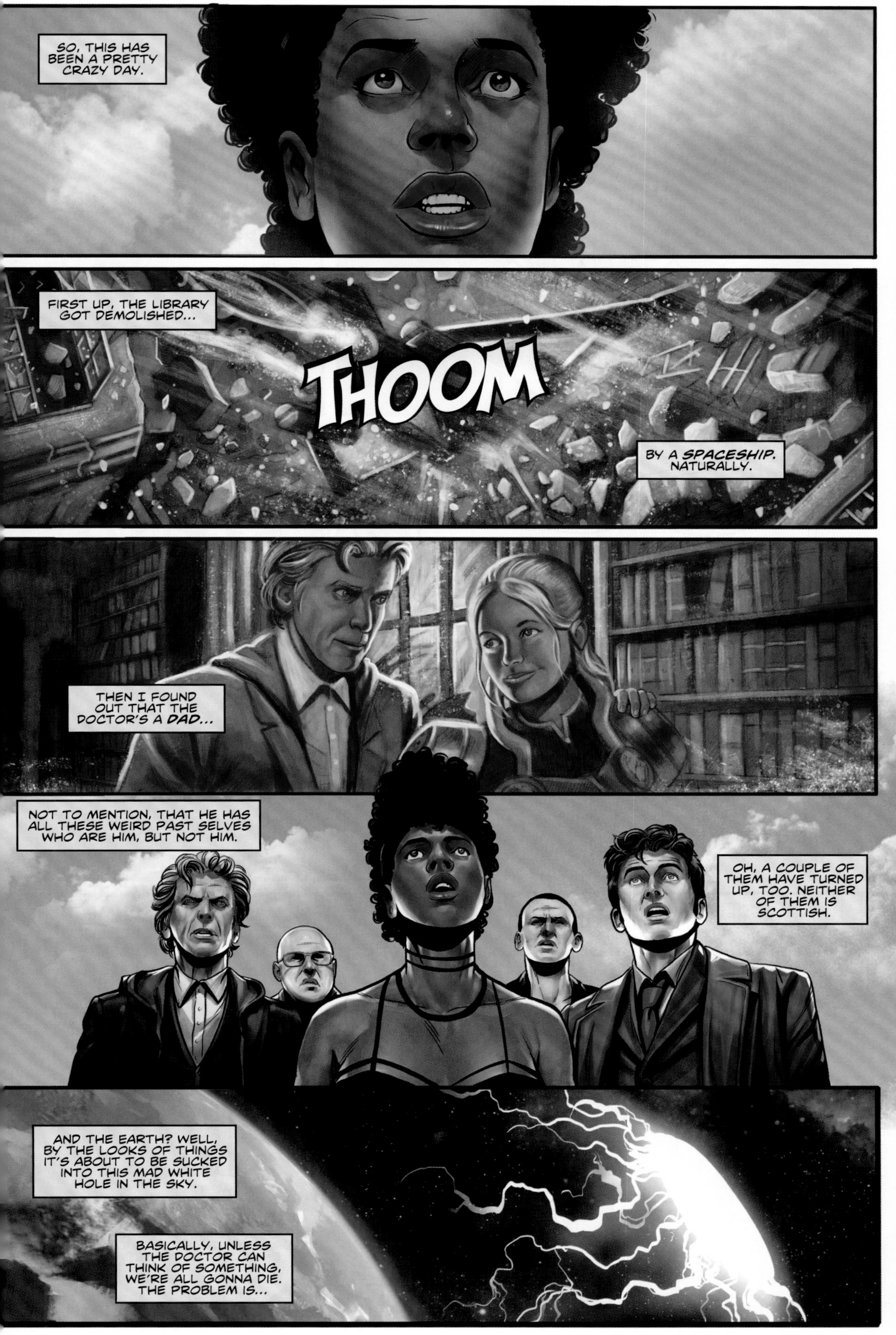
SO, THIS HAS BEEN A PRETTY CRAZY DAY.
FIRST UP, THE LIBRARY GOT DEMOLISHED...
THOOM
BY A SPACESHIP. NATURALLY.
THEN I FOUND OUT THAT THE DOCTOR'S A DAD...
NOT TO MENTION, THAT HE HAS ALL THESE WEIRD PAST SELVES WHO ARE HIM, BUT NOT HIM.
OH, A COUPLE OF THEM HAVE TURNED UP, TOO. NEITHER OF THEM IS SCOTTISH.
AND THE EARTH? WELL, BY THE LOOKS OF THINGS IT'S ABOUT TO BE SUCKED INTO THIS MAD WHITE HOLE IN THE SKY.
BASICALLY, UNLESS THE DOCTOR CAN THINK OF SOMETHING, WE'RE ALL GONNA DIE. THE PROBLEM IS...

HE'S TOO BUSY ARGUING WITH HIMSELF...

LAST TIME YOU SAW A WHITE HOLE, WHAT DID YOU DO?

WHAT DO YOU MEAN?

HOW DID YOU *STOP* IT?

WOAH, WOAH, WOAH... WHAT DID SHE MEAN BY 'DADS'?

ONE AT A TIME.

ME WITH THE EARS: SHE'S YOUR *DAUGHTER.* SORT OF. LONG STORY. HAVEN'T TIME TO EXPLAIN.

ME WITH THE EYEBROWS: I DIDN'T. I WAS BUSY TRYING NOT TO *DIE.*

WE CAN'T CLOSE THE WHITE HOLE?

PROBABLY NOT.

AND WE CAN'T STOP THE WORLD BEING SUCKED INTO IT?

NOT BY THE LOOKS OF THINGS.

VREEE

THEN WE'LL JUST HAVE TO MOVE EARTH OUT OF ITS WAY.

I'VE DONE IT BEFORE. OR AT LEAST, *HE* HAS.

YOU *WHAT?*

OI! SPOILERS.

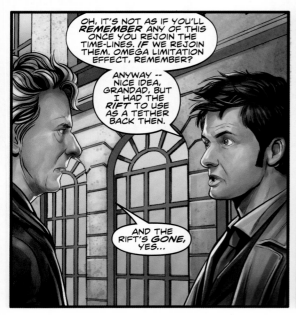

OH, IT'S NOT AS IF YOU'LL *REMEMBER* ANY OF THIS ONCE YOU REJOIN THE TIME-LINES. *IF* WE REJOIN THEM. OMEGA LIMITATION EFFECT, REMEMBER?

ANYWAY -- NICE IDEA, GRANDAD, BUT I HAD THE *RIFT* TO USE AS A TETHER BACK THEN.

AND THE RIFT'S *GONE,* YES...

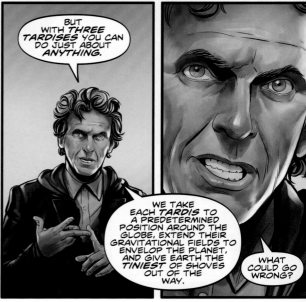

BUT WITH *THREE TARDISES* YOU CAN DO JUST ABOUT *ANYTHING.*

WE TAKE EACH *TARDIS* TO A PREDETERMINED POSITION AROUND THE GLOBE, EXTEND THEIR GRAVITATIONAL FIELDS TO ENVELOP THE PLANET, AND GIVE EARTH THE *TINIEST* OF SHOVES OUT OF THE WAY.

WHAT COULD GO WRONG?

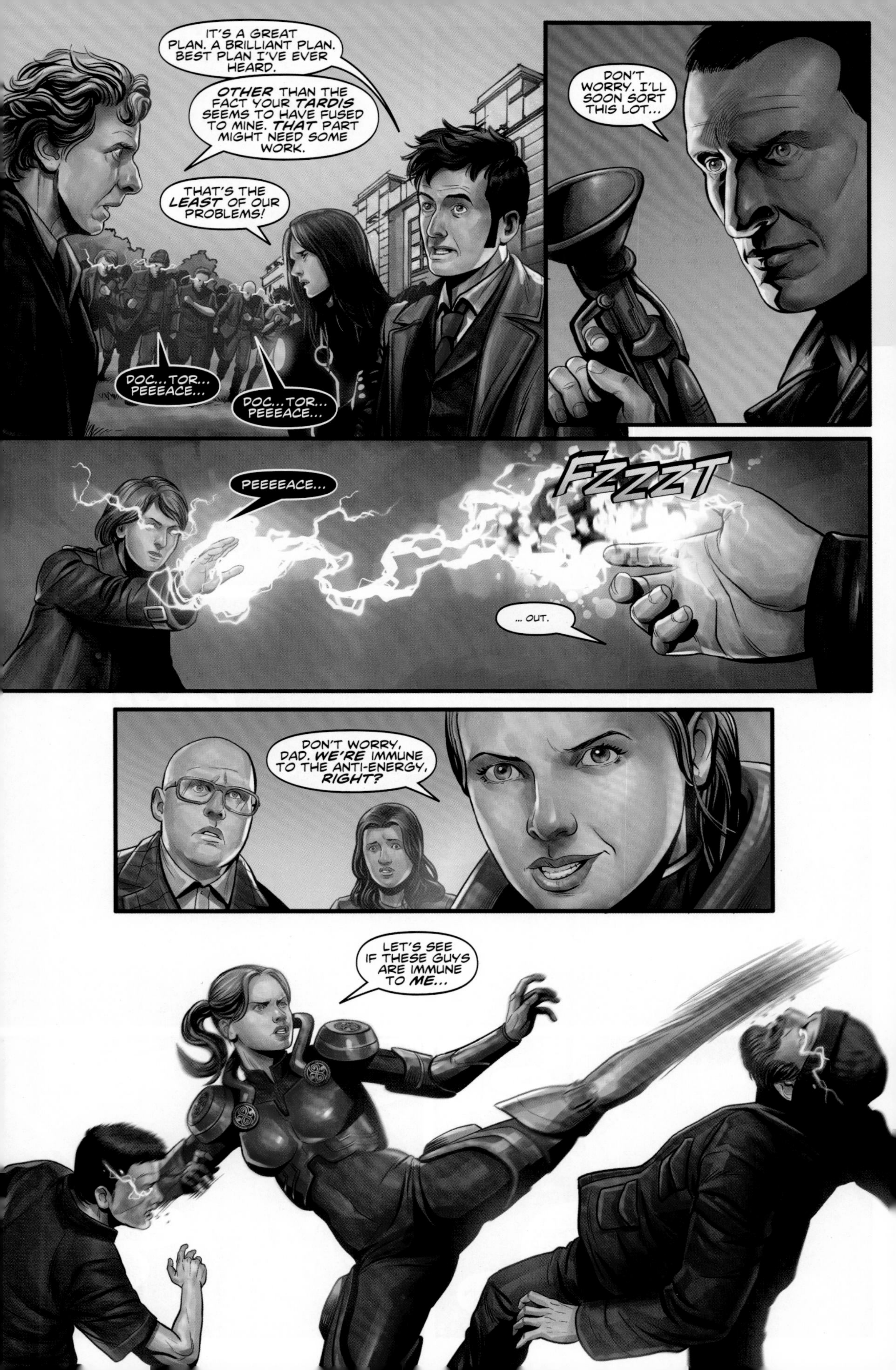
IT'S A GREAT PLAN. A BRILLIANT PLAN. BEST PLAN I'VE EVER HEARD.
OTHER THAN THE FACT YOUR TARDIS SEEMS TO HAVE FUSED TO MINE. THAT PART MIGHT NEED SOME WORK.
THAT'S THE LEAST OF OUR PROBLEMS!
DOC...TOR... PEEEACE...
DOC...TOR... PEEEACE...
DON'T WORRY. I'LL SOON SORT THIS LOT...
PEEEEACE...
FZZZT
... OUT.
DON'T WORRY, DAD. WE'RE IMMUNE TO THE ANTI-ENERGY, RIGHT?
LET'S SEE IF THESE GUYS ARE IMMUNE TO ME...

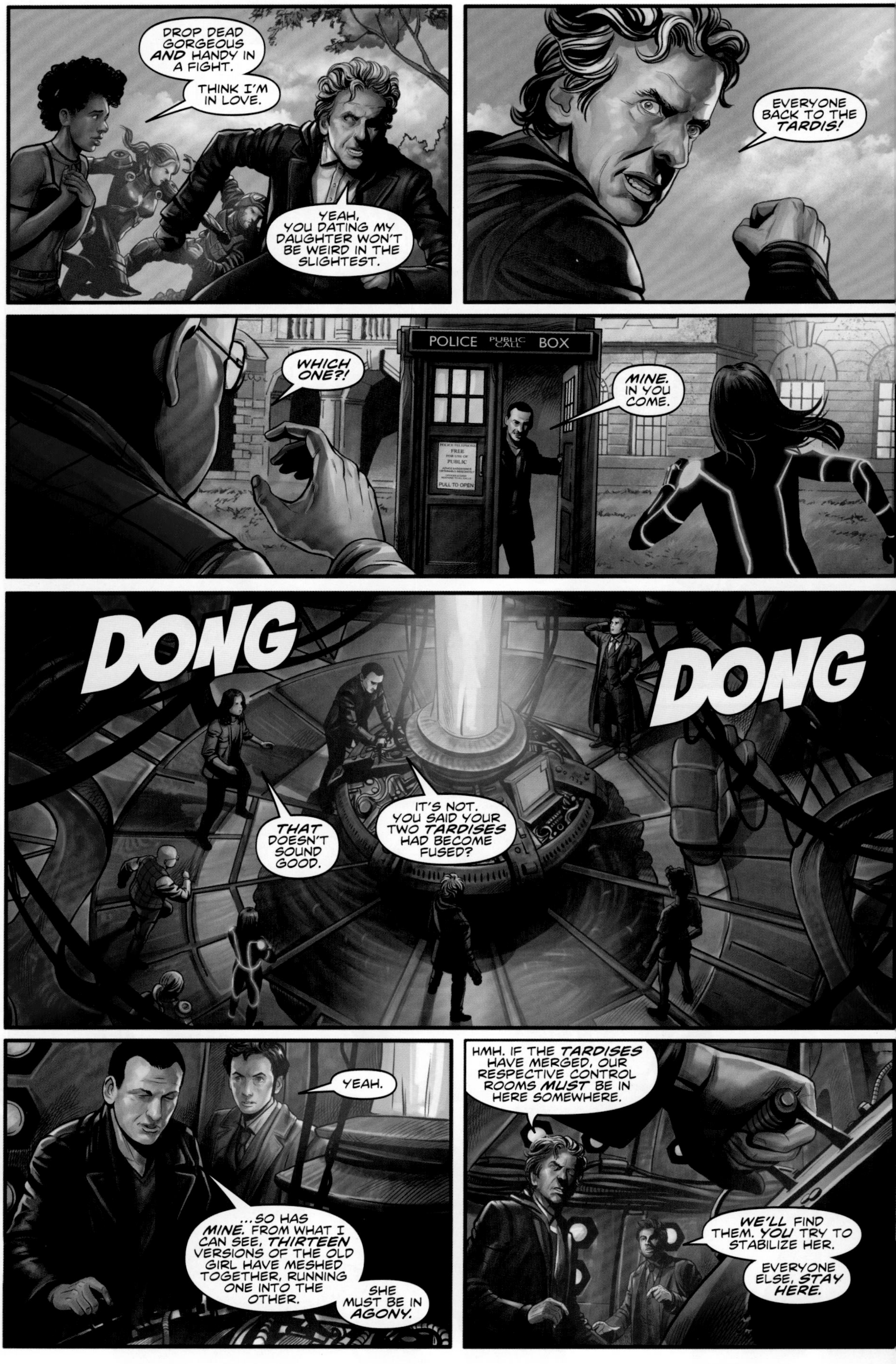
DROP DEAD GORGEOUS AND HANDY IN A FIGHT.
THINK I'M IN LOVE.
YEAH, YOU DATING MY DAUGHTER WON'T BE WEIRD IN THE SLIGHTEST.
EVERYONE BACK TO THE TARDIS!
WHICH ONE?!
POLICE PUBLIC CALL BOX
MINE. IN YOU COME.
DONG
DONG
THAT DOESN'T SOUND GOOD.
IT'S NOT. YOU SAID YOUR TWO TARDISES HAD BECOME FUSED?
YEAH.
...SO HAS MINE. FROM WHAT I CAN SEE, THIRTEEN VERSIONS OF THE OLD GIRL HAVE MESHED TOGETHER, RUNNING ONE INTO THE OTHER.
SHE MUST BE IN AGONY.
HMH. IF THE TARDISES HAVE MERGED, OUR RESPECTIVE CONTROL ROOMS MUST BE IN HERE SOMEWHERE.
WE'LL FIND THEM. YOU TRY TO STABILIZE HER.
EVERYONE ELSE, STAY HERE.

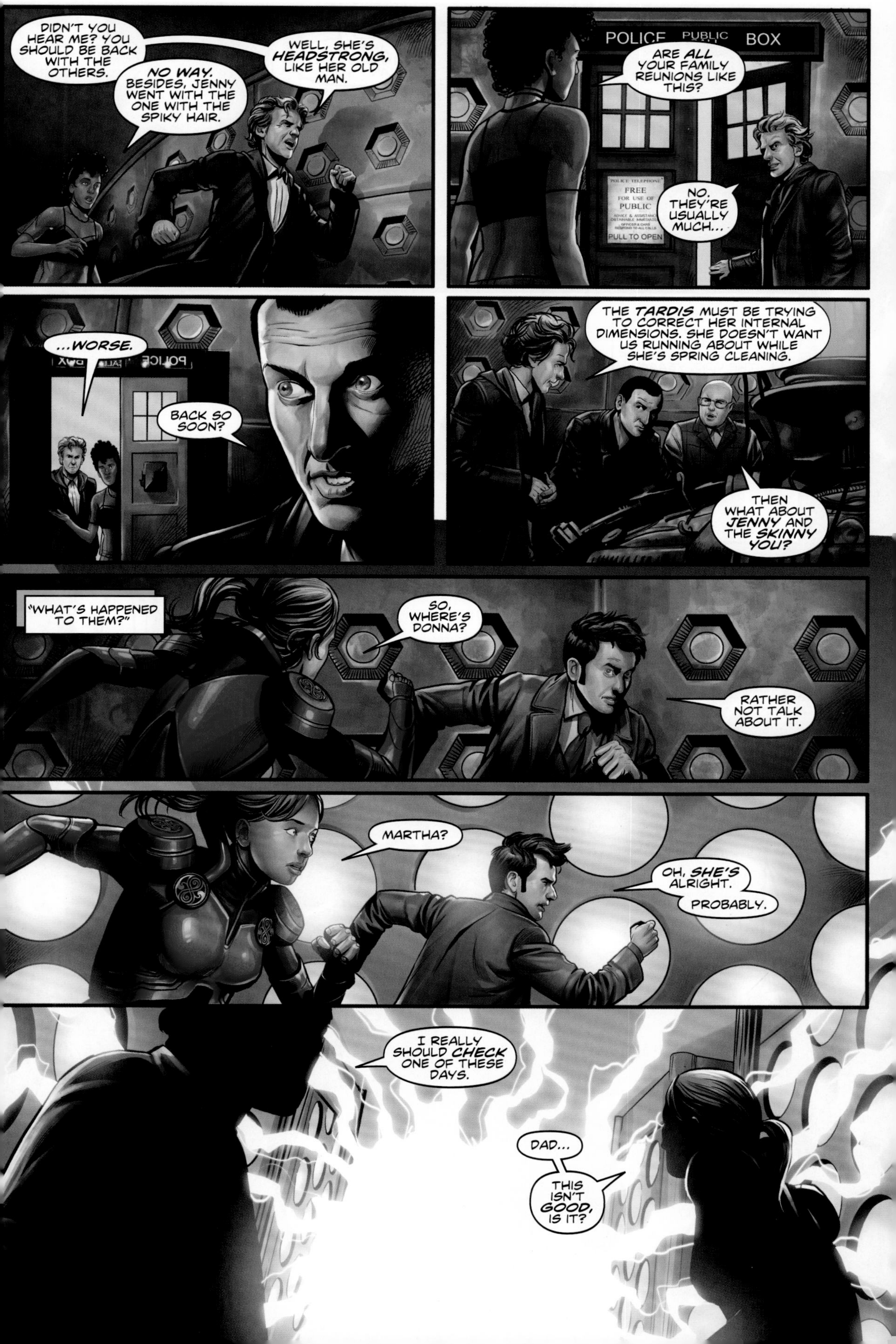
DIDN'T YOU HEAR ME? YOU SHOULD BE BACK WITH THE OTHERS.
NO WAY. BESIDES, JENNY WENT WITH THE ONE WITH THE SPIKY HAIR.
WELL, SHE'S HEADSTRONG, LIKE HER OLD MAN.
POLICE PUBLIC BOX
ARE ALL YOUR FAMILY REUNIONS LIKE THIS?
POLICE TELEPHONE FREE FOR USE OF PUBLIC ADVICE & ASSISTANCE OBTAINABLE IMMEDIATELY OFFICERS & CARS RESPOND TO ALL CALLS PULL TO OPEN
NO, THEY'RE USUALLY MUCH...
...WORSE.
BACK SO SOON?
THE TARDIS MUST BE TRYING TO CORRECT HER INTERNAL DIMENSIONS. SHE DOESN'T WANT US RUNNING ABOUT WHILE SHE'S SPRING CLEANING.
THEN WHAT ABOUT JENNY AND THE SKINNY YOU?
"WHAT'S HAPPENED TO THEM?"
SO, WHERE'S DONNA?
RATHER NOT TALK ABOUT IT.
MARTHA?
OH, SHE'S ALRIGHT.
PROBABLY.
I REALLY SHOULD CHECK ONE OF THESE DAYS.
DAD...
THIS ISN'T GOOD, IS IT?

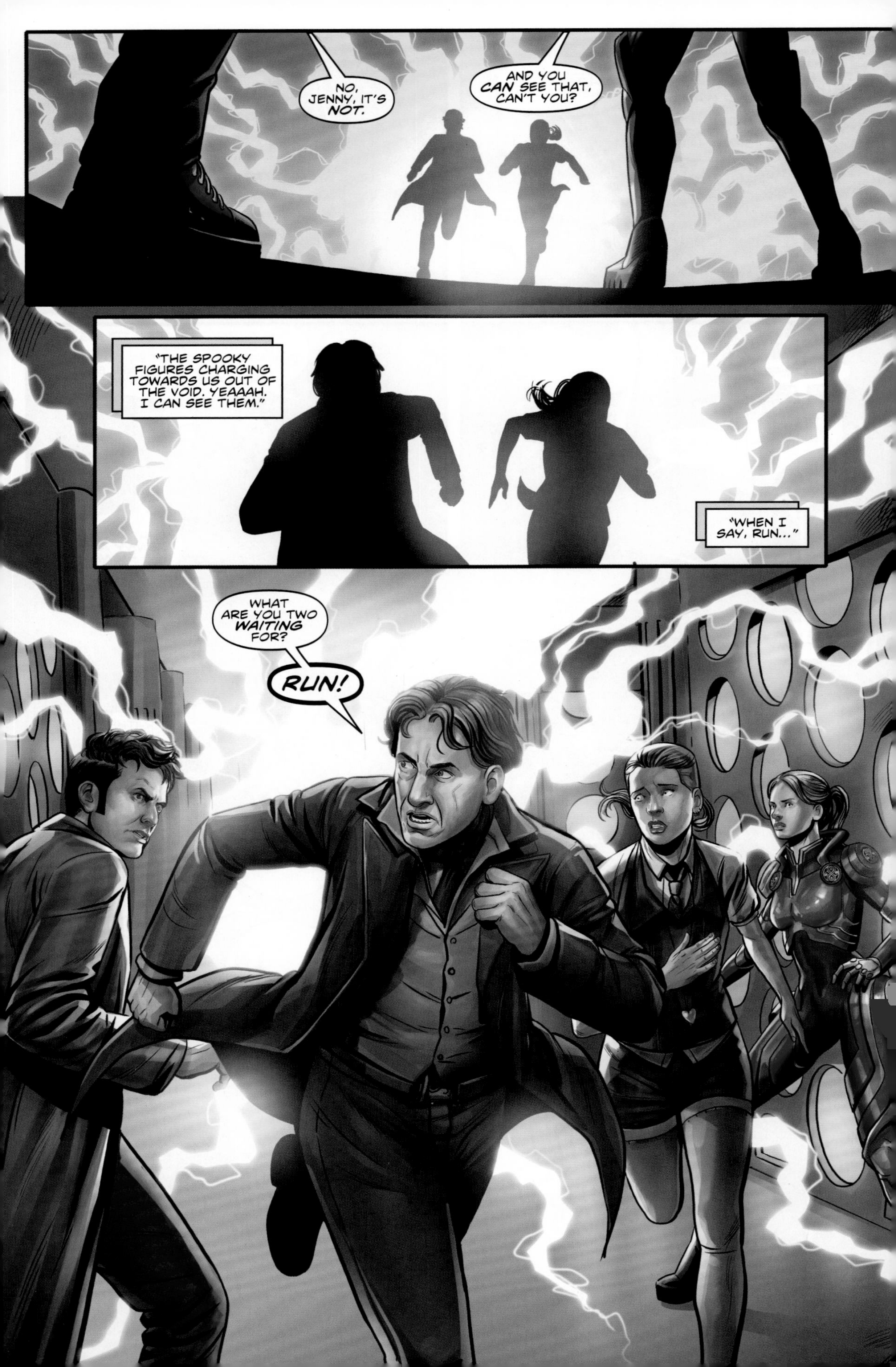
NO, JENNY, IT'S NOT.
AND YOU CAN SEE THAT, CAN'T YOU?
"THE SPOOKY FIGURES CHARGING TOWARDS US OUT OF THE VOID. YEAAAH. I CAN SEE THEM."
"WHEN I SAY, RUN..."
WHAT ARE YOU TWO WAITING FOR?
RUN!

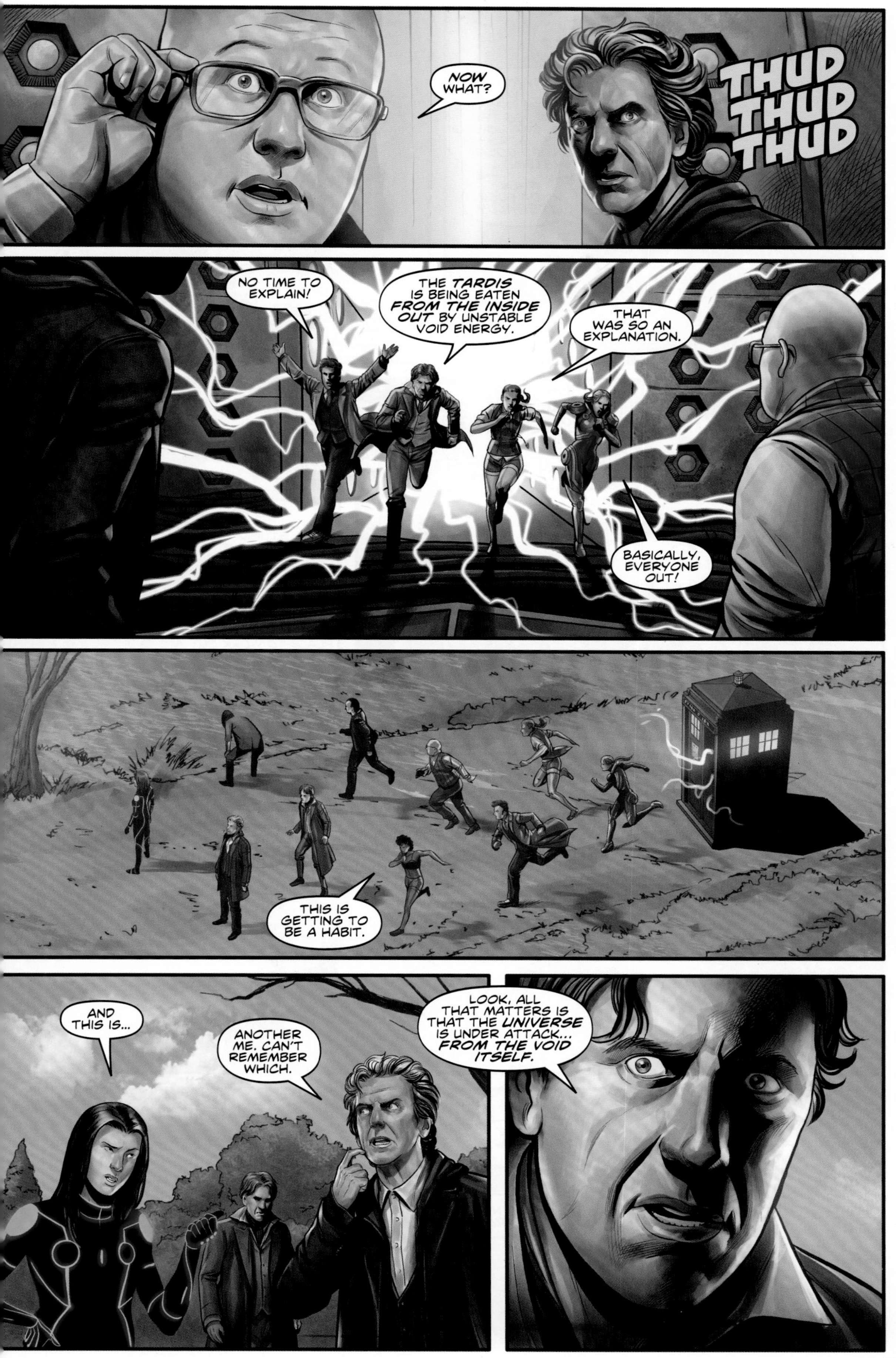
NOW WHAT?
THUD THUD THUD
NO TIME TO EXPLAIN!
THE TARDIS IS BEING EATEN FROM THE INSIDE OUT BY UNSTABLE VOID ENERGY.
THAT WAS SO AN EXPLANATION.
BASICALLY, EVERYONE OUT!
THIS IS GETTING TO BE A HABIT.
AND THIS IS...
ANOTHER ME. CAN'T REMEMBER WHICH.
LOOK, ALL THAT MATTERS IS THAT THE UNIVERSE IS UNDER ATTACK... FROM THE VOID ITSELF.

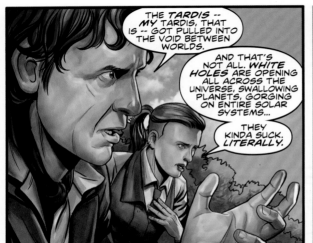

THE *TARDIS* -- *MY* TARDIS, THAT IS -- GOT PULLED INTO THE VOID BETWEEN WORLDS.

AND THAT'S NOT ALL. *WHITE HOLES* ARE OPENING ALL ACROSS THE UNIVERSE, SWALLOWING PLANETS, GORGING ON ENTIRE SOLAR SYSTEMS...

THEY KINDA SUCK. *LITERALLY.*

JOSIE, *BREATHE.* YOU'RE ALL RIGHT.

YOU KNOW MY *NAME?*

OF *COURSE* I DO. TELL ME, HOW MANY OF *US* ARE IN THE VOID?

...AT LEAST *SIX OR SEVEN.* THEY HELPED ME ESCAPE BY LINKING OUR *TARDISES* TOGETHER, FORMING A *DIMENSIONAL BRIDGE.*

STUPID. STUPID, STUPID, STUPID.

WHY WASTE ENERGY BREAKING *OUT?* DIDN'T YOU REALIZE YOU WERE IN THE *PERFECT* PLACE TO WORK OUT EXACTLY WHAT'S HAPPENING?

THE ONLY WAY TO DEFEAT SOMETHING IS TO UNDERSTAND IT, TO KNOW WHAT IT IS. WHAT IT WANTS.

HANG ON. I *KNOW* THAT FACE.

YOU WANT TO GO *INTO* THAT THING, DON'T YOU? YOU ACTUALLY *WANT* TO GO INTO THE WHITE HOLE.

SHAME OUR *TARDISES* ARE GROUNDED.

WHO NEEDS A *TARDIS*...

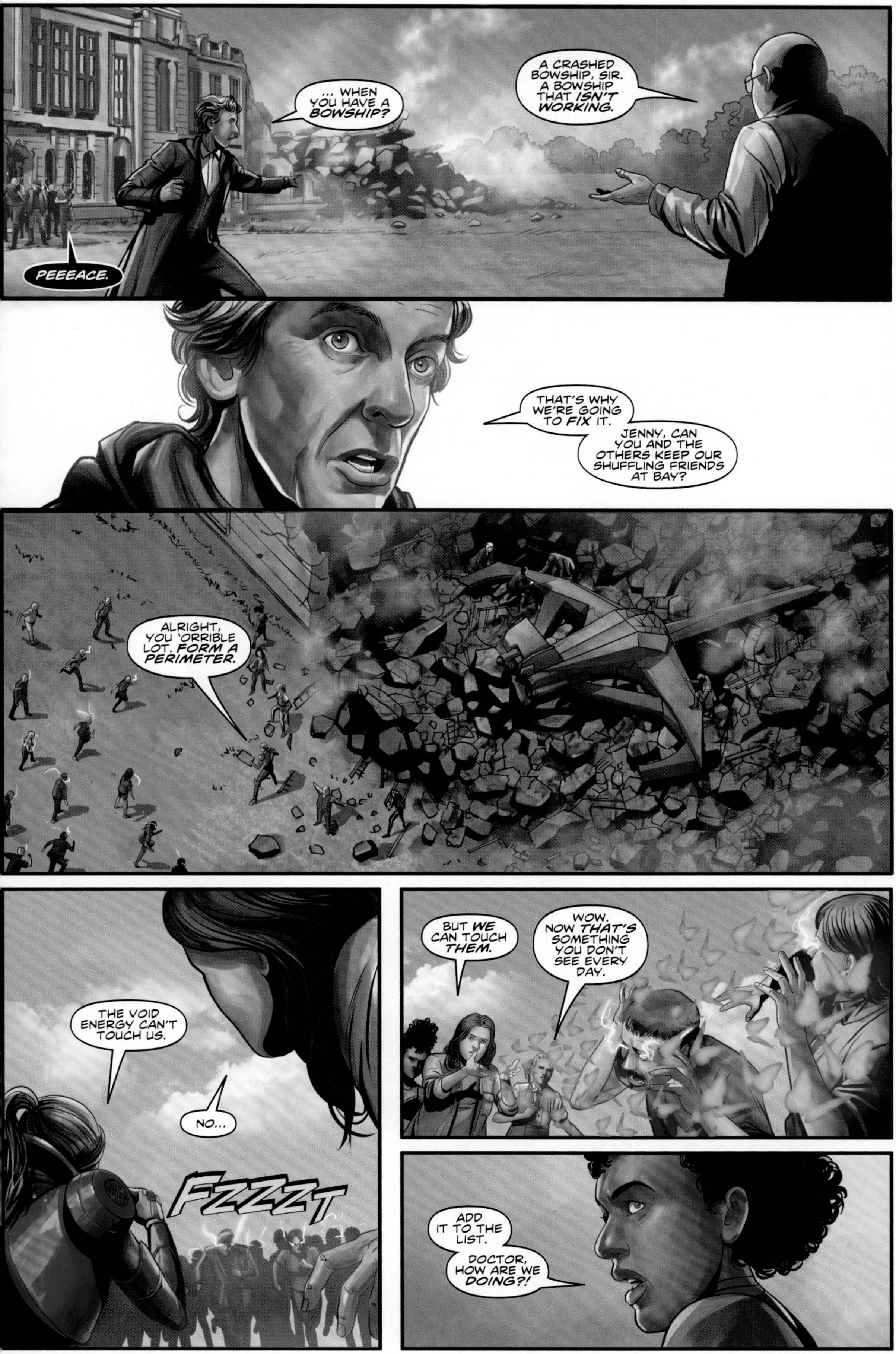
... WHEN YOU HAVE A BOWSHIP?
PEEEACE.
A CRASHED BOWSHIP, SIR. A BOWSHIP THAT ISN'T WORKING.
THAT'S WHY WE'RE GOING TO FIX IT.
JENNY, CAN YOU AND THE OTHERS KEEP OUR SHUFFLING FRIENDS AT BAY?
ALRIGHT, YOU 'ORRIBLE LOT. FORM A PERIMETER.
THE VOID ENERGY CAN'T TOUCH US.
NO...
FZZZZT
BUT WE CAN TOUCH THEM.
WOW. NOW THAT'S SOMETHING YOU DON'T SEE EVERY DAY.
ADD IT TO THE LIST.
DOCTOR, HOW ARE WE DOING?!

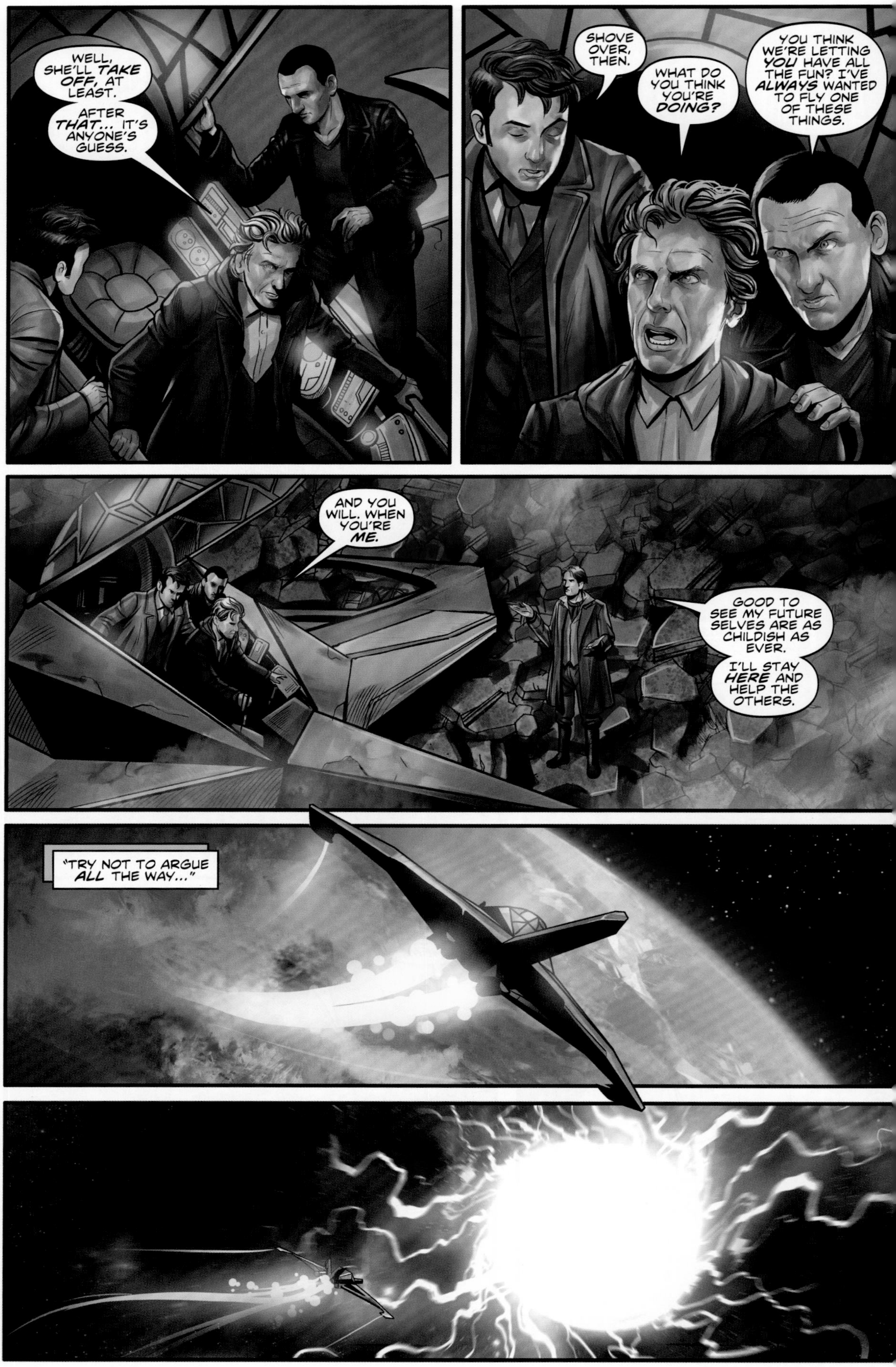
WELL, SHE'LL TAKE OFF, AT LEAST.
AFTER THAT... IT'S ANYONE'S GUESS.
SHOVE OVER, THEN.
WHAT DO YOU THINK YOU'RE DOING?
YOU THINK WE'RE LETTING YOU HAVE ALL THE FUN? I'VE ALWAYS WANTED TO FLY ONE OF THESE THINGS.
AND YOU WILL. WHEN YOU'RE ME.
GOOD TO SEE MY FUTURE SELVES ARE AS CHILDISH AS EVER.
I'LL STAY HERE AND HELP THE OTHERS.
"TRY NOT TO ARGUE ALL THE WAY..."

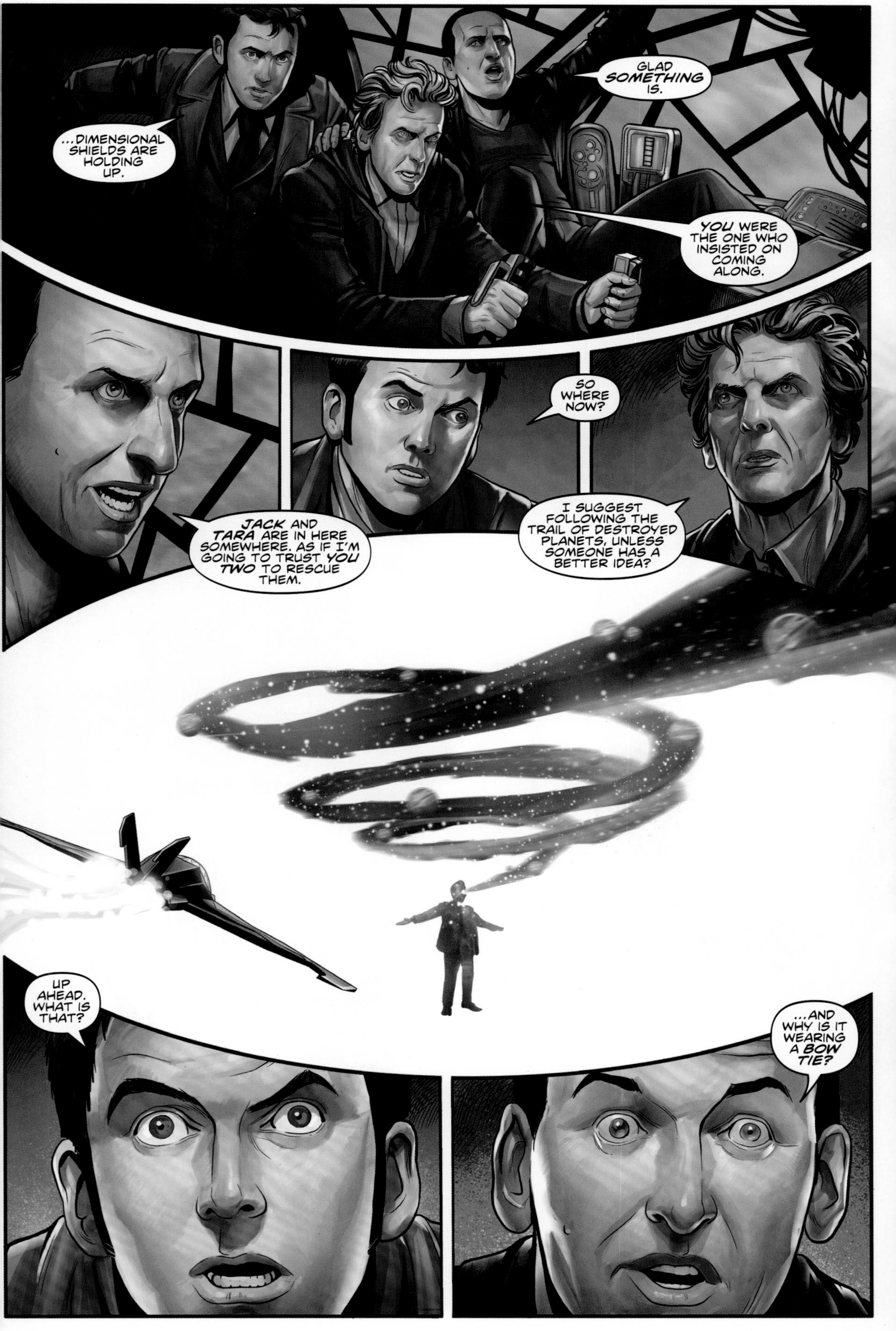
...DIMENSIONAL SHIELDS ARE HOLDING UP.
GLAD SOMETHING IS.
YOU WERE THE ONE WHO INSISTED ON COMING ALONG.
JACK AND TARA ARE IN HERE SOMEWHERE. AS IF I'M GOING TO TRUST YOU TWO TO RESCUE THEM.
SO WHERE NOW?
I SUGGEST FOLLOWING THE TRAIL OF DESTROYED PLANETS, UNLESS SOMEONE HAS A BETTER IDEA?
UP AHEAD. WHAT IS THAT?
...AND WHY IS IT WEARING A BOW TIE?

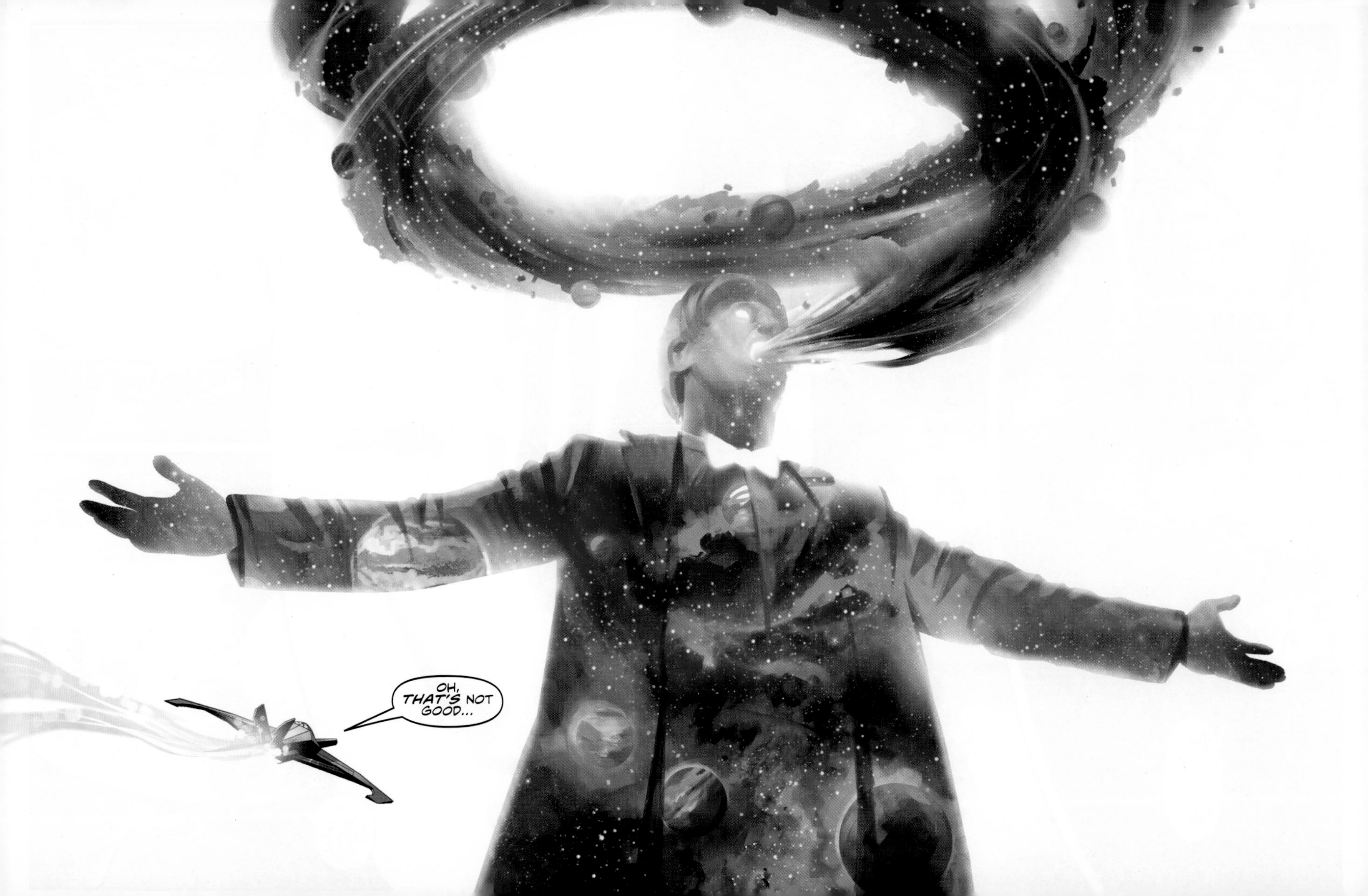
OH, THAT'S NOT GOOD...

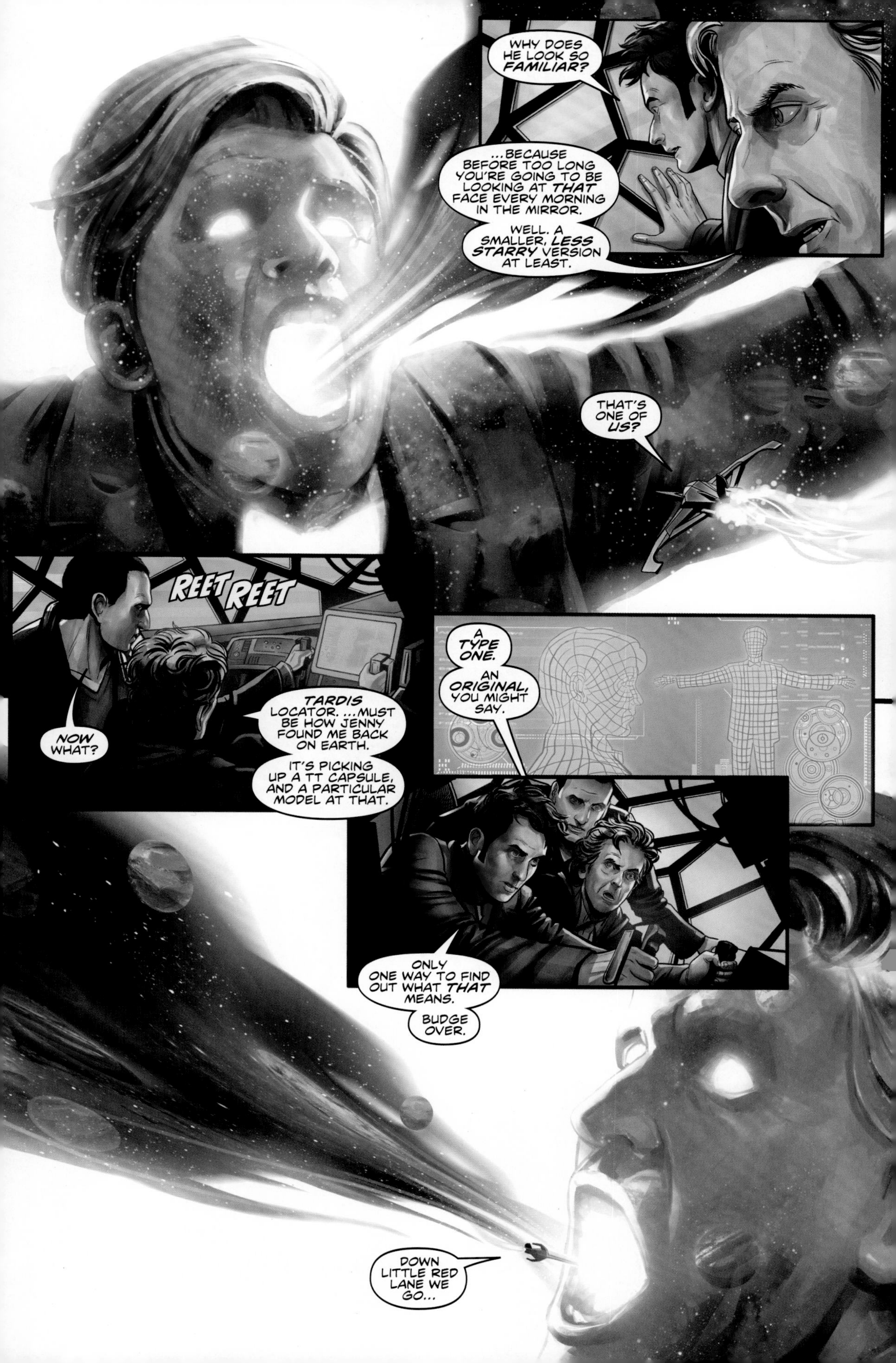

WHY DOES HE LOOK SO *FAMILIAR?*
...BECAUSE BEFORE TOO LONG YOU'RE GOING TO BE LOOKING AT *THAT* FACE EVERY MORNING IN THE MIRROR.
WELL. A SMALLER, *LESS STARRY* VERSION AT LEAST.
THAT'S ONE OF *US?*
REET REET
NOW WHAT?
TARDIS LOCATOR. ...MUST BE HOW JENNY FOUND ME BACK ON EARTH.
IT'S PICKING UP A TT CAPSULE, AND A PARTICULAR MODEL AT THAT.
A *TYPE ONE.*
AN *ORIGINAL,* YOU MIGHT SAY.
ONLY ONE WAY TO FIND OUT WHAT *THAT* MEANS.
BUDGE OVER.
DOWN LITTLE RED LANE WE GO...

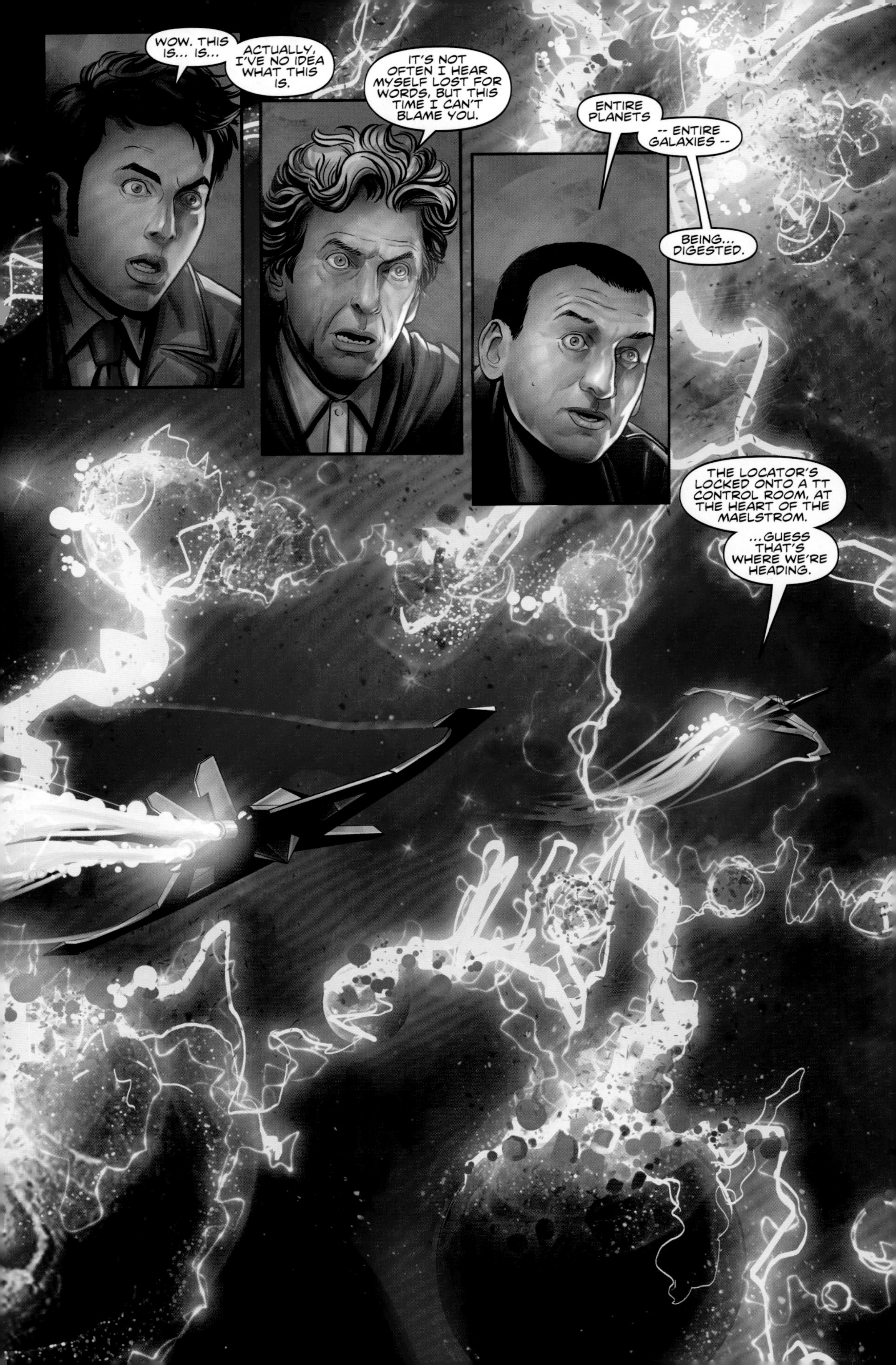
WOW. THIS IS... IS...
ACTUALLY, I'VE NO IDEA WHAT THIS IS.
IT'S NOT OFTEN I HEAR MYSELF LOST FOR WORDS, BUT THIS TIME I CAN'T BLAME YOU.
ENTIRE PLANETS
-- ENTIRE GALAXIES --
BEING... DIGESTED.
THE LOCATOR'S LOCKED ONTO A TT CONTROL ROOM, AT THE HEART OF THE MAELSTROM.
...GUESS THAT'S WHERE WE'RE HEADING.

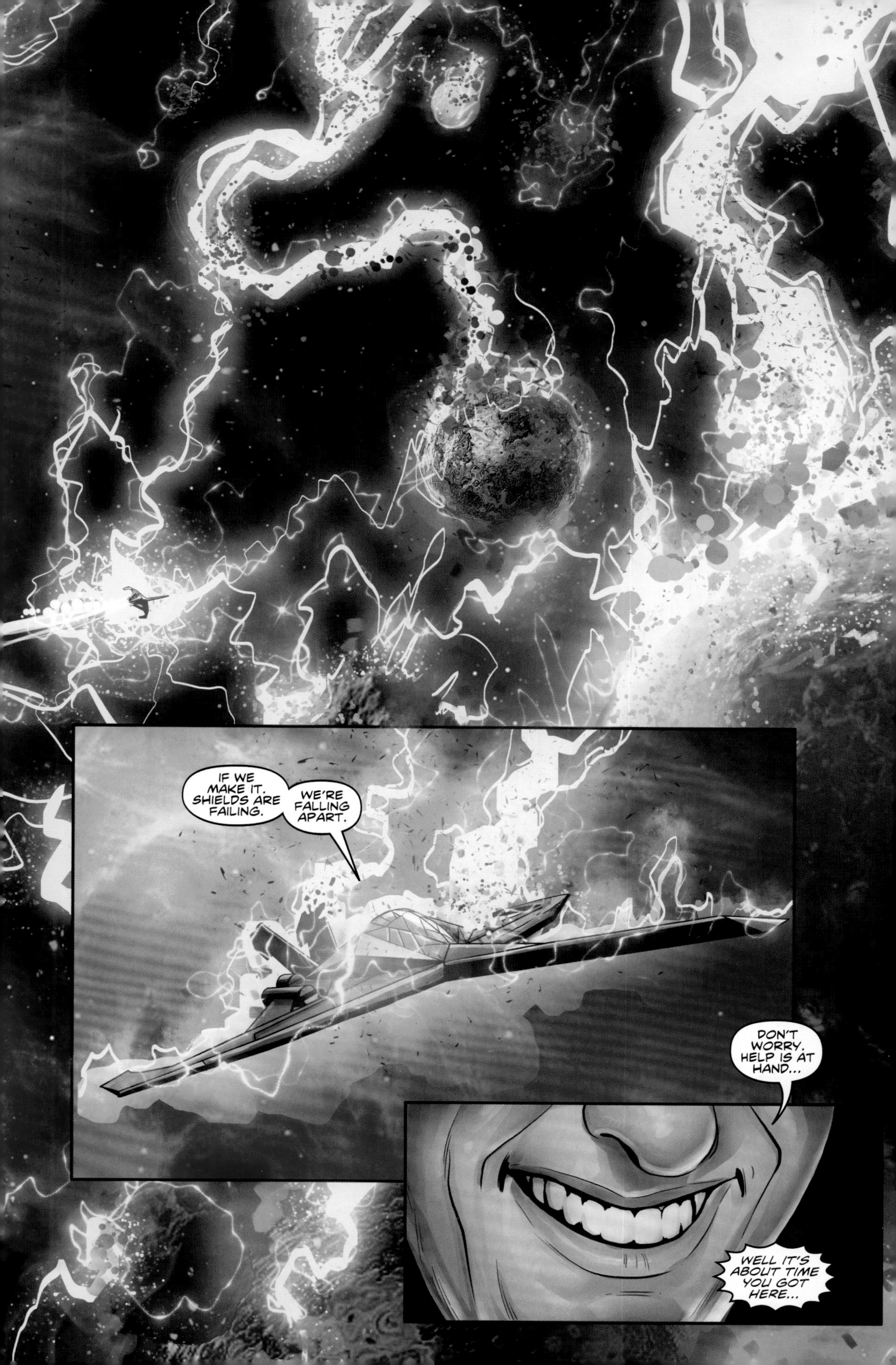
IF WE MAKE IT. SHIELDS ARE FAILING.
WE'RE FALLING APART.
DON'T WORRY. HELP IS AT HAND...
WELL IT'S ABOUT TIME YOU GOT HERE...

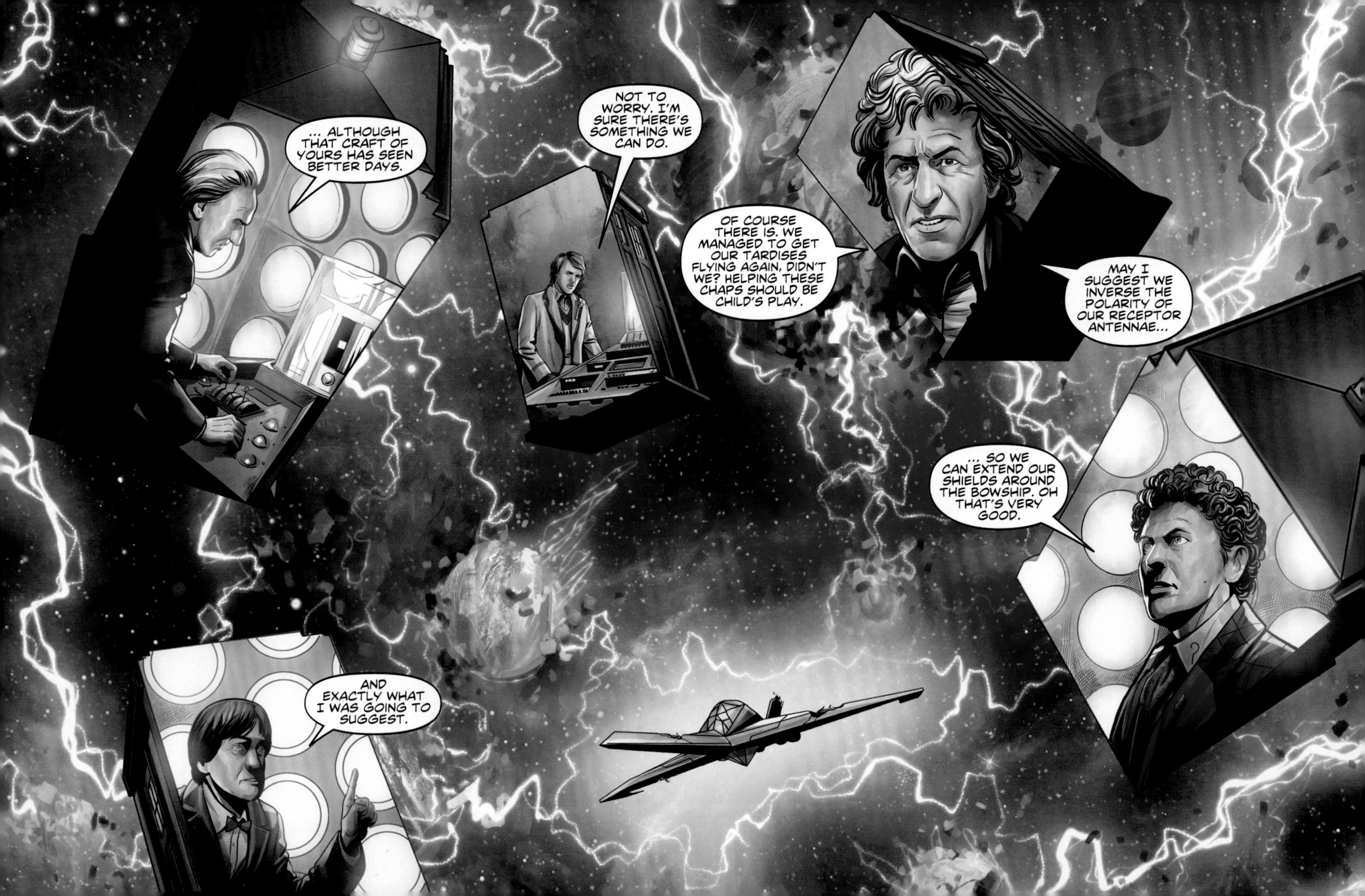
... ALTHOUGH THAT CRAFT OF YOURS HAS SEEN BETTER DAYS.
NOT TO WORRY. I'M SURE THERE'S SOMETHING WE CAN DO.
OF COURSE THERE IS. WE MANAGED TO GET OUR TARDISES FLYING AGAIN, DIDN'T WE? HELPING THESE CHAPS SHOULD BE CHILD'S PLAY.
MAY I SUGGEST WE INVERSE THE POLARITY OF OUR RECEPTOR ANTENNAE...
... SO WE CAN EXTEND OUR SHIELDS AROUND THE BOWSHIP. OH THAT'S VERY GOOD.
AND EXACTLY WHAT I WAS GOING TO SUGGEST.

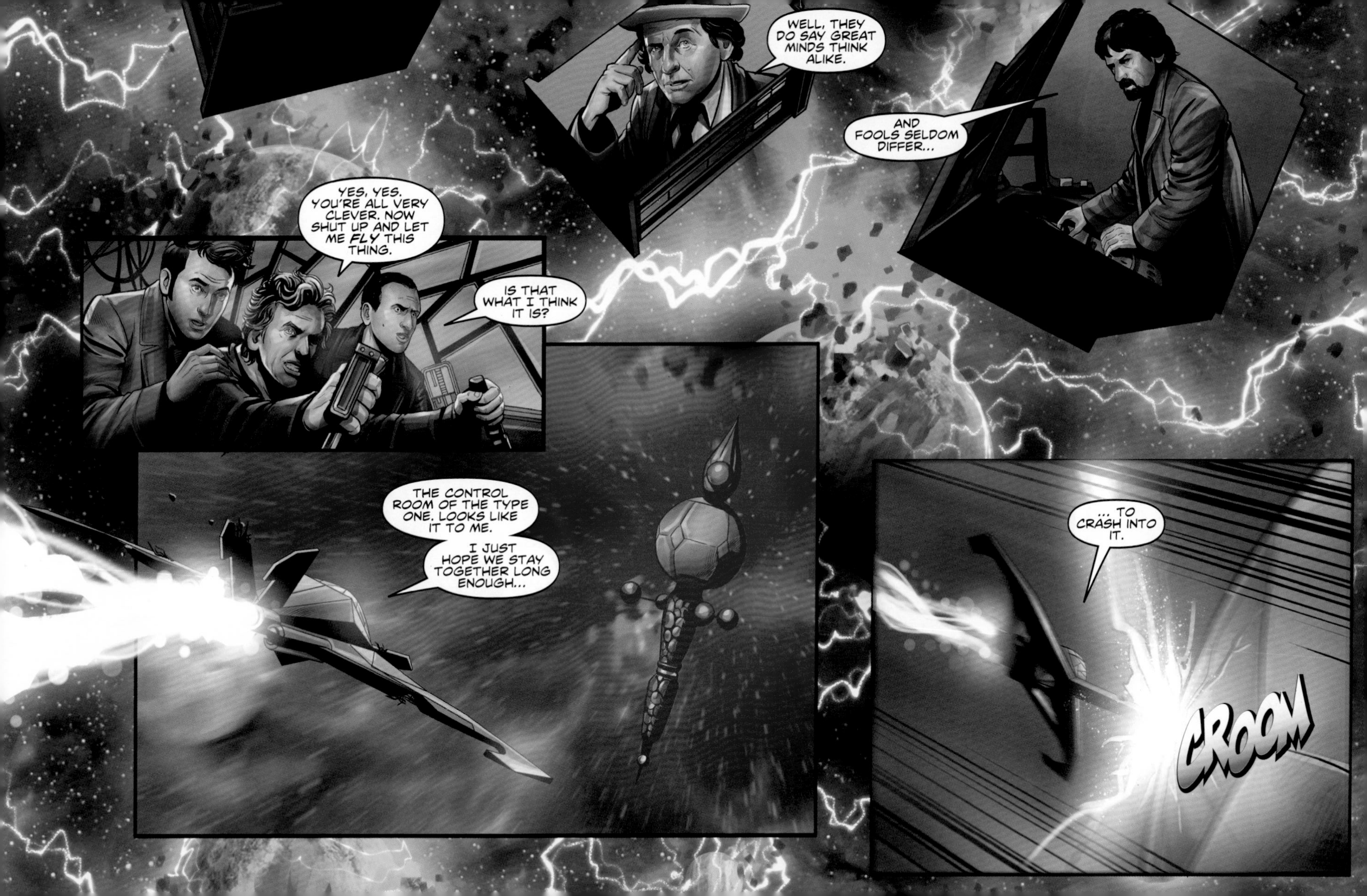
WELL, THEY DO SAY GREAT MINDS THINK ALIKE.
AND FOOLS SELDOM DIFFER...
YES, YES. YOU'RE ALL VERY CLEVER. NOW SHUT UP AND LET ME FLY THIS THING.
IS THAT WHAT I THINK IT IS?
THE CONTROL ROOM OF THE TYPE ONE. LOOKS LIKE IT TO ME.
I JUST HOPE WE STAY TOGETHER LONG ENOUGH...
...TO CRASH INTO IT.
CROOM

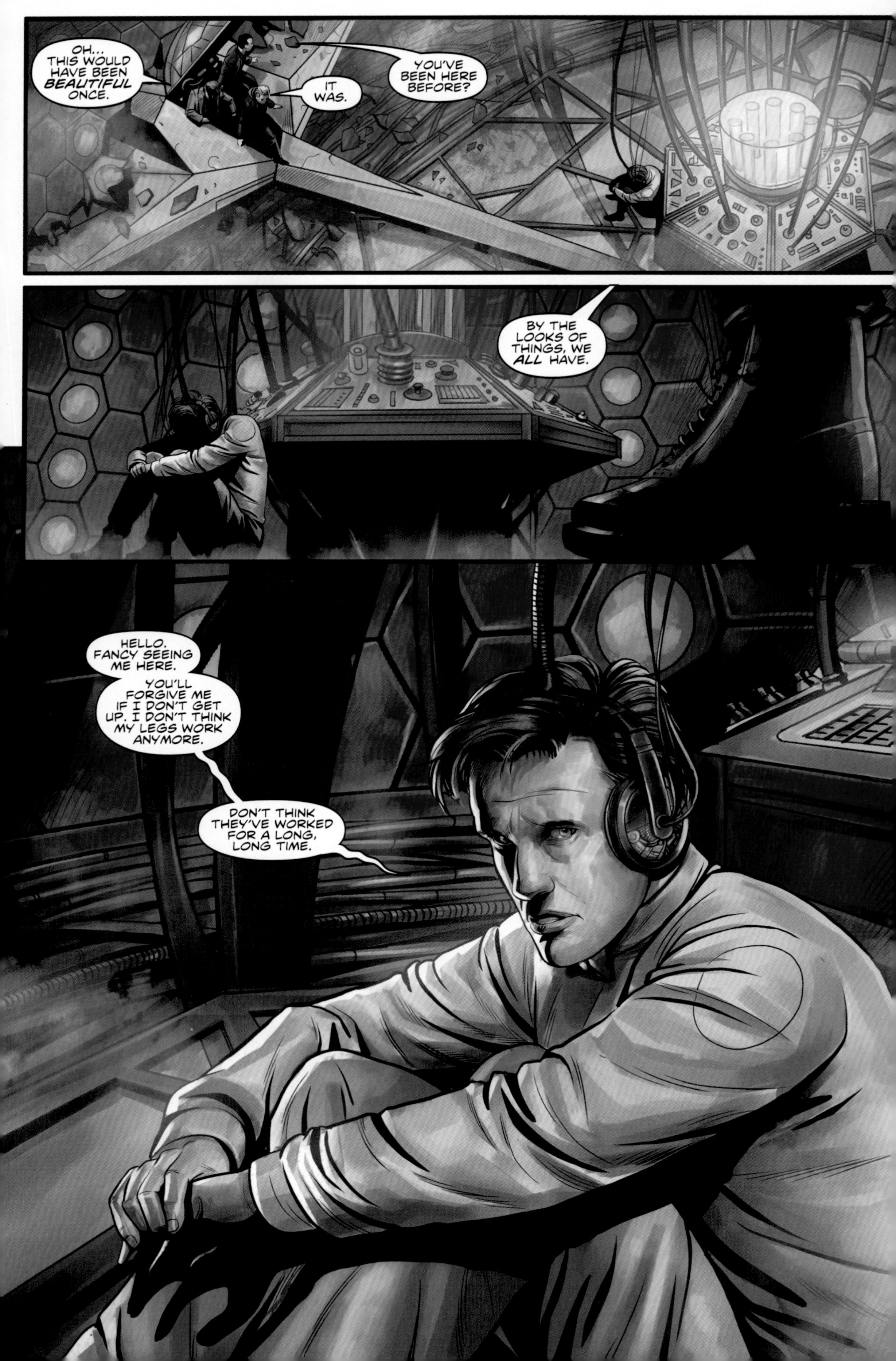
OH... THIS WOULD HAVE BEEN BEAUTIFUL ONCE.
IT WAS.
YOU'VE BEEN HERE BEFORE?
BY THE LOOKS OF THINGS, WE ALL HAVE.
HELLO. FANCY SEEING ME HERE.
YOU'LL FORGIVE ME IF I DON'T GET UP. I DON'T THINK MY LEGS WORK ANYMORE.
DON'T THINK THEY'VE WORKED FOR A LONG, LONG TIME.

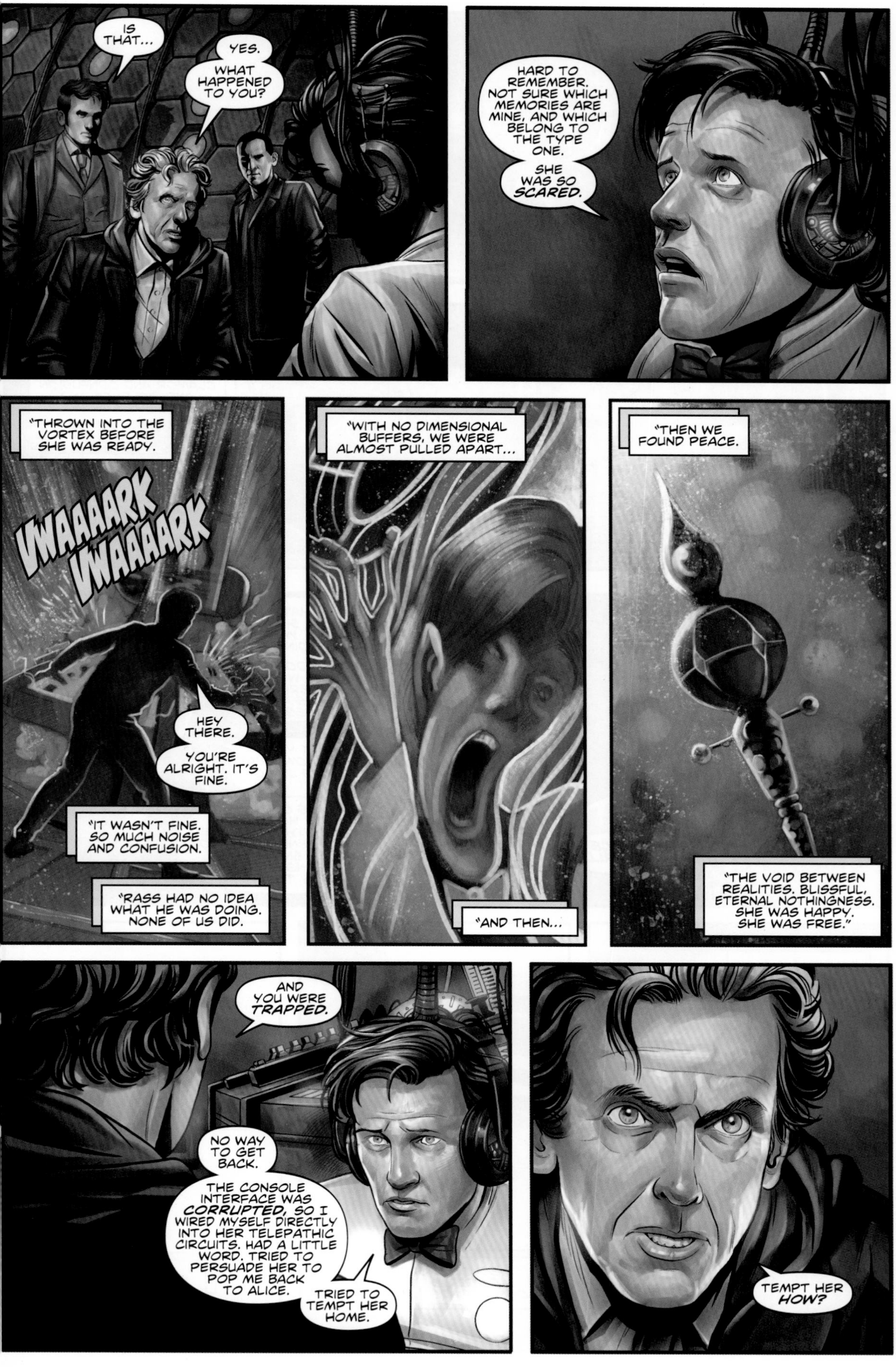
IS THAT...
YES.
WHAT HAPPENED TO YOU?
HARD TO REMEMBER. NOT SURE WHICH MEMORIES ARE MINE, AND WHICH BELONG TO THE TYPE ONE.
SHE WAS SO SCARED.
"THROWN INTO THE VORTEX BEFORE SHE WAS READY.
VWAAAARK VWAAAARK
HEY THERE.
YOU'RE ALRIGHT. IT'S FINE.
"IT WASN'T FINE. SO MUCH NOISE AND CONFUSION.
"RASS HAD NO IDEA WHAT HE WAS DOING. NONE OF US DID.
"WITH NO DIMENSIONAL BUFFERS, WE WERE ALMOST PULLED APART...
"AND THEN...
"THEN WE FOUND PEACE.
"THE VOID BETWEEN REALITIES. BLISSFUL, ETERNAL NOTHINGNESS. SHE WAS HAPPY. SHE WAS FREE."
AND YOU WERE TRAPPED.
NO WAY TO GET BACK.
THE CONSOLE INTERFACE WAS CORRUPTED, SO I WIRED MYSELF DIRECTLY INTO HER TELEPATHIC CIRCUITS. HAD A LITTLE WORD. TRIED TO PERSUADE HER TO POP ME BACK TO ALICE.
TRIED TO TEMPT HER HOME.
TEMPT HER HOW?

"WHAT WE ALWAYS DO. I SHOWED HER THE UNIVERSE, ALL THE PLACES SHE COULD VISIT, ALL THE WONDER SHE COULD EXPERIENCE."

"SHE LOOKED INTO MY MIND AND SAW... SHE SAW..."

"YES?"

"SHE SAW *CHAOS*. SHE SAW HATE. SHE SAW CLAMOR AND CONFUSION AND VIOLENCE AND DEATH. SHE SAW *WAR*."

"AND SHE HEARD WORDS REPEATED OVER AND OVER AGAIN, WORDS SHE TOOK AS AN IMPERATIVE..."

SILENCE WILL FALL.

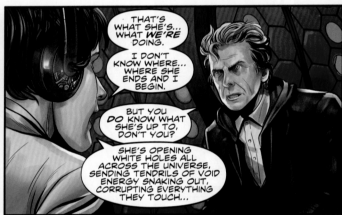

THAT'S WHAT SHE'S... WHAT *WE'RE* DOING. I DON'T KNOW WHERE... WHERE SHE ENDS AND I BEGIN.

BUT YOU *DO* KNOW WHAT SHE'S UP TO, DON'T YOU?

SHE'S OPENING WHITE HOLES ALL ACROSS THE UNIVERSE, SENDING TENDRILS OF VOID ENERGY SNAKING OUT, CORRUPTING EVERYTHING THEY TOUCH...

"DRAWING ALL OF CREATION INTO HERSELF...

"...CONSUMING *ALL MATTER* SO THE COSMOS FINDS PEACE...

"... BY BECOMING VOID ITSELF."

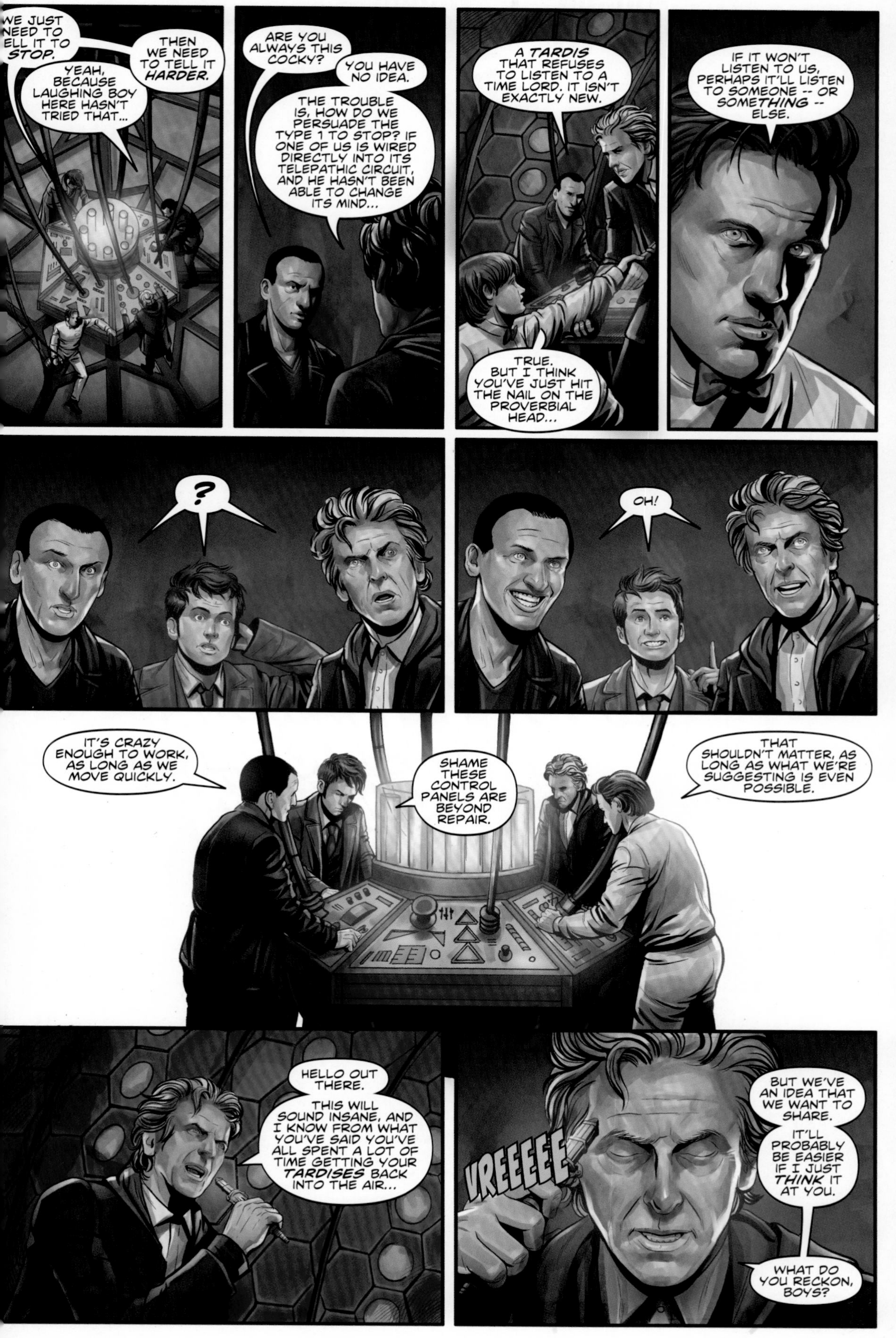
WE JUST NEED TO TELL IT TO STOP.
THEN WE NEED TO TELL IT HARDER.
YEAH, BECAUSE LAUGHING BOY HERE HASN'T TRIED THAT...
ARE YOU ALWAYS THIS COCKY?
YOU HAVE NO IDEA.
THE TROUBLE IS, HOW DO WE PERSUADE THE TYPE 1 TO STOP? IF ONE OF US IS WIRED DIRECTLY INTO ITS TELEPATHIC CIRCUIT, AND HE HASN'T BEEN ABLE TO CHANGE ITS MIND...
A TARDIS THAT REFUSES TO LISTEN TO A TIME LORD. IT ISN'T EXACTLY NEW.
TRUE. BUT I THINK YOU'VE JUST HIT THE NAIL ON THE PROVERBIAL HEAD...
IF IT WON'T LISTEN TO US, PERHAPS IT'LL LISTEN TO SOMEONE -- OR SOMETHING -- ELSE.
?
OH!
IT'S CRAZY ENOUGH TO WORK, AS LONG AS WE MOVE QUICKLY.
SHAME THESE CONTROL PANELS ARE BEYOND REPAIR.
THAT SHOULDN'T MATTER, AS LONG AS WHAT WE'RE SUGGESTING IS EVEN POSSIBLE.
HELLO OUT THERE.
THIS WILL SOUND INSANE, AND I KNOW FROM WHAT YOU'VE SAID YOU'VE ALL SPENT A LOT OF TIME GETTING YOUR TARDISES BACK INTO THE AIR...
VREEEEE
BUT WE'VE AN IDEA THAT WE WANT TO SHARE.
IT'LL PROBABLY BE EASIER IF I JUST THINK IT AT YOU.
WHAT DO YOU RECKON, BOYS?

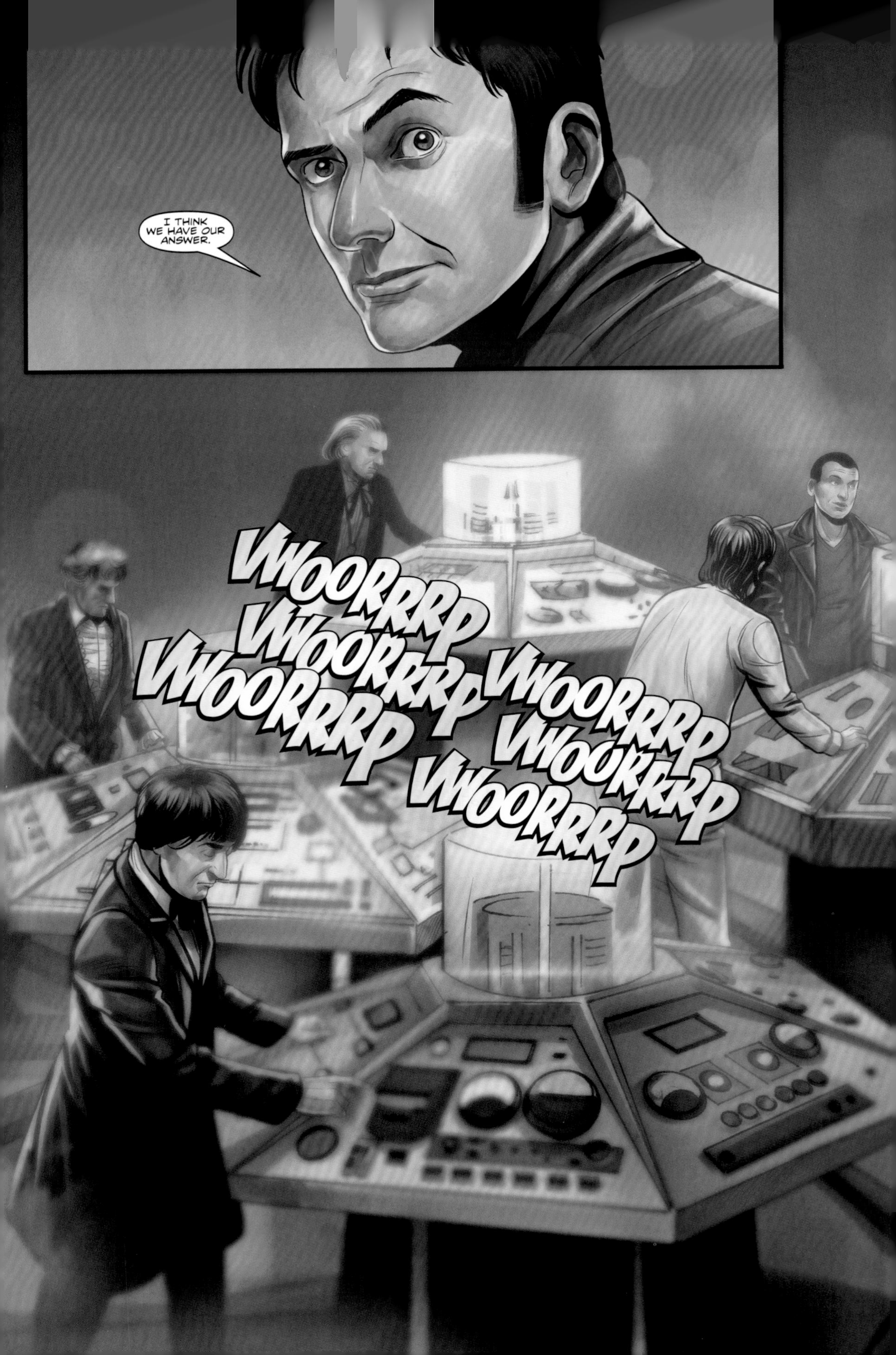
I THINK WE HAVE OUR ANSWER.
VWOORRRP
VWOORRRP
VWOORRRP
VWOORRRP
VWOORRRP
VWOORRRP

VWOORRRP
VWOORRRP
VWOORRRP
IF THE OLD GIRL SURVIVES THIS IT WILL BE A *MIRACLE!*
OH, I DON'T KNOW. SHE'S STRONGER THAN SHE LOOKS.
AREN'T WE ALL?
THAT SAID, WE DON'T WANT TO TEMPT FATE.
AGREED. THIS IS EXTREME, EVEN FOR US. THERE'S EVERY CHANCE THE *TARDIS*ES WILL RUPTURE IF WE KEEP THEM LOCKED TOGETHER LIKE THIS.
YOU'RE THE ONE GAS-BAGGING. GET *ON* WITH IT, MAN.

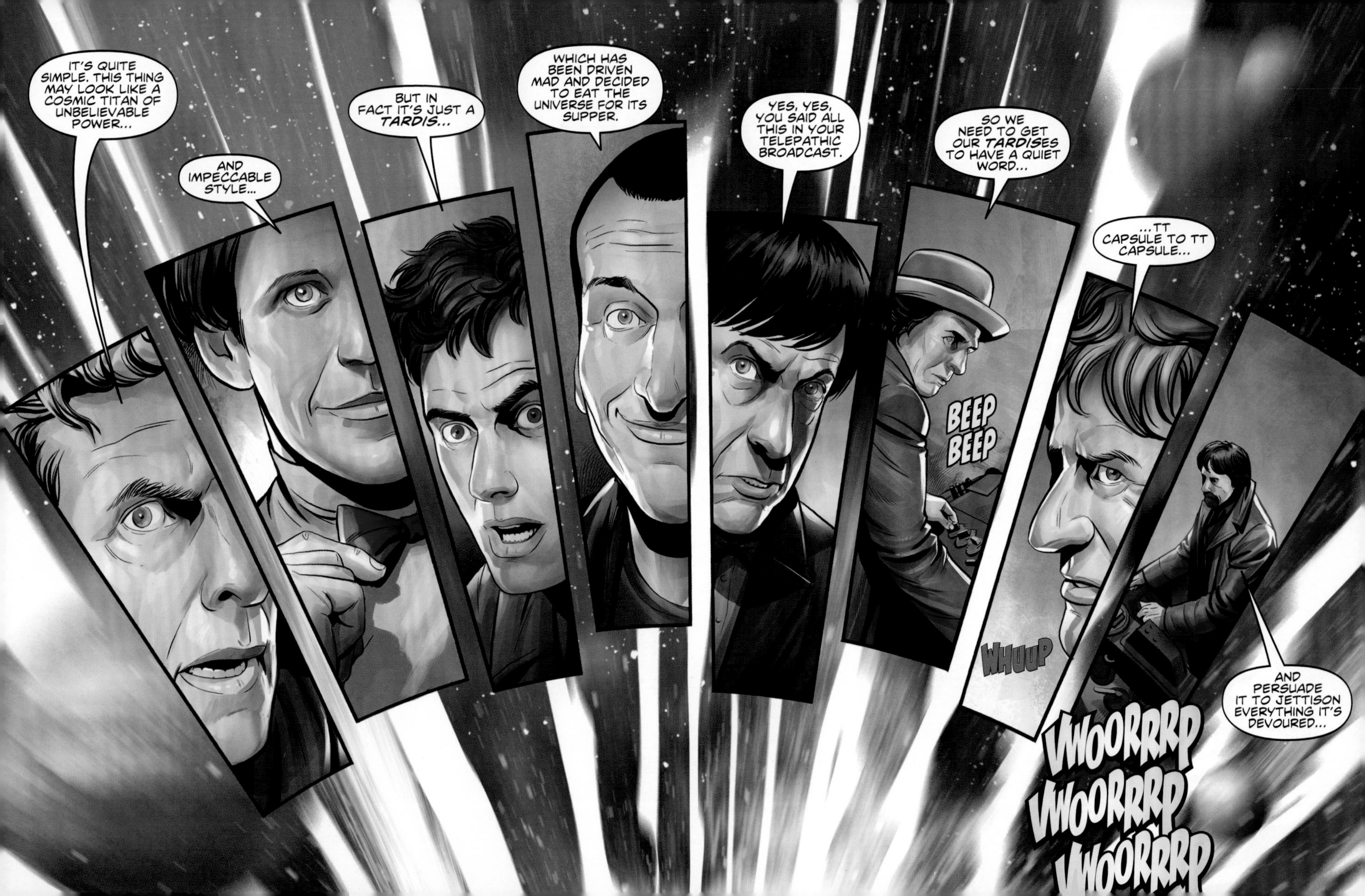
IT'S QUITE SIMPLE. THIS THING MAY LOOK LIKE A COSMIC TITAN OF UNBELIEVABLE POWER...
AND IMPECCABLE STYLE...
BUT IN FACT IT'S JUST A *TARDIS*...
WHICH HAS BEEN DRIVEN MAD AND DECIDED TO EAT THE UNIVERSE FOR ITS SUPPER.
YES, YES, YOU SAID ALL THIS IN YOUR TELEPATHIC BROADCAST.
SO WE NEED TO GET OUR *TARDISES* TO HAVE A QUIET WORD...
BEEP BEEP
...TT CAPSULE TO TT CAPSULE...
WHUUP
AND PERSUADE IT TO JETTISON EVERYTHING IT'S DEVOURED...
VWOORRRP
VWOORRRP
VWOORRRP

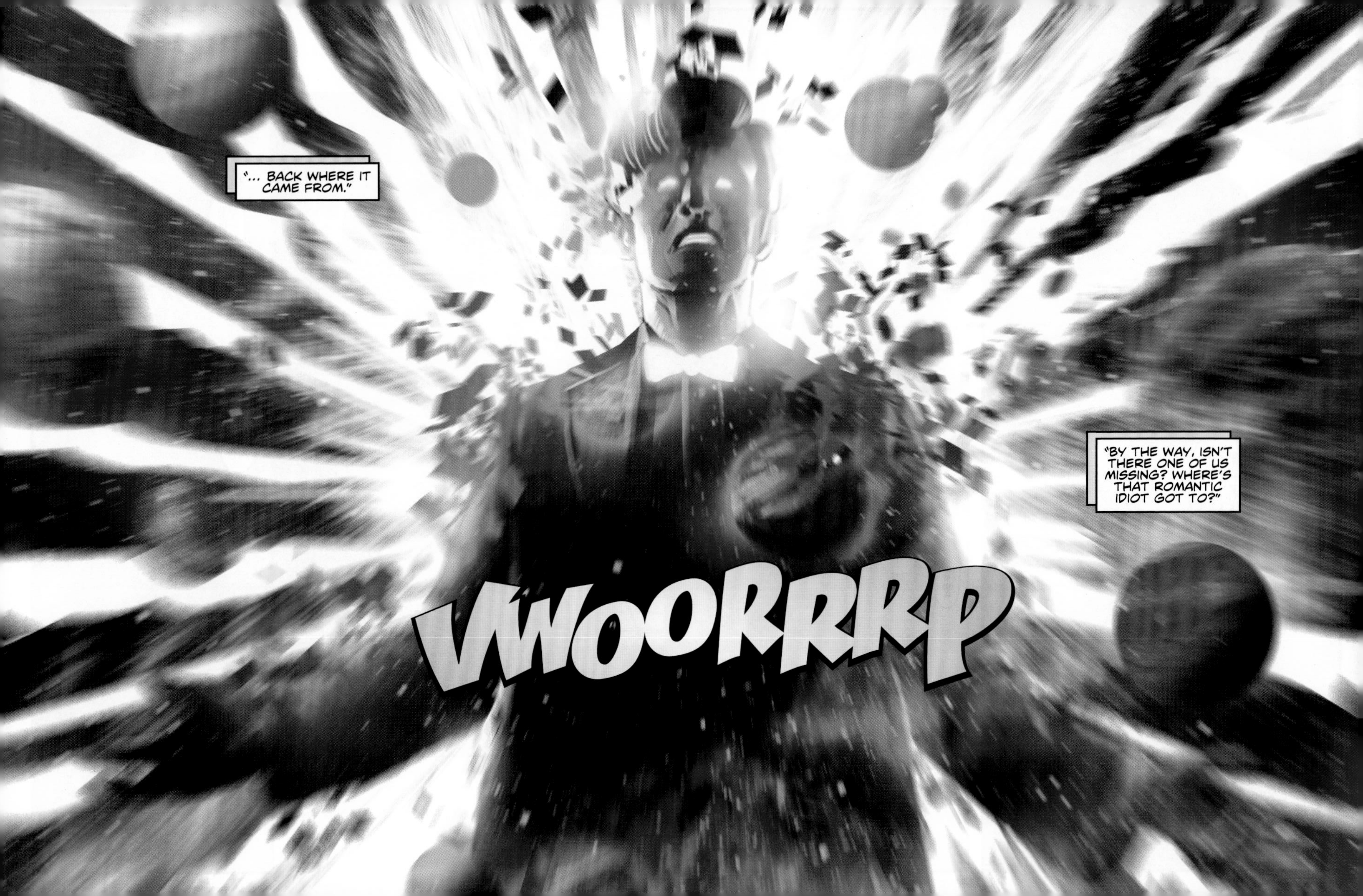
"... BACK WHERE IT CAME FROM."
VWOORRRP
"BY THE WAY, ISN'T THERE ONE OF US MISSING? WHERE'S THAT ROMANTIC IDIOT GOT TO?"

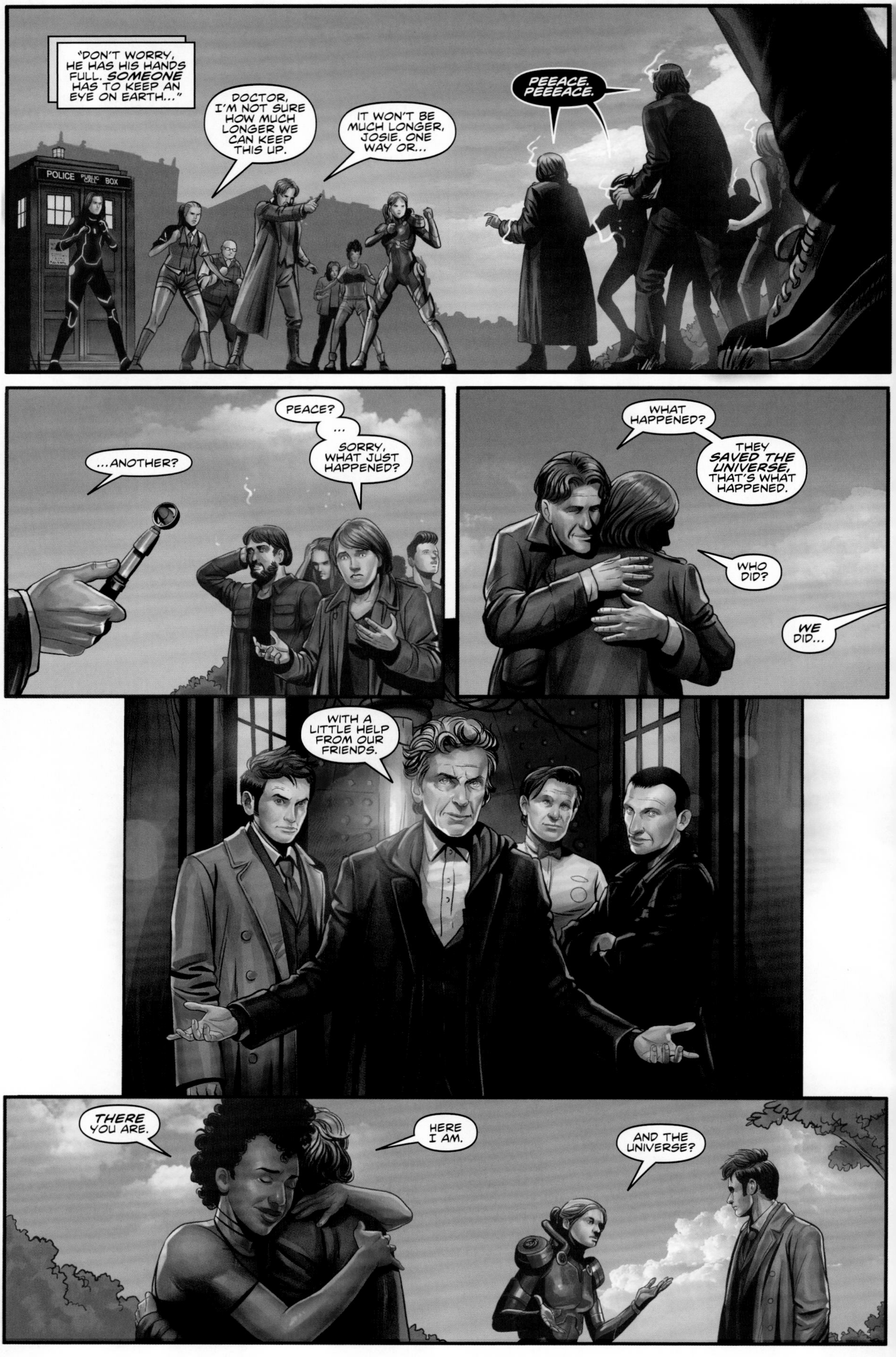
"DON'T WORRY, HE HAS HIS HANDS FULL. SOMEONE HAS TO KEEP AN EYE ON EARTH..."
DOCTOR, I'M NOT SURE HOW MUCH LONGER WE CAN KEEP THIS UP.
IT WON'T BE MUCH LONGER, JOSIE. ONE WAY OR...
PEEEACE. PEEEACE.
POLICE PUBLIC CALL BOX
...ANOTHER?
PEACE?
...
SORRY, WHAT JUST HAPPENED?
WHAT HAPPENED?
THEY SAVED THE UNIVERSE, THAT'S WHAT HAPPENED.
WHO DID?
WE DID...
WITH A LITTLE HELP FROM OUR FRIENDS.
THERE YOU ARE.
HERE I AM.
AND THE UNIVERSE?

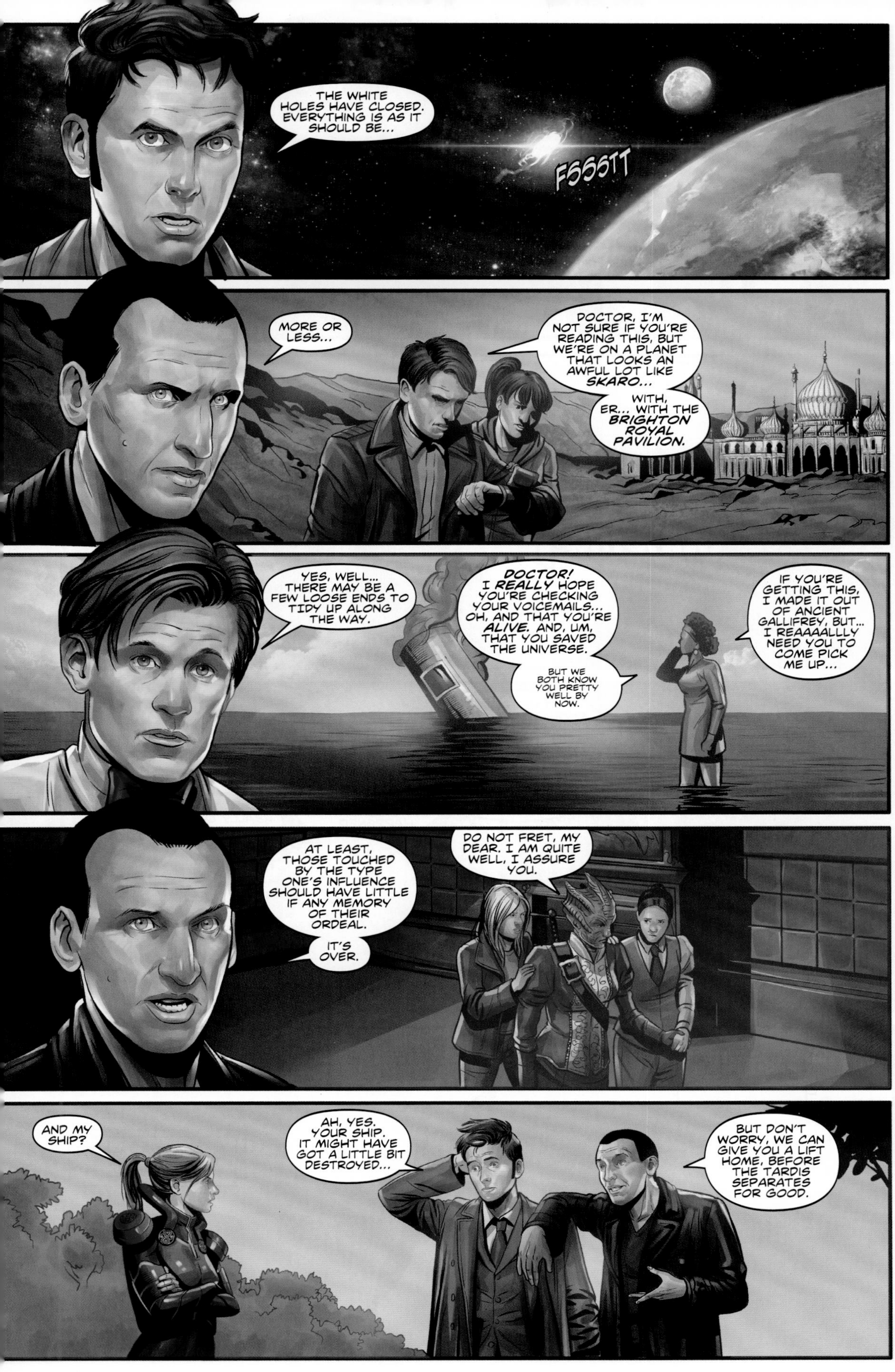
THE WHITE HOLES HAVE CLOSED. EVERYTHING IS AS IT SHOULD BE...
FSSSTT
MORE OR LESS...
DOCTOR, I'M NOT SURE IF YOU'RE READING THIS, BUT WE'RE ON A PLANET THAT LOOKS AN AWFUL LOT LIKE SKARO...
WITH, ER... WITH THE BRIGHTON ROYAL PAVILION.
YES, WELL... THERE MAY BE A FEW LOOSE ENDS TO TIDY UP ALONG THE WAY.
DOCTOR! I REALLY HOPE YOU'RE CHECKING YOUR VOICEMAILS... OH, AND THAT YOU'RE ALIVE. AND, UM, THAT YOU SAVED THE UNIVERSE.
BUT WE BOTH KNOW YOU PRETTY WELL BY NOW.
IF YOU'RE GETTING THIS, I MADE IT OUT OF ANCIENT GALLIFREY, BUT... I REAAAALLLY NEED YOU TO COME PICK ME UP...
AT LEAST, THOSE TOUCHED BY THE TYPE ONE'S INFLUENCE SHOULD HAVE LITTLE IF ANY MEMORY OF THEIR ORDEAL.
IT'S OVER.
DO NOT FRET, MY DEAR. I AM QUITE WELL, I ASSURE YOU.
AND MY SHIP?
AH, YES. YOUR SHIP. IT MIGHT HAVE GOT A LITTLE BIT DESTROYED...
BUT DON'T WORRY, WE CAN GIVE YOU A LIFT HOME, BEFORE THE TARDIS SEPARATES FOR GOOD.

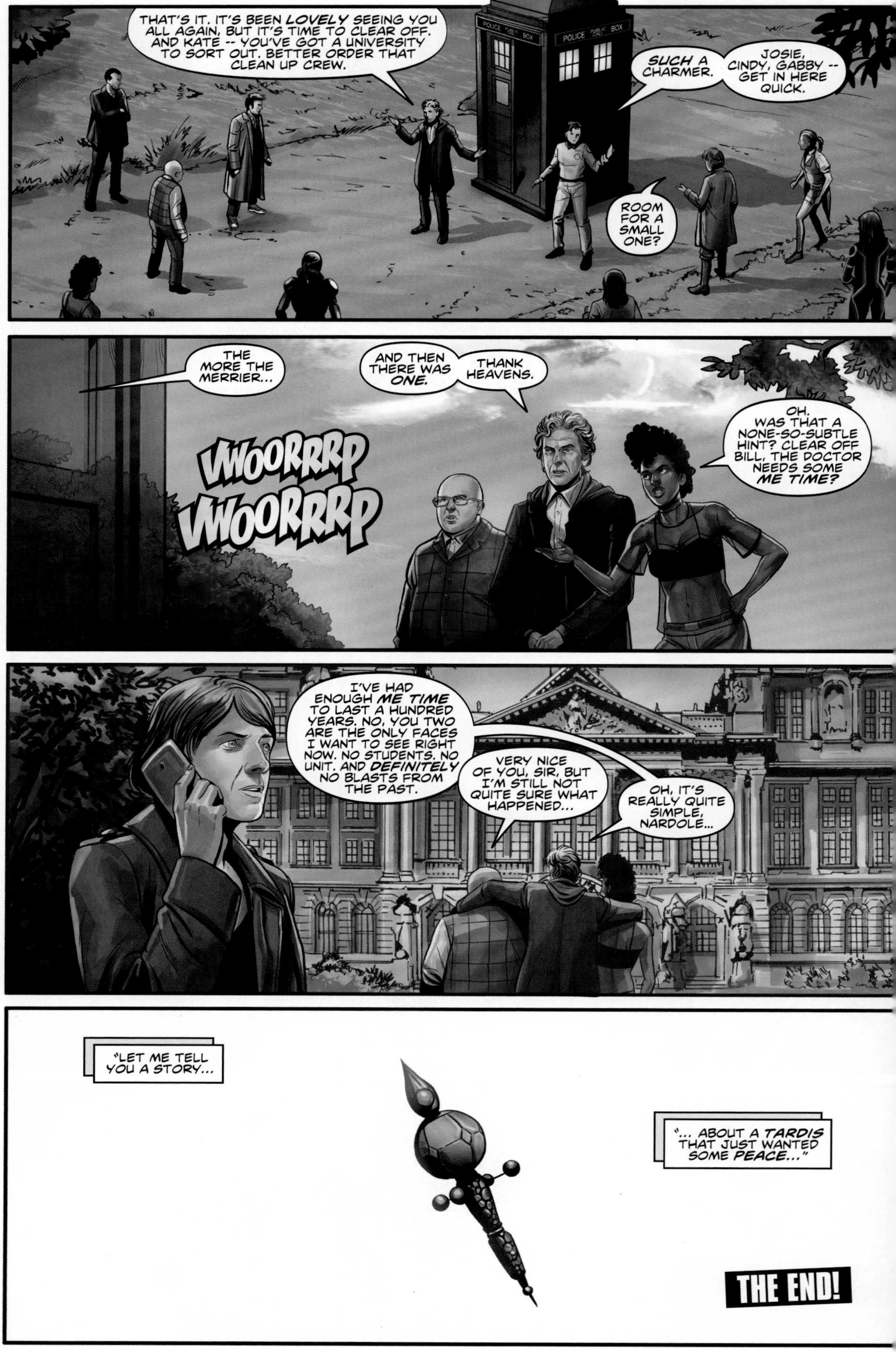
POLICE PUBLIC CALL BOX
THAT'S IT. IT'S BEEN LOVELY SEEING YOU ALL AGAIN, BUT IT'S TIME TO CLEAR OFF. AND KATE -- YOU'VE GOT A UNIVERSITY TO SORT OUT. BETTER ORDER THAT CLEAN UP CREW.
SUCH A CHARMER.
JOSIE, CINDY, GABBY -- GET IN HERE QUICK.
ROOM FOR A SMALL ONE?
THE MORE THE MERRIER...
VWOORRRP VWOORRRP
AND THEN THERE WAS ONE.
THANK HEAVENS.
OH, WAS THAT A NONE-SO-SUBTLE HINT? CLEAR OFF BILL, THE DOCTOR NEEDS SOME ME TIME?
I'VE HAD ENOUGH ME TIME TO LAST A HUNDRED YEARS. NO, YOU TWO ARE THE ONLY FACES I WANT TO SEE RIGHT NOW. NO STUDENTS. NO UNIT. AND DEFINITELY NO BLASTS FROM THE PAST.
VERY NICE OF YOU, SIR, BUT I'M STILL NOT QUITE SURE WHAT HAPPENED...
OH, IT'S REALLY QUITE SIMPLE, NARDOLE...
"LET ME TELL YOU A STORY...
"... ABOUT A TARDIS THAT JUST WANTED SOME PEACE..."
THE END!

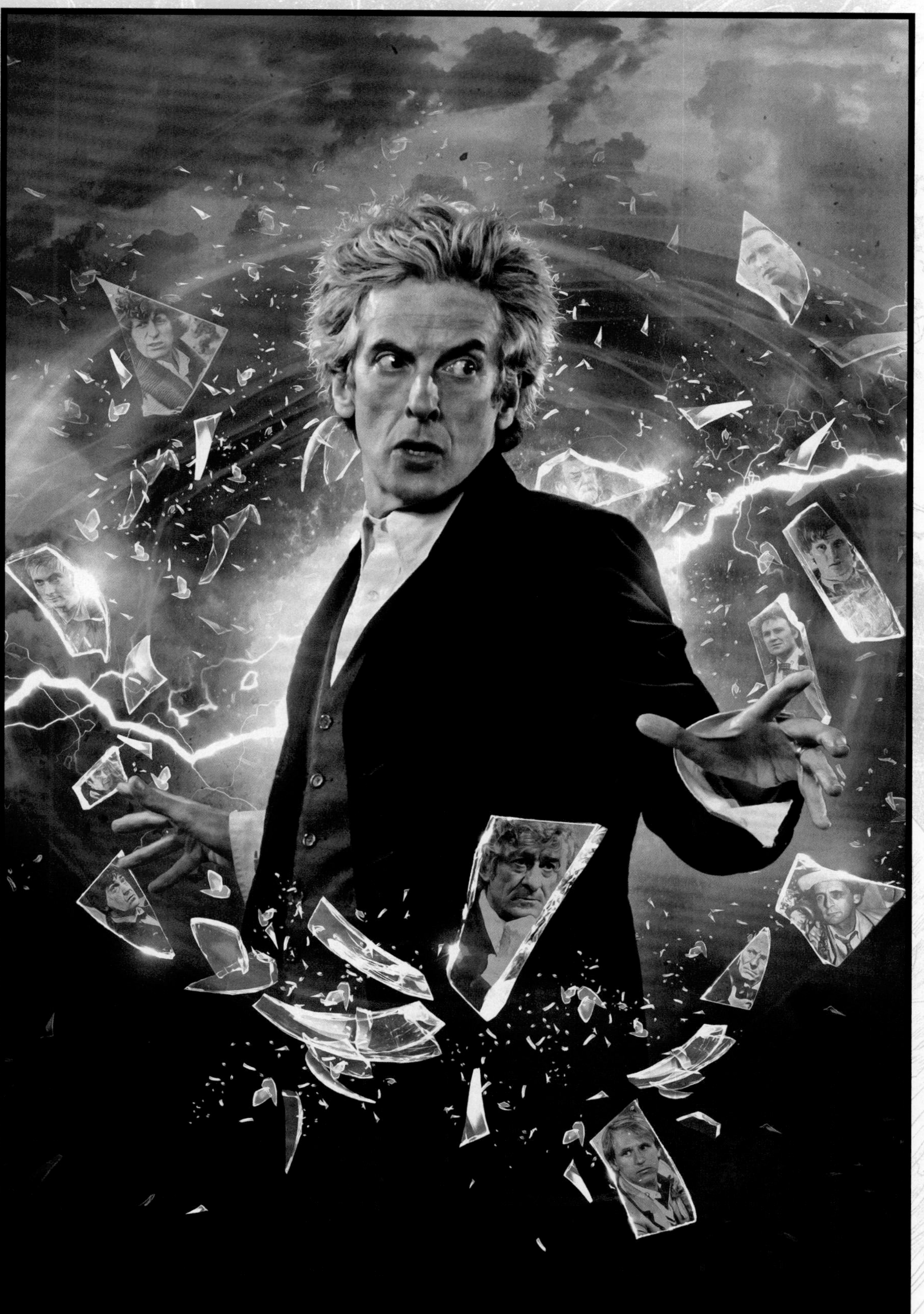

Omega Cover B: WILL BROOKS

BBC

DOCTOR WHO

READER'S GUIDE

With so many amazing *Doctor Who* comics out on the shelves, it can be difficult to know where to start! That's where this handy guide comes in.

THE TWELFTH DOCTOR – ONGOING

DOCTOR WHO
TERRORFORMER
DOCTOR WHO
FRACTURES
DOCTOR WHO
HYPERION
DOCTOR WHO
THE SCHOOL OF DEATH
DOCTOR WHO
THE TWIST

VOL. 1: TERRORFORMER

VOL. 2: FRACTURES

VOL. 3: HYPERION

YEAR TWO BEGINS! VOL. 4: SCHOOL OF DEATH

VOL. 5: THE TWIST

THE ELEVENTH DOCTOR – ONGOING

DOCTOR WHO
AFTER LIFE
DOCTOR WHO
SERVE YOU
DOCTOR WHO
CONVERSION
DOCTOR WHO
THE THEN AND THE NOW
DOCTOR WHO
THE ONE

VOL. 1: AFTER LIFE

VOL. 2: SERVE YOU

VOL. 3: CONVERSION

YEAR TWO BEGINS! VOL. 4: THE THEN AND THE NOW

VOL. 5: THE ONE

THE TENTH DOCTOR – ONGOING

DOCTOR WHO
REVOLUTIONS OF TERROR
DOCTOR WHO
THE WEEPING ANGELS OF MONS
DOCTOR WHO
THE FOUNTAINS OF FOREVER
DOCTOR WHO
THE ENDLESS SONG
DOCTOR WHO
ARENA OF FEAR

VOL. 1: REVOLUTIONS OF TERROR

VOL. 2: THE WEEPING ANGELS OF MONS

VOL. 3: THE FOUNTAINS OF FOREVER

YEAR TWO BEGINS! VOL. 4: THE ENDLESS SONG

VOL. 5: ARENA OF FEAR

THE NINTH DOCTOR – ONGOING

DOCTOR WHO
WEAPONS OF PAST DESTRUCTION
DOCTOR WHO
DOCTORMANIA
DOCTOR WHO
OFFICIAL SECRETS
DOCTOR WHO
SIN EATERS

VOL. 1: WEAPONS OF

VOL. 2:

VOL. 3:

VOL. 4:

There are currently **four** main *Doctor Who* series, each following a different modern Doctor.
Each ongoing series is **entirely self-contained**, so you can follow one, two, or all of your favorite Doctors, as you wish! The ongoings are arranged in season-like **Years**, collected into roughly three books per Year. Feel free to start at Volume 1 of any series, or jump straight to Volume 4, for an equally-accessible new season premiere!
Each book, and every comic, features a **catch-up and character guide** at the beginning, making it easy to jump on board – and each ongoing has a very different flavor, representative of that Doctor's era on screen.

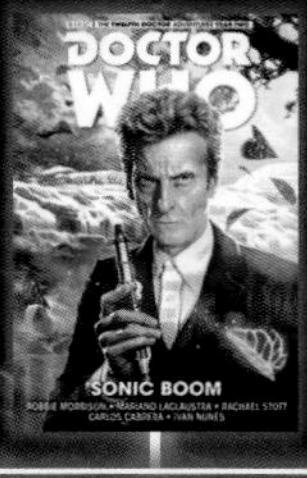
DOCTOR WHO
SONIC BOOM

VOL. 6:
SONIC BOOM

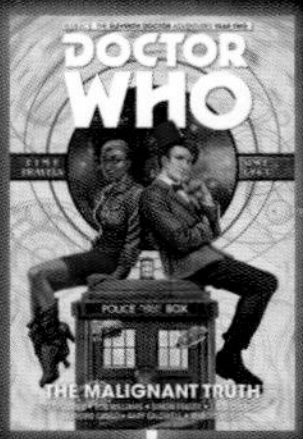
DOCTOR WHO
THE MALIGNANT TRUTH

VOL. 6:
THE MALIGNANT TRUTH

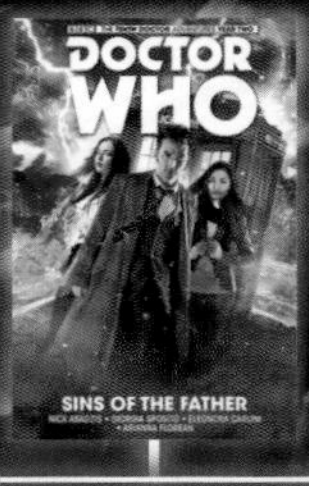
DOCTOR WHO
SINS OF THE FATHER

VOL. 6:
SINS OF THE FATHER

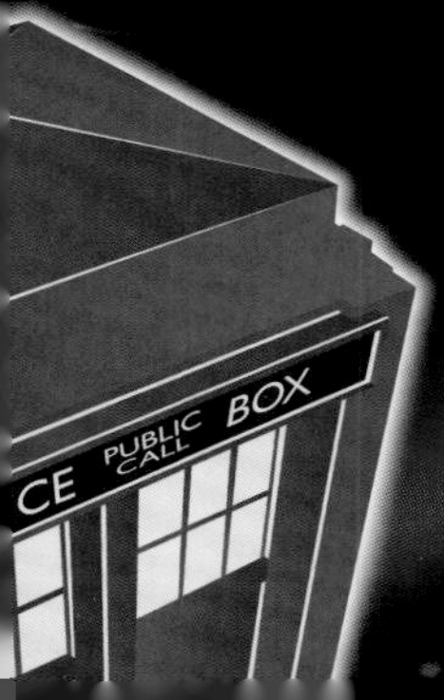
PUBLIC CALL BOX

THIRD DOCTOR

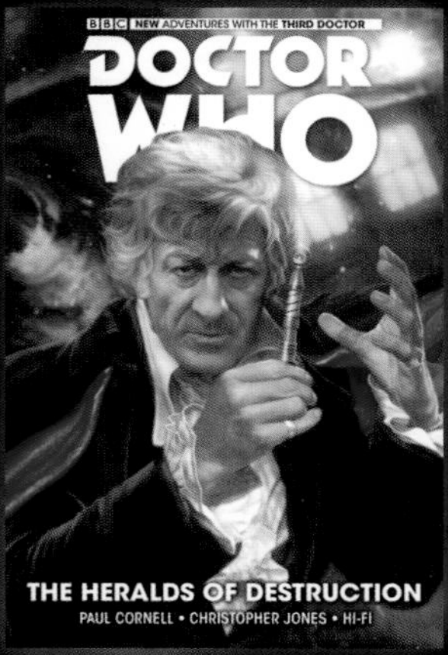
BBC NEW ADVENTURES WITH THE THIRD DOCTOR
DOCTOR WHO
THE HERALDS OF DESTRUCTION
PAUL CORNELL • CHRISTOPHER JONES • HI-FI

As well as the four ongoing series, we have published three major **past Doctor miniseries**, for the Third, Fourth, and Eighth Doctors. These volumes are each a **complete** and **self-contained** story.

There are also two fantastic **crossover event** volumes, starring the Ninth, Tenth, Eleventh, and Twelfth Doctors – the first, *Four Doctors*, sees an impossible team-up, and the second, *Supremacy of the Cybermen*, sees the monstrous cyborgs rule victorious over the universe... unless the Doctors can stop them!

FOURTH DOCTOR

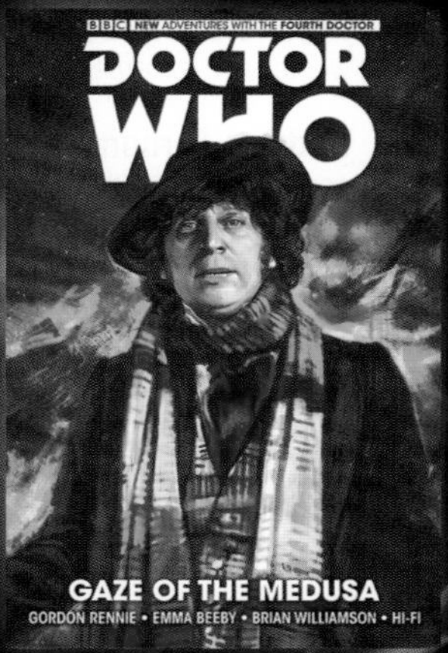
BBC NEW ADVENTURES WITH THE FOURTH DOCTOR
DOCTOR WHO
GAZE OF THE MEDUSA
GORDON RENNIE • EMMA BEEBY • BRIAN WILLIAMSON • HI-FI

FOUR DOCTORS

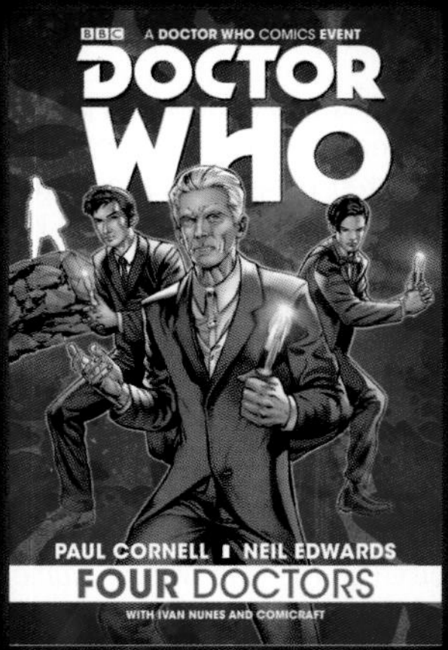
BBC A DOCTOR WHO COMICS EVENT
DOCTOR WHO
PAUL CORNELL NEIL EDWARDS
FOUR DOCTORS
WITH IVAN NUNES AND COMICRAFT

EIGHTH DOCTOR

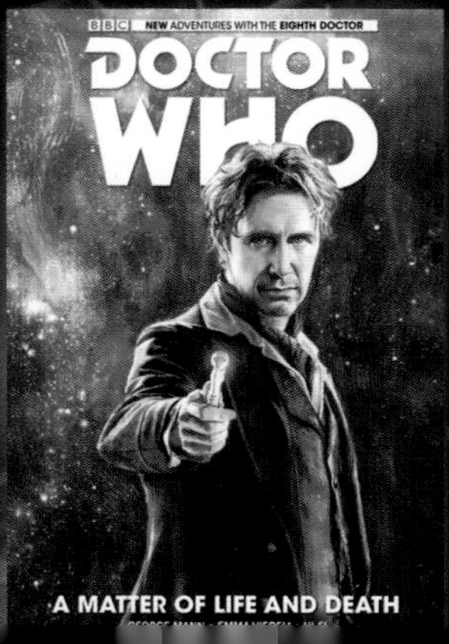
BBC NEW ADVENTURES WITH THE EIGHTH DOCTOR
DOCTOR WHO
A MATTER OF LIFE AND DEATH

SUPREMACY OF THE CYBERMEN

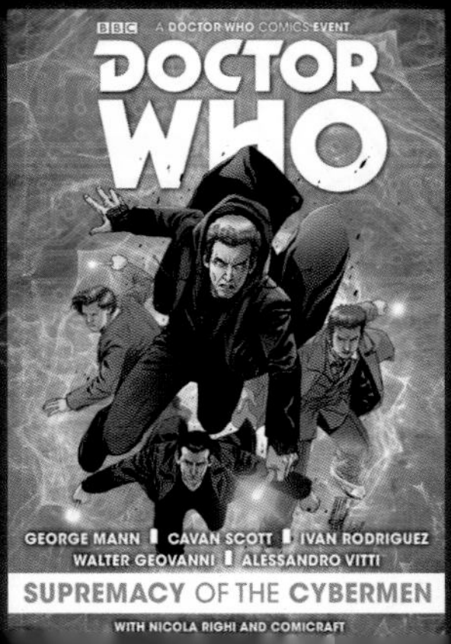
BBC A DOCTOR WHO COMICS EVENT
DOCTOR WHO
GEORGE MANN CAVAN SCOTT IVAN RODRIGUEZ
WALTER GEOVANNI ALESSANDRO VITTI
SUPREMACY OF THE CYBERMEN
WITH NICOLA RIGHI AND COMICRAFT

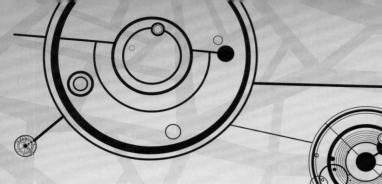

BIOGRAPHIES

Gordon Rennie is an acclaimed writer of comics, novels and video games, with titles including *Judge Dredd, Fighting American, White Trash*, and *Dishonored*. He lives in Edinburgh with his partner Emma Beeby and their young daughter.

Emma Beeby is a talented writer of titles such as *Witch Hunter, Survival Geeks*, and the forthcoming *Mata Hari*, and was the first woman to write for *Judge Dredd*.

George Mann is the comics writer behind *Dark Souls* and *Warhammer 40,000*, and the author of *Newbury & Hobbes*, as well as numerous short stories, novellas, and an original *Doctor Who* audiobook. He lives near Grantham, UK, with his wife and children.

Cavan Scott is a writer, editor, and journalist. He is known for his comics writing on *Doctor Who, Star Wars, Vikings*, and *Tekken*, as well as his many novels. He is also known for co-writing the bestselling *Who-Ology* book. He lives in Bristol with his wife, two daughters, and an inflatable Dalek named Desmond.

Ivan Rodriguez is a Brazilian artist whose work includes *The Spider, Doctor Who: Supremacy of the Cybermen*, and *The Shadow*.

Wellington Diaz is a Brazilian illustrator and inker, who has worked on *The Man With No Name, Nova*, and *Superman: Grounded.*

Rachael Stott, the winner of the Best Newcomer Artist at the British Comic Awards 2015, has worked on *Planet of the Apes, Star Trek*, and *Doctor Who*.

Mariano Laclaustra is a creator with a background in the Fine Arts. A freelance artist based in Argentina, he has worked with publishers across Europe and the United States, including for *Dark Horse Presents*. In between drawing and coloring comics, he teaches oil painting.

Thiago Ribeiro is an illustrator and colorist from Rio de Janeiro, Brazil. He has worked on titles such as *Red Sonja, Green Hornet*, and *Assassin's Creed*.

Mauricio Wallace is a Brazilian colorist who has worked on *Tekken, Blood Bowl,* and *Weird Detective*.

Rodrigo Fernandes is a colorist whose beautiful work can be seen on titles such as *Vikings, Independence Day,* and *Doctor Who.*

Carlos Cabrera is an Argentinian colorist with many diverse projects to his name, such as *Invincible Iron Man, Agents of Atlas,* and *Doctor Who.*

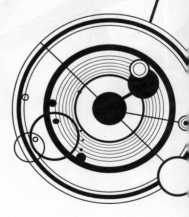

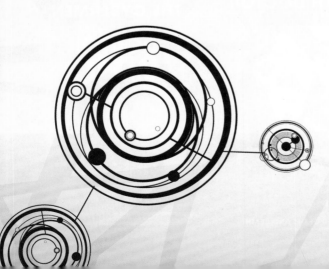